"LIFE
UNWORTHY
OF LIFE"

"LIFE UNWORTHY OF LIFE"

RACIAL PHOBIA AND MASS MURDER IN HITLER'S GERMANY

JAMES M. GLASS

BASIC BOOKS

A Member of the Perseus Books Group

Published by BasicBooks,
A Member of The Perseus Books Group

All rights reserved. Printed in the United States of America.

ISBN (pb) 0465098460

Designed by Laura Lindgren

Library of Congress Cataloging-in-Publication Data

Glass, James M.
    Life unworthy of life : racial phobia and mass murder in Hitler's Germany / James M. Glass.
        p.   cm.
    Includes bibliographical references and index.
    ISBN 0-465-09844-4
    1. Holocaust, Jewish (1939–1945)—Causes.
2. Antisemitism—Germany.   3. Eugenics—Germany—History—20th century.   I. Title.
D804.3.G587   1997
940.53'18—dc21   97-20118
                                                    r97

10 9 8 7 6

TO THE MEMORY OF THOSE
INNOCENT MEN, WOMEN,
CHILDREN, AND INFANTS
WHO PERISHED IN THE HOLOCAUST.

It is the supreme duty of a national state to grant life and livelihood only to the healthy and hereditarily sound and racially pure folk for all eternity.

DR. ARTHUR GUEST, DIRECTOR OF PUBLIC HEALTH,
MINISTRY OF THE INTERIOR IN THE THIRD REICH, 1935

I write these lines in anxiety and grief—who knows what the next several days will bring us? Thousands have already been deported, tens of thousands more will be sent away. In our present situation, too exhausted for walking on our feet—in the strictest sense of the word—deportation is obviously a mortal danger for us, for even if they don't kill us outright, we will surely die from the hardships along the way, and from starvation.

ANONYMOUS DIARY ENTRY, LODZ GHETTO, MAY 7, 1944

CONTENTS

ACKNOWLEDGMENTS

I would like to thank a number of people. This book has been enriched by my conversations with Fred Alford; his sensitivity, probing questions, and wide knowledge of group theory and dynamics contributed enormously to the theoretical and historical argument. I am deeply indebted to his presence and insights. George Quester and Victor Wolfenstein read the entire manuscript and offered valuable advice. Roger Haydon encouraged the pursuit of the project; his guidance concerning argument and thematic structure was invaluable. I am also grateful to Jane Flax, Fred Frohock, Richard Konigsberg, Roger Lewin, Bonnie Oppenheimer, Stanley Renshon, Seymour Rubenfeld, Morton Schoolman, and Linda Zerilli for thoughtful suggestions during the evolution of the manuscript. Jerrold Post provided the opportunity to present this research at his continuing seminar in political psychology at the Elliot School, George Washington University, in addition to an invitation to address the 1995 International Association of Political Psychology's annual meeting's plenary session, convened at the United States Holocaust Memorial Museum. Paul Golob, my editor at Basic Books, generously gave his support and editorial assistance.

For their invitations to present this research, I acknowledge the political science and psychiatric faculties at Syracuse University; the Student Government Association and political science department at the State University of New York, Albany; Shaare Tefila Congregation in Silver Spring, Maryland; the Eastern Regional Conference on Dissociative Disorders in Washington, D.C.; the Department of Government and Politics at the University of Maryland, College Park; and the Multiple Personality Study Group of the greater Washington, D.C., area. I am also grateful to my graduate students for feedback in courses on genocide and mass murder and the general theme of scapegoating.

My typist, Flora Paoli, in addition to providing consistently readable and flawless text and remarkable talent in incorporating the manuscript's many revisions, gave me sound advice on matters relating to organization of textual material.

Funding for the research in Poland came from the University of Maryland, College Park, Graduate School; the Department of Jewish Studies, University of Maryland, College Park; and the International Travel Fund Committee, University of Maryland, College Park. I also thank the University of Maryland, General Research Board, for a semester research grant, facilitating exclusive focus on this project.

The research in Poland would not have been possible without the excellent translations of Beate Czajkowska in the Kraków and Lublin city archives, the National University Library in Warsaw, and in the interviews themselves. Beate's work was remarkable. I am also grateful to Jacek Nowakowski, Director of the Collections and Acquisitions Department at the United States Holocaust Memorial Museum, for providing contacts and introductions. For their help in Poland I acknowledge Professors Jerzy Aleksandrowicz, Maria Orwid, and Adam Szymusik, and Drs. Jan Cieckiewicz, Andrzej Friedman, Andrzej Link-Lenczowski, Arnold Mostowicz, and Edwin Opoczynski.

And finally, to my wife, Cyndi, and children, Jason, Jeremy, and Justin, my love and gratitude for your patience, understanding, and support.

THE GROUND
OF KILLING

German society, particularly the professions, enthusiastically pursued genocide because of a culturewide phobia against touching Jewish flesh, a perception forged by the biological and medical sciences and by a firm belief in the absolute necessity of maintaining racial purity. Ghettos (way stations on the ultimate journey to the death camps) had been established primarily in Poland, with the specific intent of concentrating and segregating Jews. However, in the ghettoes themselves hundreds of thousands of Jews perished from disease, hunger, and physical and psychological brutalization. Ghettoization in Poland and elsewhere had been provoked by the German fear of the Jewish body and the belief that Jewish flesh and blood polluted the health of the German *volk*, its genes, and its cultures.

A great number of Germans, in addition to members of the Nazi Party, participated in and supported murderous actions, accepted race ideology as truth, and contributed—as nurses, engineers, physicians, industrialists, research scientists, land use specialists—to the logistics of concentration, transport, ghettoization, and murder of Jewish adults, children, and infants. Race ideology dominated the thinking and action of the entire society. Anti-Semitism, embraced and elaborated by Nazism, was generalized throughout the culture, defining the Jew as a threatening, dangerous, and poisonous Other. While sporadic resistance to the isolation of the Jewish population and the killing in the death camps occasionally appeared within Germany, it never impeded any of the regime's genocidal aims. Race ideology, and its medical implications, dominated the thinking and action of the entire culture.

The term *Kultur*-group, as it is used in this book, refers to a group constituted by a set of common or shared beliefs. What unites and gives common meaning to the *Kultur*-group are the ideas that dominate the period, the belief inventory functioning as the society's major ideational context, the internalization of ideology as unquestioned imagery of "good" and "bad," and the broad cultural consensus regarding the regime's political practices. Biomedical science, in conjunction with other major professions in German society and the Nazi party, created this ideational context, what Daniel Jonah Goldhagen[1] calls "eliminationist anti-Semitism," and is particularly responsible for its biological inventory of beliefs.

The following chapters examine the belief structure that led to Auschwitz, Majdanek, Sobibor, Treblinka, and Belzec, and the psychological and political forces that made mass murder a normal part of day-to-day politics and administrative life in the Third Reich. The Final Solution, played out primarily on Polish soil, produced the death of more than six million Jews, four million in a nine-month period. Ghettos established in Warsaw, Lodz, Kraków, Radom, Lvov, to name a few, accounted for the deaths of hundreds of thousands from starvation, disease, forced labor, and the random brutality of the German occupier.

As part of a research project in Poland in the summer of 1995, I explored the perception of the Jewish body as diseased and infectious, in an interview in Kraków with the son of Dr. S, who had served during the German occupation as secretary to the Polish Chamber of Physicians, roughly the equivalent of the head of the American Medical Association, with administrative power to direct medical activities and implement German directives.

The German Health Office, supervising medical administration in occupied Poland (the "General Government") with headquarters in Kraków, devised policies instrumental in concentrating the Jewish populations into ghettos and transporting Jews to forced labor and death camps. The ideology driving this process is central to this book: the ideological imperatives that lay behind the construction of ghettos; the professional sectors that defined and extended the process;

the beliefs in the culture that supported policies of concentration, transport, and annihilation.

Dr. S regularly corresponded with and carried out the directives of Dr. Kroll, the chief German medical and health official, or *Sanitäts-oberführer*.

Dr. S's son repeatedly argued that his father's relationship with the Germans was one of "dependence, not collaboration." While in a literal sense this may have been true, extensive correspondence and communication regularly passed between Kroll and Dr. S. The Kraków city archives contain correspondence covering the entire occupation; communication between the two administrators involved primarily carrying out German orders regarding contact with Jewish doctors, the levying of fines and taxes, the administration of the Polish National Health Service, and the establishment of ghettos. But it is also clear Dr. S carried out these orders without equivocation.

Judging from the sheer volume of work required of the head of Polish medicine, the line between dependence and collaboration appears to have been crossed several times: administering questionnaires, keeping track of the addresses of Jewish doctors, implementing the ghettoization process, enforcing public health ordinances requiring the quarantine of Jewish populations, levying taxes against Jews, implementing race laws regarding Jews practicing medicine. No evidence suggests Dr. S actively collaborated in the killing of Jews, but, as well, there is no evidence that he offered help to Jews or resistance to German plans.

Much of the communication between Dr. S and Kroll had to do with organizing the city's public health services to prevent epidemics, specifically typhus. The Germans insisted on segregating the Jewish population largely because they believed that Jews, by nature, carried and transmitted typhus and other infectious diseases. No other "subhuman" races or types found themselves saddled with this particular "trait"; ghettoization of the Jews, then, was a special form of quarantine.

Dr. S's son spoke of the German "schizophrenia" in this regard: the paranoid fear of typhus epidemics created conditions in the ghetto—overcrowding, hunger, lice, and illnesses—that made the ghettos themselves a threat to health and life. This contradiction never troubled the German administrators because it reinforced the stereotype of the Jew as a carrier of disease. Ghettoization, then, had a twofold purpose: to isolate disease and to kill Jews. Although it is impossible to be precise, at least 35 to 40 percent of Jewish deaths in Poland were due to disease, malnutrition, and hunger. Ghettoization killed as effectively, if not as efficiently, as the death camps.

The Germans in the occupation of Poland were hardly schizophrenic; starvation and hunger constituted part of a deliberate policy to kill all Jews who were regarded as a mortal threat to public health and blood purity. Posters throughout Poland proclaimed the ghetto to be a place of disease and sickness. No Pole, it was ordered, should attempt to enter. The Jews in Kraków were forced to move from the old Jewish quarter to a ghetto about one-quarter its size. I walked the length of the ghetto in seven minutes, and took three minutes to walk its breadth. This area, primarily two-story buildings, contained twenty to thirty thousand people.

It was not that the Germans were unaware of typhus as a disease process; their approach to treatment and containment indicate a knowledge of its connection with public health. But the German mind-set did not link unsanitary living conditions ruthlessly imposed on the Jewish population with disease. Jews contracted typhus and sickness not because of being forced into intolerable physical environments—very few physicians admitted to this fact as causative of ghetto typhus—but because Jewish blood and genes predisposed Jewish bodies to infection.

If typhus and disease were innate to the Jew, no amount of public health in the ghetto would clean it up, in spite of protests by Jewish doctors, *Judenrat* administrators, and some Polish public health officials. Dr. S persistently faced this argument in dealing with Nazi officials: the need to exterminate Jewish bodies as a problem in sanitation management. In fact, typhus caused a relatively small percentage of total deaths in the ghetto, approximately 3 percent. Diseases linked to unsanitary conditions—typhoid fever, dysentery, tuberculosis, and starvation—killed the vast majority of Jews. As for the burning of bodies: "Everyone knew what was going on in Plaszów [the infamous labor camp just outside Kraków]; you could see the smoke; if you were anywhere near the camp, you could smell it."

Dr. S's son concluded our interview with the following observation: "German doctors looked at racial subtypes almost like a veterinarian would look at different species of animals." The Poles had a different, but also negative, attitude: "I may hate the Jews, but they are my Jews and you have no right to kill them," although he adds this sentiment applied to very few Poles. "It is unfortunate, but many Poles either did not do enough or at least in the early days of the occupation helped themselves to Jewish goods and beat up Jews on the streets as they fled their homes. It's a sad story, and, as you know, Poles are very defensive about it." Only 8,000 doctors remained in Poland after the war; almost none of them Jewish. Before the war Jewish doctors made up nearly half of the practice of medicine and dentistry.

From the earliest days of the occupation, the German administration issued edicts requiring all professions to be divided into specific racial "teams": Germans administering to Germans, Poles to Poles, and Jews to Jews. Each team was segregated from the others; hospitals were to be kept separate. Jews were not to receive any medical service at Aryan hospitals; and the public administration of health was to be kept separate.

The following are excerpts from race-driven edicts issued early in the occupation.[2]

March 6, 1940:
It is commonly known that typhus and other infectious diseases are spread by the Jewish population. Therefore, if sick Jews are treated by Aryan doctors, the doctors pose a danger to the Aryan population which may be infected directly or indirectly through the doctors by Jewish illness or sickness.

On November 18, 1940, a directive was given that Jews could not prescribe drugs or medicines for Aryans. Jewish prescriptions needed to include the Star of David on the bottle. Poles could not be treated or touched by Jewish doctors. In June 1940, local Polish officials were asked to identify all Jewish health professionals; special taxes were placed on Jewish physicians and dentists. Polish doctors were required to inform the German medical administration which of their fellow doctors were Jewish. District doctors were asked about health professionals who refused to fill out questionnaires. Jewish health professionals were required to give "donations" to a fund for Polish families that had suffered a loss. Only Jews were asked to contribute.

In the spring of 1940, the German head of the health office in Lublin sent a letter to the health office in Kraków insisting that a Jewish midwife, who in assisting an Aryan birth contributed to race pollution, should be "brought to justice [death]." On April 18, 1942, a directive ordered that a Jewish sector be established in Kraków to facilitate "health care" and to improve "traffic."

These documents pertaining to the German Health Administration contain numerous lists of doctors, taxes, forced contributions; lists of Jewish health workers in various districts; lists of who was treating whom; reports of Jewish doctors treating Aryan patients; signed and unsigned letters describing various Jewish peccadilloes regarding medical and health practice, from unsanitary treatment conditions, to the dispensing of inferior medicines, to the charging of exorbitant fees.

Meticulous counts were kept of diseases making up ghetto hospital populations; typhus patients were kept strictly separated. "Effective" sanitation required burning houses and personal effects and quarantining inhabitants for weeks at a time, often without food or water. One document from a local police official in Lublin to an official in the General Government requested that no more Jews be sent to the Lublin ghetto because of the difficulty in "processing" Jews at the Majdanek death camp. German officials persistently sent memos on health regulations and ghetto "processing."

Lacking sewage systems, the inhabitants often dug their own latrines. On the infrequent occasion that the sewage pits were emptied, small children pulled the waste wagons. Since running water had been cut off along with the sewage systems, the ghetto inhabitants dug wells, often in close proximity to the primitive toilets.

The links between Jews and disease were regularly made explicit in the German-run daily newspaper, *Nowy Kourier*:[3] "Cleanliness is a measure of a cultured society; everyone stand up and fight dirt . . . cleanliness is a postulate of modern society." As the German propaganda equated Jews with uncleanliness, the implications of this association could not be mistaken. "In the quest for hygiene and health, the entire society must take part. [There are] three rules of hygiene: (1) personal hygiene, clean clothes; (2) lack of contact with dirty people; and (3) avoiding places that do not stand up to proper hygiene."

In Spring 1943, an anti-Jewish/typhus exhibit opened in Warsaw. Its primary theme equated the Jew with typhus. More than fifty thousand people toured the exhibit; school children were required to attend. Lectures, films, programs, and demonstrations equated Jews with typhus and lice. A Polish professor of Jewish history, at the time around seven or eight, remembers attending the exhibition. "It was quite amazing. All sorts of posters, tables, settings, films, literature showing how the Jew had to be feared because of an inborn disease potential. Jews, we were told, were the primary carrier of lice; and Jewish flesh poisoned you if you touched it. Coming anywhere near a Jew caused illness, fever, possibly death."

A *Nowy Kourier* article noted: "Lice is a murderer of humans . . . dirt is the father of epidemics." A little boy at the exhibit was heard screaming: "Jewish army, Jewish army!" Someone asked him why he was so frightened, where was this "Jewish army?" He pointed to lice in an exhibit case and said, "There you see it, that's the Jewish army! If you had lived on Franciszkanska Street before the war, you would have known it; you would see what a Jewish army looks like!"[4] The association of Jew, disease, typhus, and threat to the German cultural and spiritual body dominated political and medical policy of the Final Solution. Isolating the Jews in ghettos and then exterminating them in death camps required a vast and enthusiastic cooperation of major segments of the German political, medical, scientific, legal, bureaucratic, and manufacturing professions. How to interpret and understand the feeling that the Jew could infect and destroy the German body politic is the objective of this inquiry into the Holocaust.

"LIFE
UNWORTHY OF
LIFE"

ONE

THE ENTHUSIASTS OF DEATH

Elie Wiesel, a survivor of Auschwitz, writes:

> This, this was the thing I had wanted to understand ever since
> the war. Nothing else. How a human being can remain indif-
> ferent. The executioners I understood; also the victims,
> though with more difficulty. For the others, all the others,
> those who were neither for nor against, those who sprawled
> in passive patience, those who told themselves, "The storm
> will blow over and everything will be normal again," those
> who thought themselves above the battle, those who were
> permanently and merely spectators—all those were closed to
> me, incomprehensible.[1]

The argument of indifference is vastly overstated. What Wiesel
and others call indifference was more than acquiescence. It was a
willed desire, throughout the German population, for the elimination
and extermination of persons of the Jewish race.

What appeared to be indifference, patience, spectatorship above
the fray, was not at all silent protest or passive acceptance of the Nazi
persecution of the Jews, but an active embracing of actions to rid the
Kultur and nation of what was psychologically experienced as a racial
infection. Arguments that the German populace was ignorant of or

isolated from the killings and slave labor camps, or generally apathetic to the fate of the Jews, are common to this line of interpretation. For example, the German historian Martin Broszat argues that the extermination of the Jews "could largely be concealed and kept quiet." The relative invisibility of the mechanics, therefore, made the fate of Jewish bodies a "little noticed matter of secondary importance for the majority of Germans during the war." Further, he rejects the argument that Auschwitz be understood as "the cardinal point, the hinge on which the entire factual complex of historical events of the Nazi period turns."[2] With most Germans, "out of sight, out of mind" meant not only a lack of preoccupation with the Jewish presence or its absence but a willing blindness to the facts of their extermination.[3]

Given the widespread demand for slave labor—a fact dramatically present in the Nuremberg trial reports—the presence of hundreds of labor and concentration camps inside Germany itself, the participation of industry, administration, medicine, law, engineering, architecture, and manufacture, and the use of five to six million foreign workers, most of them "conscripted" from occupied territories, to maintain ignorance of these crimes or to suggest that acquiescence to these practices derived from "indifference" is a narrow reading of the psychological forces impelling mass murder and enslavement. Further, this reading minimizes what Jürgen Habermas sees as the interlacing of responsibility, guilt, and crime in the population as a whole, "the complex connections between criminality and the ambiguous normality of daily life in Nazi Germany, between destruction and vigorous productivity, between a devastating systemic perspective and an inconspicuous-ambivalent nearsightedness on the local level."[4]

The indifference argument is deceptively simple. One could equally well argue that individuals enjoy killing or being in proximity to the killing machine, that the Final Solution demonstrates a group thirst for sadistic violence, and that it shows how close to the surface are primitive and atavistic drives for vengeance, retribution, and annihilation. While indifference played a role in the Holocaust, while sadism accurately describes actions undertaken by specific groups and individuals (for example, the SS, concentration camp guards, party officials, physicians involved in medical "experimentation"), these arguments or observations alone do not explain the seemingly culturewide consensus on the killing and absence of moral, ethical, or epistemological protest. The lack of protest, notably the lack of a concerted reaction to the notion that Jews constitute "life unworthy of life," suggests more than indifference or apathy unifying German society in the pursuit of mass murder.

Moral apathy certainly existed, somewhere, someplace in the Third Reich. Many Germans simply did not care what happened to their Jewish neighbors. Even studies quantifying indifference from available historical archives may not be sufficient to unravel the complex reality of psychological intent and unconscious motive. Efforts to generalize the indifference hypothesis, however, as a blanket approach to complicity are troubling. For example, Yehuda Bauer states, "[T]he attitude of the German population was characterized more by apathy, indifference, discomfort . . . than by active agreement with Nazi policies whose general content was either known or correctly guessed."[5] To assert indifference as a societal state of mind based on the fact of inaction does not bear on whether ordinary citizens or practicing professionals actively desired—or better, emotionally consented to—what the regime sought to accomplish by destroying racially inferior or defective populations.[6]

What historical and social psychological literature on the Final Solution has called "indifference" may be more accurately identified as an unwillingness to see or experience the suffering of the victims. The suffering was not seen because Jews and other racially inferior bodies were not understood as human beings, but, in the words of Nazi racial theory, as "life unworthy of life."[7] Not to see does not necessarily describe indifference; indeed, a more accurate indication of the feelings and perception of the German populace is in the actions of enslavement and murder, beginning with the exclusionary legislation of the early thirties and culminating in the Holocaust.

BLINDNESS TO SUFFERING

In an account of the escape of Russian prisoners of war from the Mauthausen concentration camp, Gordon Horwitz interprets this willingness to kill as a blindness to a "recognition [that] bespeaks care for one's fellow man." If one truly cared about the suffering of others, the psychological impulse would be "wanting to see and know in order not to turn one's back." Concern for the other "entails an open-ness not only to the unexpected encounter—the sudden appearance of a column of inmates before one's eyes, the smell of the smoke as one walks by the river—but a desire to see," indicating a desire to make contact with suffering and to help. But nothing of the sort came from the vast majority of the German population and their sympathizers in the occupied territories, no evidence of "a desire to see, a choice of preparing oneself to see in order to make contact, at the least to leave a morsel by the roadside or toss an apple into the ranks."[8] What Horwitz calls the "concerned vision" seizing "the opportunity to act" did not exist, and the minuscule resistance to the murders and concern for the victims was dwarfed by the massiveness of the cooperation in the Final Solution.

Resistance to mass murder requires a "concerned vision." But Germans had been told for years, through literature, popular media, political speeches, and the medical establishment, that Jewish bodies constituted a threat to the *Kultur*'s blood, to its genetic purity. And if one sees others as polluted, infected matter dangerous to the culture, one sees not human beings with feelings, capable of pain, and elicit-ing pity and empathy. Instead, one sees a being who elicits fear, anxi-ety, and uncertainty.

If one does not acknowledge the other as a sentient human, then primitive emotional responses, such as pity and compassion, possess no context in which to function. If the other becomes a phobic object in the group unconscious mind, then the reaction is to keep it away, to not see it, to not acknowledge it. Further, if the phobic object threatens the culture's sense of its own physical and psychological integrity, there is a pressing need to rid the environment of this infec-tion, in other words, an enthusiasm to kill and remove the object pro-voking such intense fear.

Hate and fear may be equally as important as indifference and banality in explaining the seeming objectivity and bureaucratic rou-tine of the Final Solution, how within a very short period of time, millions of human beings, an entire race, could be killed, without so much as a murmur from the host population. As Harold Kaplan puts it, the term *Final Solution* sounded to the Nazis like a "moral appeal."[9]

By no stretch of the imagination can the Final Solution be consid-ered politics as usual; nor can all responsibility for the deaths of millions of Jews be laid on the surrounding population's moral indifference or on bureaucrats following orders. It may be useful to look at psychological components, particularly group-psychological dynamics, for explanations of racist motivations behind the killing process. To this extent, I disagree with Hannah Arendt's well-known thesis of the Holocaust as an illustration of the "banality of evil."[10] She is right in describing the bureaucratic mentality of thousands of administrators engaging in unimaginable evil. What is lacking in Arendt's argument, and the line of interpretive literature following her, is a sensitivity to psychological dynamics, specifically the power of phobia in defining perceptions and attitudes toward an object regarded as a lethal source of racial poisoning.

BUREAUCRATIC ENTHUSIASM
AND THE NORMALITY OF DEATH

It was not cultural propagandists who organized the infamous "special treatment" of the Jews; it was the public health officials, the scientific journals, the physicians, the administrators, and the lawyers, who feared that the very presence of the Jews would endanger their families, their bodies, and ultimately their lives. To think of the Jew in such terms is insane from our perspective, but it was held to be sane in the culture caught up in the phobic projection of infection onto the Jews and the scientific authority legitimizing such beliefs.

Hannah Arendt rightly argues that bureaucrats and administrators were major participants and far more responsible for the magnitude of the killings than the psychologically twisted who constituted the SS. The work of Arendt and historians such as Raul Hilberg demonstrates how important bureaucracy and administration, in addition to the party officials, were in the dynamics of the Holocaust, and suggests that the Holocaust itself might be a phenomenon radically different from historical methods of exclusion and discrimination characteristic of German society in the past. The civil service, Hilberg argues, contributed "sure-footed planning and bureaucratic thoroughness." The army gave the machinery of destruction its "military precision, discipline, and callousness." The influence of industry was evident in the "great emphasis on accounting, penny saving, and salvage, as well as in the factory-like efficiency of the killing centers."

And the Nazi Party contributed "a sense of 'mission,' and a notion of 'history making.'"[11] Thus, he concludes, four major bureaucratic institutions agreed not only on what the task at hand was, but also on how to go about it. The extermination process involved "a sprawling, diverse, and—above all—decentralized apparatus. . . . [T]here was hardly an agency, an office, or an organization that did not at one time or another have an interest in anti-Jewish measures."[12]

Yet something is missing in this explanation. Why would bureaucracies cooperate to such an extent? What would create such a nationwide consensus on what to do about the "Jewish problem?" Auschwitz suggests more than the effort of like-minded bureaucrats to follow out a rational policy of administered death. Key to the explanation is what the victims meant both consciously and unconsciously to the Kultur-group's fears, to the imminence of its own fantasized disintegration and its obsession with blood. German society chose to eliminate an entire race from its midst, and conscious administrative rationality does not fully explain its actions. A society does not initiate such suffering to so many human beings without fear being a part of the motivational complex.

Violence of the magnitude of the Holocaust indicates that the Jews had to be both hated and feared as infected, polluted objects. This persistent demonstration of intense fears and hates is indicative of a phobic reaction. Or as Yitzhak Arad describes the German state of mind in his account of Operation Reinhard, the plan to exterminate all Jews in central Poland, "under the regime of Nazi Germany . . . perfectly ordinary people were turned into something extraordinarily inhuman."[13] Murder could be justified because "the Jew is a sub-human, a germ that attempts to infect the pure German blood."[14] At Treblinka, a Professor Doctor Pfannenstiel, Professor of Hygiene at the University of Marburg–Lahn, told the SS: "Your work is a great work and a very useful and very necessary duty. . . . When one sees the bodies of the Jews, one understands the greatness of your work!" Pfannenstiel saw Treblinka as a place of "kindness," a "humanitarian establishment."[15] Not only did Germans feel they had been chosen morally to accomplish this massive sanitation project, they also saw themselves as the agents of a history defined by biological purpose.

The broad reach of murder required not only bureaucratic rationality, but individual enthusiasm and relief at the segregation of the Jew. Hilberg speaks about the anticipation and excitement accompanying the sales of Jewish apartments and auctions of furniture, objects of art, and clothing.[16] The recipients knew the origin of these goods. Like Arendt's, every page of Hilberg's historical analyses is filled with the horror of the process. Yet the historical recounting of the facts brackets, but does not elaborate on, the equally important psychological dimension of the slaughter.

Franz Stangl, commandant of Treblinka, described the moment he began to think of the Jews under his supervision not as humans, but as "cargo": "I think it started the day I first saw the *Totenlager* [burial pits] in Treblinka. I remember Wirth [who oversaw exterminations in Belsen, Sobibor, and Treblinka] standing there, next to the pits full of blue-black corpses. It had nothing to do with humanity—it couldn't have; it was a mass—a mass of rotting flesh. Wirth said, 'What shall we do with this garbage?' . . . I rarely saw them as individuals. It was always a huge mass."[17] Gitta Sereny found similar observations among the administrators and planners of the various programs for murder. They claimed "they were simply administering the 'public health' of the nation and were in no way directly concerned with violence or horror."[18] Several euthanasia institutes—for example, those at Hartheim, Hadamar, Sonnenstein, and Grafeneck—were set up as medical schools, conducting classes not in curing but in killing mental and genetic "defectives." One ex-Nazi, interviewed after the war, observed with some indignation that his psychiatric professors "believed in euthanasia, not as Nazis, but as responsible physicians,"[19] medical ethics being defined as the willingness to kill.

Hilberg describes how central to the *system* of extermination was the belief in Jewish disease, and how the Jews were seen as "carriers of sickness." The ghettos were horrible places of suffering. People lived fifteen to a room, with insufficient water for cooking, much less bathing. Families would descend like vultures on vacant buildings and rip them apart for fuel. Coal was scarce enough to be referred to as "black pearls." Such places could breed real, not fantasized, diseases.[20] One of the biggest tasks of both the *Judenräte* and the JSS lay in taking care of the thousands of orphans living in these dismal conditions. (The *Judenräte*, or Jewish councils, administered the ghettos; their leaders or heads were appointed by the Germans. The Jewish

Social Self-Help [JSS], an organization independent of the Jewish councils, provided relief and welfare services to ghetto inhabitants. Its branches were ordered disbanded by the SS in October 1942.)[21]

An observer of the deportation of children from the Warsaw ghetto notes, "The smaller children did not consider the fate that expected them and only feared the congestion and panic en route, and were affected by the outcries of the adults. They would draw close to their teachers and would not part from them for even the briefest moment. Some children cried and asked: 'Will they drown us there?' This form of death frightened them more than anything else."[22] Janusz Korczak, a pediatrician who helped to establish hostels throughout the Warsaw Ghetto for thousands of homeless orphans, and who ultimately went to his death with the children in his care, described the plight of the children of the ghetto:

> Help for those vomiting, moaning with pain, was adminis-
> tered in near darkness—with limewater. An injection of caf-
> feine for a hysterical new inmate following a collapse. His
> mother, wasting away of ulcerated intestines, was unwilling to
> die until the child had been placed in the Home. The boy was
> unwilling to go until the mother had died. He finally yielded.
> The mother died propitiously, now the child has pangs of con-
> science. In his illness, he mimics his mother: he moans . . . ,
> complains of pain, then gasps, then feels hot, finally is dying of
> thirst. [He screams] 'Water!' I pace the dormitory to and fro.
> Will there be an outbreak of mass hysteria? Might be![23]

On March 21, 1942, in a dry, objective accounting of conditions in the ghetto, the Propaganda Division of the Warsaw German administration reported:

> The death figure in the ghetto still hovers around 5,000 per
> month. A few days ago, the first case of hunger cannibalism
> was reported. In a Jewish family the man and his three chil-
> dren died within a few days. From the flesh of the child who
> died last—a twelve-year-old boy—the mother ate a piece. To
> be sure, this could not save her either, and she herself died
> two days later.[24]

Reports like these constantly coming out of the regional offices of the ghetto administration could not help but reinforce the Germans' vision of the disease-carrying Jew, requiring rapid extermination. Death was omnipresent, but the suffering of the dying was of utterly no concern to the Germans: the very flesh of these "diseased" people constituted an immanent threat demanding drastic measures. Serious illness in the ghetto generally afflicted at least 40 percent of the population and more as conditions worsened. One ghetto physician wrote in 1942:

> Active, busy, energetic people are changed into apathetic, sleepy beings, always in bed, hardly able to get up to eat or go to the toilet. Passage from life to death is slow and gradual, like death from physiological old age. There is nothing violent, no dyspnea, no pain, no obvious changes in breathing or circulation. Vital functions subside simultaneously. Pulse rate and respiratory rate get slower and it becomes more and more difficult to reach the patient's awareness, until life is gone. People fall asleep in bed or on the street and are dead in the morning. They die during physical effort, such as searching for food, and sometimes even with a piece of bread in their hands.[25]

Adam Czerniakow, Chairman of the Warsaw Judenrat, describes in his diary "utter misery and dire poverty. [Children who] are living skeletons [are among] the ranks of the street beggars. . . . Damned be those of us who have enough to eat and drink and forget about these children."[26]

Annihilation like this does not occur in a vacuum. It is impossible to eliminate an entire race of people from the landscape without the host population noticing or asking questions about the absence. People may will blindness to the facts, but it is inconceivable to escape the fact of absence and the stories circulating about the fate of former associates, friends, and neighbors. It cannot be argued that no one knew what was happening; still, very few chose to do anything about the facts. Stories about Jewish mothers eating their children must have reinforced the popular stereotype about the depraved Jew. Yet, it was the perpetrators who engaged in limitless, amoral behavior; who transvalued historical conceptions of morality.

Arnost Lustig describes a soldier in the so-called model ghetto, Theresienstadt, whose eyes "went cold" during the brutalization of an old woman.[27] This going cold, this loss of any empathic connection with victims, was evident throughout the German *Kultur* in its approach to its "Jewish problem." Hitler himself expressed it in his vision of the new German nation: "A violently active, dominating, intrepid, brutal youth—that is what I am after. Youth must be all those things. It must be indifferent to pain. There must be no weakness or tenderness in it. I want to see once more in its eyes the gleam of pride and independence of the beast of prey."[28]

THE ARGUMENT OF INDIFFERENCE:
MORALITY AND ITS FATE

It is one thing to be indifferent to the fate of one's neighbor. It is an entirely different matter to acquiesce not only in the killing of one's neighbor, but in that of every single member of your neighbor's ethnic community. The status of the Jews in Nazi Germany is described literally by Kaplan as "damned in nature." Jews found themselves associated with lice and typhus. Killing, therefore, affirmed "life against death, a medical sentence beyond appeal." It was as if the Jews had "truly sinned with the 'original sin' of their biological nature." In ridding the nation of this pollution, the extermination of insects and the disposal of toxic wastes were used as models for "the Nazi way of death."[29]

Zygmunt Bauman's moving and passionate analysis of the Holocaust focuses attention on technology and its role in distancing the perpetrator from the victim.[30] But distance does not explain why large groups of human beings chose to kill other large groups of human beings. The indifference and banality of technology form only one piece of the explanation. The other piece is a collective group psychological phenomenon, a psychotic dimension, and the elevation of the psychotic to "rational" levels of state and public health policy.

In her diary of Westerbork, the concentration camp for Dutch Jews destined for Auschwitz, Etty Hillesum describes the absence of pity for the suffering body: "Oafish, jeering faces in which one seeks in vain for even the slightest trace of human warmth . . . the disparity between the guards and the guarded is too absurd."[31] The scenes of dislocation and physical and psychological pain testify to the victimizers' ability to make invisible the other's degradation. "You should see these poor mothers sitting beside the cots of their wailing young in blank and brute despair, . . . abandoned children whose parents have been sent on transport, and who are ignored by other mothers."[32] Chaim Kaplan writes of crowds of desperate children everywhere in the streets of Warsaw: "Mothers take up positions on the sidewalks with their children's cradles, and they lean against the sides of buildings all along the street."[33] Children sing for bread, a cigarette, some money; it is music "permeated with Jewish sorrow and grief." Kaplan grimly concludes: "There is no barbarism of which the conquerors are incapable."[34]

An elderly survivor of Auschwitz-Birkenau, a retired physician, stepped out of his car with me onto the site of the death camp. Only survivors are allowed to drive onto the grounds of Auschwitz-Birkenau. The light breeze through the trees and the heavy summer sun seemed incongruous with the blown-up gas chambers and crematoria, a huge disinfection building, a field and pond layered with human ashes, empty barracks still standing, row after row, and chimneys, scores of them, rising from the weed-strewn ground. "Whenever we saw the sky, we never saw blue. Whenever we looked at the ground, what we could see was mud, pools of dirt, up to our knees, all the time. For us the camp was always muddy and full of filth: no trees, nothing green. Even if a plant were there, we did not see it. Nothing but the color of the living dead, hemmed in by mud, barbed wire, black smoke everywhere—in the sky, on top of us, in our clothes, our nostrils. And that smell, the odor of burning flesh. And the guard towers, behemoths in the sky."

"It's beautiful today, not a cloud in that sky. But even if we had such days, which I do not remember, all I could see was mud, grayness, stretching out to whatever horizon met my eyes. Living in Birkenau was like living in a hell, always dark. No sun, no warmth, just the ice-cold knowledge of death."

THE INVISIBLE VICTIM AND THE *KULTUR*-GROUP

The term *invisible* does not mean that the body is not there; rather, the body's suffering is not noticed as suffering. The *Kultur*-group, defining the group through the common set of shared scientific and popular beliefs, demonstrates a striking lack of empathic connection with suffering and pain in individuals identified as "life unworthy of life" or as genetically and hereditarily flawed or diseased. Invisibility refers to not seeing or noticing what would otherwise be seen or noticed as extreme suffering, deprivation, anguish, and pain.

What made the death camps possible was that those individuals who actively herded up Jews, as well as their neighbors who passively accepted the Final Solution, did not experience the suffering of the victims as being there, visible and present to consciousness. The victim ceased to be a sentient body registering real, viable emotions eliciting even the most rudimentary pity. Instead, the victim's body, and what the body's surfaces registered as pain, appeared as infectious disease, noxious matter requiring immediate disposal. The body was seen as a public health menace.

This is not to say that everyone in the culture saw the Jewish body as invisible or that there were not isolated cases of resistance to this understanding of Jewish flesh. No group is static; no group is so tightly constituted as to preclude individuals who resist the group consciousness or who simply are not affected by it. Yet, given the power of knowledge, particularly scientific knowledge, to define reality and perception, such instances were rare in the Third Reich. Isolated protests against the crimes of the regime—for example, the White Rose group in Munich—elicited little response from the surrounding civilian population. What was striking about Germany during the Nazi period was the power of the professions to set the ideological parameters of group consciousness and define the values that various groups— lawyers, judges, doctors, industrialists, scientists, chemists, engineers, and so on—internalized as self-evident truth.

In this sense the *Kultur*-group may be thought of as being constituted by the set of ideals represented by the professions and their practices. These ideals are absorbed into the knowledge inventory of the culture as the truth about self, race, heredity, and genetic health.

CONCEALMENT OF CRIME

It has been argued that the Nazis went to great efforts to conceal the death camps and the policy of mass murder because they knew such actions would be repudiated by the general population and would not be widely supported. Such an argument makes little sense, given the vast logistical enterprise mobilized by the Final Solution. The concealment argument is belied by the facts of participation: the reports of *Einsatzgruppen* commanders, whose death squads followed the German army into the Soviet Union; letters home from soldiers on the Eastern Front; the special equipment that required the cooperation of industrialists, engineers, chemists, and pharmaceutical and medical supply companies; the active involvement of the air force and navy in concentration camp medical experiments; the use of statisticians, land use specialists, economists, and public health officials in planning and carrying out the establishment of the ghettos; the deliberations of finance and health offices, railway and transport systems; the widespread involvement of physicians in the administration of the death camps and in "scientific" reports of medical experimentation presented at numerous conferences held throughout the Reich.

While the SS, for obvious reasons, never publicized the death camps, the disappearance of German Jews, the participation of professional sectors in the operation and construction of the camps themselves, the extensive use of slave labor from places such as Auschwitz to labor camps inside Germany, and the tens of thousands of individuals directly and indirectly contributing to the extermination process expose the argument of concealment as absurd.

The everyday cultural life of the Reich made clear to its citizens the ramifications of the Final Solution. "Up the chimney" was a common figure of speech in wartime Germany. The constant shipments of ownerless jewelry, clothes, and other goods from the death camps to the Reich could not be concealed. Bars of gold flowing out of Poland had an origin—Jewish artifacts and gold teeth melted down in Nazi smelting plants—and a meaning.

Note the following description by Rudolf Hoess, commandant of Auschwitz, of the fate of personal effects of murdered Jews:

> All of the left-over clothing and effects were sorted by a group of prisoners who worked all the time and were quartered in the effects camp. Once a month valuables were sent to the Reichsbank in Berlin. After they had been cleaned, items of clothing were sent to armaments firms for the east-

ern labour working there or to repatriates. Gold from the
teeth was melted down and likewise sent once a month to the
sanitation office of the Waffen–SS.[35]

Concealment never worked. In fact, it was never a serious policy
of the Third Reich; the SS spent relatively little resources on concealment. Families of medical and administrative officers stationed in
Poland could not help but know the functions of Auschwitz, Mai-
danek, Sobibor, and Treblinka. German manufacturers, officials, transport officers, Reich functionaries, and suppliers visiting Poland on
business could not avoid the facts of the breaking up of Jewish communities and the establishment of ghettos for the concentration of the
Jews. Concentration and slave labor camps inside Germany could
hardly be disguised.

Given, then, the enormous logistical demands and efforts to
exterminate millions of people within a relatively short period of
time, the argument of concealment, to suggest less than willing German collusion and knowledge of the Holocaust, makes no realistic
sense.

THE ROLE OF THE PARTY

Hitler and the party drove the political process. However, the belief
structures necessary to undertake the Final Solution had been initiated
before the National Socialist takeover of power. Most important, ancil-
lary power centers in the professions, rather than resist the Reich with
their prestige, knowledge, and professional codes, instead implemented
much of the psychological and physical groundwork for the techniques, technologies, and emotional energy of mass extermination.

Race hygiene arguments, while popular during the 1920s, came
to dominate the scientific, engineering, legal, and medical paradigms
of the Third Reich. The Nazis legitimated and pursued race theory
through the construction and maintenance of political, legal, administrative, and cultural institutions. The Nazi Party put race hygiene
theory into action, but the professions contributed the ideological
imperatives at the core of race hygiene theory.

Hitler's violent anti-Semitism gave to the scientists and biologists
a political legitimacy to undertake the measures necessary for cul-

tural purification. The perception of the Jew as a genetic threat to the nation's health, the role of the physician as doctor to the *Volk*, and the vast scope of sterilization and euthanasia imparted an action component to race hygiene theory. Hitler authorized race ideology in terms of state sanctions and legitimacy; the Nazi Party gave the *Kultur*-group a political, constitutional, and ethical context grounded in the authority of knowledge, history, and scientific practice.

INDIVIDUAL RESPONSIBILITY

The individuals constituting the rogues gallery of prominent Nazi Party and SS officials—Heinrich Himmler, Adolf Eichmann, Rudolf Franz Hoess, Franz Stangl, Otto Ohlendorf, and countless others—all bear enormous individual responsibility for vicious crimes. Further, the defense of following orders or doing one's job fails as exoneration of individual acts. Assenting to group perceptions seeing the Jew as blood threat, to practices supporting such culturewide perceptions, do not negate individual culpability in the actions of the Final Solution. Obviously, someone like Franz Stangl, commandant of Treblinka, assumed a degree of responsibility different from the worker on the Zyklon B production line.

Rudolf Hoess, hanged by the Poles in 1947; Eichmann, captured, tried, executed by the Israelis in 1961; Stangl, Himmler, Mengele, convicted of individual crimes against humanity—all pursued race hygiene ideology with a ferocity exceeding any known moral or historical limits.

The worker on the Zyklon B production line, the Reichsbahn administrator, the accountant in one of the ministries, the statistician figuring out land-use and resettlement ratios, the train engineer transporting Hungarian Jews from Budapest to Auschwitz—these individuals contributed to the genocide, too. But their participation brought no legal reprisal. No public trials examined any crimes of complicity in sectors of the population not directly connected with the Nazi Party, the SS, the state apparatus, or the direct administration of the death camps and slave labor camps.

It is naive to suggest only a few thousand individuals were responsible for the deaths of millions.

Moral culpability and legal responsibility are two entirely different issues. Should the Zyklon B worker have been tried for war crimes? Should such a person have been placed before the judges at Nuremberg? Relative degrees of individual culpability can be assessed; and responsibility, moral and legal, can and should be assigned for individual acts of complicity. Many sectors of German professional and cultural life were caught up in a group dynamic obliterating historical distinctions between right and wrong.

Such issues touch on questions of moral responsibility, the obligation of civil disobedience, and the extent to which knowledge of a crime and acts supporting that crime place perpetrators, of all degrees of participation, within the reach of legal responsibility. Even trials conducted subsequent to Nuremberg (for example, the so-called Auschwitz trials of the early 1960s) did not extend their reach far enough.

Many have argued the scope of Nuremberg was too narrow; that the trials held too strict a view of who should be considered a participant in the machinery of death. To determine what level of participation was sufficient for punishment, the Allies drew specific legal distinctions, many for the sake of expedience in prosecution. However, it has been remarked enough, and rightly so, that many who should have been punished were not. Ordinary citizens—professionals, laborers, shopkeepers, nurses—who actively contributed to the regime and the ends of its theories found their way back into the professional networks of postwar Germany. Many who deserved severe punishment, given the magnitude of the crimes of the Third Reich, escaped for legal, political, and geopolitical considerations that have been well documented.

Understanding the forces driving the Final Solution through a group psychological approach does not preclude individual responsibility. It is therefore critical to insist that individuals be held responsible for crimes that run counter to all principles, ethics, and morals of human decency, and that such individuals be judged and punished accordingly.

KILLING OUTSIDE THE CULTURE GROUP

People all over Europe murdered Jews for a variety of reasons. Many individuals in Vichy France, Greece, Holland, Hungary, Rumania, Yugoslavia, Lithuania, and elsewhere cooperated with the Germans in the rounding-up and killing of Jewish populations. Anti-Semitism in collaborationist regimes allowed a broad range of fascist movements to implement racist agendas that had existed for centuries. Hatred of the Jew had not been invented by the Nazis. What was new was the pursuit of mass murder legitimized as normal politics through the active collaboration of professionals, bureaucrats, and contractors. Paramilitary fascist and racist police groups, townspeople in cities and countryside, and anti-Semitic partisan groups indiscriminately killed Jews throughout the areas under occupation. The Germans gave them the excuse and, more often than not, provided them the logistical means.

While historic anti-Semitism throughout Europe might have found a means of expression in the Nazi occupation, the focus of this book is the German *Kultur*-group, its perceptions and acts that in Germany and Poland led to the mass murder of Jews, gypsies, and countless others deemed unworthy to live. It is not inconsistent to have multiple motives for killing Jews running alongside the public health and sanitation rationale behind the German intent.

A *Kultur*-group *Geist* resting on theories of biology and public health was widely supported in Germany. Because Jews were killed by the Vichy French, Hungarians, Italians, Rumanians, Slavs, and others for reasons ranging from voluntary cooperation to sheer dislike and opportunism, does not diminish the more general group psychological dynamic as it applies to German science and the role of German medicine in legitimizing Nazi aims.

The image of the Jew as carrier of pestilence appeared in anti-Semitic diatribes outside of Germany. Paul de Lagarde, a notorious French anti-Semite who wrote in the late nineteenth century, equated Jews with bacilli needing to be expelled from the nation.[36] In 1904, Anatole Leroy-Beaulieu observed: "To one and all, Slav, Latin, German, and Magyar, the Jew, that odious parasite, was the deadly microbe, the infectious bacteria, that poisoned the blood of modern states and societies."[37] Paolo Montegazza, an Italian physiologist, in an 1893 essay reviewing the conditions of European anti-Semitism, deplored how the Jews were seen as intruders on "our European body, no sinews of our flesh, no veins filled with our blood, but knotty excrescences, tumours which afflict the body all over, impeding the free circulation of our vital humours. They are called, in one word, the swollen and strutting (*die feisten und dreisten*) parasites of European life."[38]

The imagery of the Jew outside of Germany in some instances conformed to the German *Kultur*-group stereotypes; those of other victim groups did not. Whatever the impulse that led to the acceptance and encouragement of mass murder, the results were identical. When Miron Cristea, Patriarch of the Rumanian Orthodox Church, proclaimed, "One has to be sorry for the poor Romanian people, whose very marrow is sucked out by the Jews," and that "defending ourselves is a national and patriotic duty," the concept of defense itself sanctions mass killing.[39]

No single nation, tribe, or group has a monopoly on mass murder as a form of political policy. What occurred in Nazi Germany possessed certain properties that distinguished the public policy of mass death from the more diffuse and episodic hate that propelled earlier anti-Semitism, and that in many instances characterized the violence of fascist groups toward Jews in the occupied territories. To kill because of sadistic pleasure in getting even with a hated scapegoat; to kill because of a desire for a neighbor's goods; to kill because of the stereotypes and myths—all these impulses found release in occupied Europe. But the Germans took the death encounter between anti-Semite and Jew to another historical level: They removed the victim from the human community, reduced the body to the status of poisoned, diseased matter, industrialized the process of death, and transformed living beings into public refuse that required imminent sanitizing. Ghettoization was central to this process.

Perhaps the only dubious relief that came with being confined to the ghetto, according to a physician who survived the Lodz Ghetto, was in keeping the Germans out. All Germans—whether physicians, industrialists, accountants, train engineers, or SS—came to be associated in Jewish minds with uncertainty, suffering, transport, deportation, and "selection."

> Our degradation, those of us in the ghetto from the very beginning, was gradual over time. The situation progressively became more desperate; we went through stages of disintegration. We tried to adjust to starvation diets, radical changes in circumstance, sudden impoverishment, and primitive sur-

vival conditions. Our minds and bodies had sufficient time to adapt; everything of course was unexpected, but not nearly as abrupt as it was for assimilated Jews resettled in the Lodz Ghetto. Removed from what had been relatively normal lives, these Jews found themselves immediately treated as subhumans and slaves. Their minds and bodies fell apart within six months. Resources ran out; they lost contact with reality. They got sick. Most of them died.

Imagine coming to Lodz and expecting a nice work camp, with little wooden houses and comfortable workshops. The German and Austrian Jews had no idea what was coming. It was an understandable naiveté. Before leaving, the Germans assured them their social benefits would continue, living quarters would be clean and comfortable, work would match skills, medical care would be available. But the first encounter with the ghetto must have been demoralizing. People were thrown into despair.

German policy, and much of the cause of illness, could be summed up as degradation through hunger. Doctors received a few more [food] coupons. You see, Lodz was a giant slave labor camp; Biebow [commandant of the ghetto] made millions from our labor. Corruption amongst Germans and Jews became a matter of daily life. For example, I believe the motive behind killing children, the old and sick, lay in the Germans' wish to remove from the ghetto anyone not capable of working. What better way to do it than to offer the deal: your children for your adults. In the world of the ghetto, which truly was insane, to many that exchange seemed reasonable, particularly for those who had no children under ten or whose teenage kids worked. Fewer mouths to feed, less unproductive life to support. It was crude, cold—but ghetto life produced its own set of rules. Some children during the *aktion* tried to escape by hiding in privies, literally holes in the ground behind buildings. But someone—the Jewish police, the Germans— always found them. This effort to avoid selection, by those small enough to fit into these reeking holes, was well known. There could be no "right way," no "good road" to escape selections: all that mattered in the ghetto was survival.

Why couldn't the ghetto organize more resistance? Why no support for those who wanted to fight? Simply too much corruption. Life itself was the pursuit of corruption, and survival makes you do anything. Hunger fragments community, no matter how cohesive. In the face of incessant hunger, physical debilitation, illness, human weakness, and despair it was impossible to organize anything except labor brigades, soup kitchens, and orphanages. People lacked energy or will for political resistance. Broken in body and spirit, families stealing bread from each other, everyone retreated in their own grim shell. It was regarded as a miracle to be alive in the morning. You walk out of your apartment, which you share with five or six families, and literally climb over bodies dying the previous night. People collapsed in the street. They would do anything to stay alive—steal food from their own children, parents, sisters, brothers, cousins. The stench of sewage and filth in the street, stinking, lice-ridden bodies, begging, starving ghosts, wandering to nowhere, falling in doorways, gutters: what we had to live through and the shame of it, you cannot imagine. It stays inside me, the nightmares. I will live with them till the day I die.

THE INDIFFERENCE
THESIS AND
SCIENCE AS POWER

In its effort to diminish the role of ideology, indifference research focuses on the party, on public opinion, on the lack of overt expression of anti-Semitism in Germany, on party membership and its exclusivity, and on the primacy of the SS in the organization and administration of the death camps.[1] But perhaps these are not necessarily the only indices for understanding the Holocaust. Ideology can be absorbed into social value, into cultural percepts governing the sense of the group body, its integrity, and its boundaries, the demarcation lines between clean and dirty, pure and impure. In this respect, a more fitting index for understanding lies in the fact that only Jews and gypsies were singled out from all over Europe to be transported to death camps. Only Jewish and gypsy children were singled out to be destroyed so as to prevent retribution from future generations.

Millions, including Russians, gypsies, and Poles, died as a consequence of Nazi barbarism. It is essential not to understate the suffering experienced by many groups at the hands of Germans and their collaborators during World War II. But it was only Jews who in the racist policies of the Third Reich were designated to be wiped from the face of the earth—every last man, woman, child, and infant. While the German armies were razing the Warsaw Ghetto, a few kilometers away Polish citizens led relatively normal lives, patronizing cafes, shopping, riding streetcars. Diarists of the Lodz Ghetto

record Jewish children, with tears in their eyes, watching Polish children on the other side of the wire fences playing and laughing. As
early as 1938, a judge in the Nazi administrative hierarchy remarked,
"The Jew is not a human being. He is a symptom of putrefaction."[2]

It is necessary, then, to ask: What forged this state of mind? Why
only Jews down to the last one? Why the enormous use of resources
to eliminate Jewish flesh? This insistence on Jewish extermination
went far beyond indifference. An entire culture experienced the Jewish other as so poisonous that concrete actions to exterminate the carriers of this disease found expression through the actions and
practices of the major professions throughout the culture. Rather
than moral indifference motivating action, one finds considerable
moral *enthusiasm*, a commitment to an epistemology obsessively,
phobically preoccupied with the status of blood and its purity. A political, ideological, medical, and logistical process that produces remem-
brances like the following begs for more in the way of explanation
than the theoretically opaque terminology of indifference.

> With brutal frankness he [the block elder] told us what it was
> like there. "This is a K.L.," he said. "Remember those two ini-
> tials, K.L. . . . Konzentrationslager. This is a death camp, a
> Vernichtungslager. You've been brought here to be destroyed
> by hunger, beating, hard labor, and sickness. You'll be eaten
> by lice, you'll rot in your own shit. . . . [F]orget who and what
> you were . . . Everyone here is the same. . . . All are going to
> die."[3]

ON MAKING THE BODY DISPENSABLE

What makes a human being so dispensable that actions can be undertaken against the self, stripping it not only of all dignity but of its very
corporeality, its embodied being? Moving oneself psychically away
from the field between one and the other, deadening the space
between one's own consensual understandings and the other's physical presence are operations we commonly undertake with people we
don't like, who make us terribly uncomfortable, even occasionally
with our children and associates whom we do not, depending on the

moment, want to recognize or acknowledge. It is a relatively complex psychological process to make the other not there; to make the other's embodied self invisible through various methods of dissociation and distancing.

This kind of operation on the other's self is violent, not only on cognition and consciousness but on emotion and body. It is particularly violent on the body because the unacknowledged body ceases to possess human qualities and therefore exists outside any moral universe of care. The body possesses no meaning; it is perceptually transformed into waste; it may be broken up into parts for "scientific" experimentation.

Now, this process of denying body or corporeality is a powerful *political* theme. To make the other into meaningless waste—to so radically distanciate body—makes it possible to kill the other's body and to dispose of what that body contains as filth. Extermination is the public or political plane of the tragedy of destroying an empathic relation to the body's humanness.

The dehumanization of the Jew during the Holocaust reduced the body to the status of poisoned matter, making annihilation a matter of sanitation. The Jews found themselves situated in the same category as industrial waste.[4] Accorded not the place of victim, but of refuse or parasite, the Jewish body, purged through the technologies of gas and fire, lacked any moral or empathic context for the German killers.

Ghettos established by the Germans in Poland for concentrating resettled Jews were seen as places for isolating vermin. Chaim Kaplan writes in his extraordinary diary: "The genius of Nazism is in hatred of the Jews, a hatred as deep as the abyss." Germans and Poles refer to Jews as "excrement . . . filth . . . epidemic-causing bacilli."[5] Kaplan confesses his own helplessness at this madness: "I haven't the strength to hold a pen in my hand. I'm broken, shattered. My thoughts are jumbled. I don't know where to start or stop. I have seen Jewish Warsaw through forty years of events, but never before has she worn such a face. A whole community of 400,000 people condemned to exile" and finally death.[6] George Kren and Leon Rappoport note that the ideological reason behind constructing death camps outside Germany proper lay in the fear of contaminating German soil with "inferior" blood.[7] Sobibor, Treblinka, Belzec, Chelmno, Auschwitz, all these places were in Poland, although it was also the case that hundreds of thousands of Jews died from disease, starvation, brutality, murder, and medical experimentation in the concentraton and labor camps established inside Germany.

The diaries of Hans Frank, the governor-general of occupied Poland, reveal the peculiar German penchant for de-realizing the Jewish body.[8] Random samplings from the entries illustrate how the mass murder of Jews was carried out with the mundanity of other petty details of his everyday life.

A typical administrative meeting might include discussions of the increasing crime rate in Lublin, the planned liquidation of Jewish ghettos in the General Government, the obligation of German administrative employees to belong to SA units, the relocation of German citizens to areas formerly occupied by Poles and Jews, and the pleasures Frank had in playing the piano.

On May 3, 1942, Frank traveled to Lublin. His diary records he toured the city and the ghetto, visited a park, received a phone call confirming a transport of Jews, attended a meeting about liquidating the Lublin ghetto, listened to music, and met with a group of local chess players.

On another occasion, he addressed the issues of partisan activity, the liquidation of the Jews, the relocation of Poles to Germany, food rations in the Warsaw district, and the extermination of the Warsaw ghetto to prevent food speculation and the spread of typhus. Throughout the diaries he mixed descriptions of these conversations with his reflections on culture, music, and the piano.

On June 18, 1942, Frank discussed the liquidation of the Radom Jews because of insufficient housing and rampant disease in the Kraków Ghetto. But transporting Radom Jews to Kraków would cause serious "overcrowding," he noted, as if twenty to thirty thousand people in an area scarcely thirty city blocks was not already overcrowded. Extensive discussion of possible death camp destinations took place. It was the general consensus of those present that liquidation would prevent a housing shortage. At a meeting three or four days later, the use of thirty to forty thousand Jews as slave laborers was discussed.

Frank's attitude reflected a general state of mind throughout the entire German administration. It is not a dissociation or de-realization of Jews peculiar to Frank himself. A contemporary photograph of Hans Biebow, the commandant of the Lodz Ghetto, shows a handsome young SS officer lounging in a sumptuous armchair beside a table full of oysters, clams, canapes, lobster, and sausages. Biebow gorges himself on oysters and kielbasa, while daily hundreds of Jews die in the ghetto workshops.

TECHNOLOGY AND INVISIBILITY

The Third Reich's use of technology allowed the perpetrator to kill without acknowledging the victim as a person. Killing in gas chambers and crematoria created a vast gulf between killer and victim. In technologizing death, the perpetrator shifts to another level of connection with the victim, one of organization, techniques, the victim important only insofar as he or she presents a problem in organizing death. Not important as a living, sentient being, the victim's relevance to the killer is logistical: how to dispose of the body in the most efficient way possible.

The Jew becomes dehumanized, an object without distinction, and the whole community of Jews is pushed out of prevailing normative-moral discourse. Moral language no longer applies to this object. Broken down to statistics, these humans lose their moral referents, becoming objects requiring disposal. This sense of dehumanization appears in a remark scribbled on the pages of an anonymous diary found in Auschwitz: "We're not human beings anymore, nor have we become animals; we are just some strange psycho-physical product 'made in Germany.'"[9]

It is a peculiarly modern phenomenon, this ability to reduce the individual to the non-being of an object and to completely cancel out moral discourse. How can one possibly engage in moral discourse with an object? One relates to objects as entities in a bureaucratic process, the Jew relevant only insofar as the Jewish body submitted to the imperative of organizational functioning, which was to kill. If the Jew resisted these efforts, that resistance held significance only as recalcitrance constituted a technical problem to be overcome. Bureaucratic rationality was employed to neutralize human will and transform it into the deadness of object-existence.

Concern for the Jew as object takes on purely technical properties. A dehumanized object lacks a moral context. The object elicits utterly no empathy from the surrounding culture and becomes significant only as a presence requiring efficient bureaucratic action. Biological science guided bureaucratic rationale and explanation, and any religious or cultural disgust for violence proved ineffective in preventing the Final Solution.

That technical efficiency supplanted moral responsibility rests upon the assumption that the victim did not matter to the participant because the victim's body was part of the larger technical calculus of elimination and disposal. Therefore, for example, the worker who produced Zyklon B gas never had to worry about its use. Consciousness distances itself from other parts of what the system undertakes. The self literally wills blindness, and therefore becomes indifferent to the fate of work's object. Yet the worker in the gas factory also participates in other cultural and psychological narratives that enthusiastically support the reduction of the Jewish body to polluted waste.

The worker knows the destiny of the gas. It is essential in his view, as soon as possible, to rid the larger community of the pestilence threatening it. While indifference may be part of his actions, to the extent that he knows the consequences of his role his actions equally involve a belief in the popular and scientific notions that the preservation of the social body from disintegration would be better served by an elimination of the Jewish body. Complicity may be both a matter of indifference and a willed belief in the *Kultur*-group's theories.

The killing drew in countless numbers of individual Germans with graphic direct knowledge of the consequences of Germany's activities during the Holocaust. Leon Poliakov remembers:

> The SS formations stationed in the camps; the German workers, the cadres, the heads of the numerous yards and plants in which they rubbed shoulders daily with the Jewish slaves who worked there; the railroad men who, from one end of Germany to the other, serviced the innumerable shipments of deportees in trains which they saw return empty or loaded up with underwear and used clothing for distribution to the needy by all the welfare agencies in the country—these represent a very incomplete listing of the people who can truthfully be designated as eyewitnesses.[10]

The work of the professions, industries, and crafts of Nazi Germany reflected not blindness but a wide-ranging enthusiasm, despite the half-hearted efforts of the SS to keep the activities of the death camps secret. It bears repeating that considerable participation, from a variety of professional and industrial sectors, was required in the construction, maintenance, and supply of the camps. Keeping these activities secret was impossible, particularly in view of the use of slave labor and the hundreds of slave labor camps within the Reich itself. Ordinary citizens could see the skeletal figures of laborers dressed in ragged, shredded clothing. It would have been natural to ask where such people came from and who they were. To kill so many people in such a short period of time would be impossible without the zealous participation of physicians, lawyers, accountants, builders, and engineers, from the earliest days of the regime to the last.

Berel Lang sees the peculiar status of the Jew as consistent with the German army term *Kadavergehorsam,* or "cadaver obedience," a gruesomely accurate description of what was expected of the Jews.[11] Jews lacked the moral and legal rights assigned to human beings. Without even the status of animal, prisoner, or victim, they were expected to cooperate with the readiness of dead bodies.

The Germans invented a new language to describe actions taken on Jewish bodies.[12] For example, the tattooing of numbers removed the real victim from the *Kultur*-group's perception of the victim; annihilating a number is an entirely different operation from annihilating a person. Lang notes that for those who died, statisticians or public health authorities in charge of recordkeeping frequently would use not the word *corpse,* but *figures* or *pieces* (*Figuren*). "[T]he number itself would commonly serve as a means of direct address or reference." Political purpose defined and rationalized language and "subordinate[d] it to authority."[13] The bureaucrats and professionals who organized the mass killings did not live by conventional Judeo-Christian moral standards. They lived by a different kind of morality, involving the German biomedical vision that justified killing in the interests of preserving the blood and genetic integrity of the *Volk.* In the words of Rudolph Hoess, commandant of Auschwitz: "National Socialism is nothing but applied biology."[14]

This ideological/psychological construction, deriving from the obsession with racial hygiene, lay behind the Nazis' political vision of

purifying the nation through the Holocaust. This is a psychotic interpretation of reality taking hold of the imagination of an entire society.
In individual psychosis the self may generate hate-defined constructs
and project inviolable interpretations of reality; consciousness creates
bizarre realities that represent complete breaks with consensual reality.
In the case of the *Kultur*-group's attitudes toward and responses to the
Jews, a similar process occurred at the group level.

Indifference leads to a lack of respect for historical canons of
moral value. It does not, however, lead to indifference to *morality*, in
this case the self's attitude toward the nation. The venue of morality
for the group shifts from a historical, traditional context to a set of
images embracing a new construction of reality. The new morality is
far removed from its traditional foundations, resting instead on *technical* responsibility. But technical responsibility in the Third Reich also
went hand in hand with a newly constructed moral vision supported
by the scientific community, specifically medicine, and its power over
the social construction of value, meaning, and perception. Jewish and
gypsy victims generated a group-based fear of pollution; their elimination became something more than a technical act of disposal. It
developed as an enthusiastic effort to protect the group's cultural,
physical, and psychological boundaries from disintegration. Further,
the murdering of bodies was impelled by the delusions of science
and the efforts of scientific administrators and the professions to
defend the group's boundaries. It was essential therefore to destroy
the other before the other's presence eroded the group's sense of its
own integrity.

KILLING AND THE
FRAMEWORKS OF SCIENTIFIC BELIEF

German science created a very special type of conscience that
enabled killing to proceed without significant resistance from any of
the ordinary German men and women who participated in the project in various capacities. If killing were a matter of sanitation, why
worry about the fate of those persons German biology designated as
"life unworthy of life?" Why show any moral concern over the suffering of individual bodies and what the surfaces of these bodies
showed? Infected matter required disposal. In his notorious Nazi

phase, Konrad Lorenz described the link between race phobia and biological science: "There is a certain similarity between the measures which need to be taken when we draw a broad biological analogy between bodies and malignant tumors ... and a nation and individuals within it who have become asocial because of their defective constitution."[15]

It is much easier to dispose of polluted matter than live, sentient individuals. But if the bodies have no human existence, no capacity to provoke hate or pity, then the killing of this matter becomes that much easier. To kill is not murder to the perpetrator, but a technical problem in the fulfillment of a public health policy. What is frightening is that ordinary people willingly engaged in such acts of distanciation and disposal. It is this facility in killing, the analogy Lorenz draws between the public health physician and the surgeon removing gangrenous material, that German science so conveniently supported.[16] More specifically, biomedical science defining the Jew as vermin gave scientific plausibility to the phobia against any kind of contact with Jewish flesh.

As early as 1922, political parties encouraged the teaching of eugenics. Racial hygiene and eugenics united in a national and professional discourse that defined values, perceptions, and the approach to racial characteristics. German universities were filled with lectures, studies, and research regarding race and the fear that certain races would pollute and destroy the Aryan strain. The dialogue preoccupied practitioners in law and administration, as well as professionals in anatomy, anthropology, psychiatry, public health, human heredity, genetics, engineering, and family research. Race provided the focal point of concern for the professions in the decade preceding the National Socialist victory over Weimar Germany.

It was not by chance this fear of infection and disintegration came to be linked to the Jewish presence. German officials seemed obsessed with rebuilding a genetically fit race decimated by losses in World War I. Many officials, administrators, and scientists in the postwar government feared the genetic effects of chronic disease, mental disorders, and sexual decadence. Adherents of the new science of genetics stretched across the German professions, state administrations, and bureaucracies. A belief common to all administrative strata saw the biological integrity of the race under siege; corrective action was required. There appeared to be widespread support for the teaching of eugenic values and practices as healthy responses to the historical facts of social disorder and wartime defeat. The Imperial Health Office issued pamphlets speaking of progressive social degeneracy, the deleterious effects of genetic corruption, and the polluting of healthy individual bodies and minds. Administrative, scientific, and medical opinion seemed to be in general agreement with the desirability of eugenic cures.

Nazi racial theories did not just drop out of the sky; nor were they the effect of crazed racial ideologues. Hugh Gregory Gallagher writes: "It has been said that the madness of Adolf Hitler produced Nazi Germany, but it is as true, surely, to say that it was the madness of the Germany of the twenties and thirties which found its expression in Hitler."[17] The identification of ethnic groups as racially impure had been growing as part of the culture's national and historical consciousness. By 1925 the dialogue of eugenics and racial theory joined both private and public discourse. Medical alarm at genetic disease found a responsive audience in political parties controlling parliamentary assemblies. Increasingly the political dialogue defined itself through the language and values of eugenics.

It should be emphasized that certain variations of eugenic theory espoused by Weimar democrats and socialists in the 1920s disavowed radical measures, such as euthanasia or sterilization, and focused primarily on research to understand the effect of heredity in making social conditions more receptive to healthier living. The political ideals of Weimar called for a eugenics that could regulate the population and make it more receptive to cleaner lifestyles.[18] Improvements in public health measures, less crowded living conditions, regular exercise programs, and sexual moderation were ingredients of this so-called positive eugenics. By the early 1930s, however, the eugenics that emphasized collective health gave way to a eugenics focusing on the dangers of racial and blood pollution.[19]

Given the inherent exclusivity of eugenic theory and its underlying racism, the shift from social welfare measures to fears about genetic pollution did not provoke much of an outcry, apart from a few socialist and liberal democratic scientists whose voices were quickly silenced. Negative eugenics took on the task of figuring out the approach to administering and implementing racial exclusion.

Theories of identifying and containing the racially impure were the subject matter of racial hygiene lectures through the 1930s. By the early 1940s it took little psychological effort for public health administrators to shift from focusing on cleaning up ghetto environments to cleaning them out.

The majority of the attendees at the Wannsee conference, at which the strategy of the Final Solution was explained, had advanced degrees. Decision makers were not composed of rabid SS officers clamoring for the destruction of the Jews, but officials of the party and government convened by Reinhard Heydrich, head of Reich Security (RSHA) and Chief of the Security Police (SD). State Agencies were represented by deputies and State Secretaries administering occupied territories in the East and the General Government; bureaucrats from the Justice and Interior ministries, the Reich Chancellery, and the Foreign Office; and officials of the Gestapo also attended.[20]

Science had established its dominance over the belief structure of Nazi Germany. Race lay at the center of this scientific edifice; and racial hatred elaborated itself as a set of scientific principles obsessed with blood cleanliness, genetic purity, and a phobic reactivity to the potential of race contamination. These beliefs exercised an enormous influence over scientific, professional, political, and administrative practices.

EARLY COLLABORATION

As early as the 1920s, municipalities set up extensively administered programs in support of racial hygiene. Between 1921 and 1925, eugenically trained doctors and social workers rapidly advanced in the social services.[21] Enthusiastic support was given to groups such as the Reich League for Child Rich Families, which, in the late 1920s, called for measures to regain the health of the *Volk*. By the time of Hitler's ascent to power, the socialist-democratic approach to public health had largely lost influence in German society as a significant scientific and public discourse.

The Prussian Cripples Welfare Law of 1920, arguing that physical abnormalities were signs of genetic illness, became, later in the decade, symptomatic of the more narrowly construed focus on race preoccupying the scientific community and popular culture. By the

1930s, the study of eugenics had come to include hereditary data banks, criminal biological surveys, "psycho-biograms," the analysis of defective genetic traits, latent pathogenic gene analysis, Mendelian ratio configurations, campaigns against "cripples," the Pan-German League, the German Emergency League Against the Black Curse (which agitated against the children, the so-called Rhineland bastards, born in the aftermath of World War I of occupation soldiers of African descent and German women), calls for the voluntary sterilization of the hereditary sick, laws requiring registration of psychological "defectives," and some eugenicists calling for the destruction of "incurable idiots."[22] Aggravated by the bitterness of Versailles, these movements and attitudes contributed to a group state of mind making the society extremely nervous about anything that might be called eugenic deviance.

Pockets of society, notably socialist Jewish doctors in Berlin, argued against the ramifications of this cultural obsession with eugenics. By 1936, however, most of these voices had been silenced. The major professions and governing institutions, standing on values of the culture, demonstrated widespread sympathy for legal measures to enforce racial exclusion.

Medical killing of the racially defective was proposed by some physicians and lawyers as early as the 1920s. The lawyer Rudolf Binding and the psychiatrist Alfred Hoche, widely read and quoted by proponents of negative eugenics, argued that euthanasia defined a national duty, that society incurred an obligation to do away with valueless lives, and that physicians should be required to sacrifice useless life to preserve the integrity of the racially healthy.[23] The genetically deformed, constituting a biological embarrassment and a danger to future generations, were a burden on the nation and its productive machinery. According to Paul Weindling, many in the medical profession agreed "the unfit were a morally unjust burden on the fit, and that the state might kill 'valueless life' that had degenerated to the level of a plant or animal."[24]

Eugenic discourse demonstrated through legal and medical measures the power of biologistic opinions arguing for racial hegemony. The socialist welfare concerns of the early 1920s gave way to the rightwing political agenda, and the professional and social ideologies growing out of the eugenics movement embraced an exclusionary and vicious assault on sick bodies, disabled limbs, and individual lifestyles that ran counter to *Volk*ish ideals.

Even in the intellectual and liberal brilliance of the Weimar period, racial nationalism flourished in the form of the German League for National Regeneration and Heredity, which called for the protection of German genes. In 1926, the Dresden Hygiene Museum established a national reputation with exhibits centered on racial heroes and archetypes. It inspired the creation of a National Hygiene Exhibition, the Gesolei, in the summer of 1926, which over the next few years attracted seven and a half million visitors. In the 1920s a *Volksmuseum* under the name of "Man" traveled the country. Its exhibits emphasized the dangers involved in defective embryology, hereditary deviancy, subnormal racial types, and homosexuality as a form of criminal behavior.

The practice of biological science during this period was distinguished by its absorption in politics. Professional practice and political power came to share mutual assumptions about race and eugenics. Biological laws of development, natural selection, and inheritance were used to guide legislation, social and economic programs, and psychological assumptions regarding health and illness. This eugenics obsession through the entire political spectrum—left to right—during the 1920s, and its increasing stridency and repudiation of the socialist concern for living conditions and environment laid the foundation for a delusional epistemology of race. Science projected resolutions of racial contradictions, including the violent elimination of selected groups as a public health policy.

With the ascendence of National Socialism in the early 1930s, racist sentiment advanced to the forefront in the professions, particularly medicine and law. The concepts of racial hygiene already had been planted in the public mind. Groups seen to be impure found themselves encircled in a medical language filled with images of pollution and infection. With the victory of the National Socialist Party in 1933, solving the problem of eugenic imperfections by eliminating the sources of racial pollution came to be seen as a form of scientific truth.

From this perspective, the Final Solution embodies a delusional projection of a concept that by the late 1930s had taken on the status of normal science: the administrative and scientific delusion that Jews were useless biological matter. That belief, no matter how much a part of the normal scientific discourse of the times, is psychotic. This version of the normal is consistent with the violent and apocalyptic fantasies of paranoid schizophrenics.

This psychotic version of normality, filled with the assumptions, values, and most importantly images of a twisted eugenics, became the norm for a whole range of professional practices dedicated to mass murder. The most prestigious scientific institute in Germany, the Kaiser Wilhelm Institute for Anthropology, Human Genetics, and Eugenics, the German Research Council, and their extensive biomedical and eugenics research programs, had no qualms about the killing of so-called inferior and polluted races. Under the Nazis, the SS spearheaded what had been developing as a cultural and national consensus: saving racial purity by eliminating infected racial matter. Scientific institutes in the 1930s guarded the *Volk* against poverty, decadent morality, feminist sexual mores, and tainted blood and genes. Such respected scientists as Eügen Fischer and Otmar von Verschuer participated in this convergence of biology and politics.

STERILIZATION: THE FIRST PILLAR
OF A PSYCHOTIC SCIENCE

During the period 1929–33, with the Great Depression decimating German economic and social life, the medical profession seriously regarded the arguments for sterilizing the socially and culturally "unproductive." It was not a fringe position but a state of mind that dominated research agendas and funding of major biological and eugenics institutes. Public attention and popular culture, in addition to state treasuries, focused on the positive benefit of sterilization and on the socially functional consequences of euthanasia. It was a period of policy preparation, public planning, and psychological attunement to the normalcy of taking life "already crippled."

The economic depression of 1929 initiated intense interest in racial genealogy and negative eugenics. A number of racial biologists established societies for the analysis of blood purity. Scientific laboratories tracked down genetic data processed by an extensive use of early IBM computers. These studies tracked a number of racial categorizations, from blood type to ancestry and heredity. Efforts were made in some research projects to establish biochemical indices of race, with extensive cross-sectional surveys of blood types. Anthropologists performed analyses of blood purity. A national blood survey was taken of more than eight hundred districts in Germany and Austria, with blood drawn from five hundred children in each research domain.

In 1928 a journal for racial physiology was established by prominent German scientists. In the early 1930s, Himmler enlisted a staff of biological and medical professionals whose efforts to synthesize Nordic romanticism, agricultural economics, and Mendelian hereditary biology culminated in a proposal for a national program of race resettlement. Numerous policy papers were issued on the advantages of resettlement. The intellectual corpus deriving from this research and cross-professional and political collaboration provided the ideological core of a world view that throughout the 1930s absorbed and defined professional practice.

While Hitler's rabid anti-Semitism certainly contributed to intolerant racist actions, equally important was the professional sector's embracing the values and perceptions of racial science. This included large segments of the engineering profession.[25] Nazi health and social policies responded to the stress of urban and industrial growth with an increasingly conservative professional ethos and a scientific technocracy closely attached to political bureaucracies and administrators.

While the racial hygiene arguments of the 1920s were adapted to Nazism, their message of exclusion and destruction remained central to the research agenda of mainstream German science. The connection between a negative hygiene movement and engineers, administrators, physicians, lawyers, and scientists became increasingly significant in constructing a cultural consensus on eliminating abject elements of definable racial types. Racial values were at the heart of German education in the 1930s. The public health profession had a sound basis in negative eugenics. It was therefore relatively easy, from a moral point of view, to expel Jewish influences from medicine, the universities, and the professions. What was being excluded were not persons but infectious dangers to the *Kultur*-group's physical integrity.

The racial hygiene research of the 1920s sprang to action in the 1930s. Research protocols no longer only explained hereditary differences and racial subtypes, but now directed public policy on how to screen for the racial quality of given populations and rid the society of subnormal racial categories. The 1933 Law to Prevent Hereditarily Sick Offspring (the "Sterilization Law") aided this screening through sterilization and other exclusionary measures. The law sanctioned the assault on "inferior" blood and genes by professional practices without acknowledging it as a gross violation of the human body. Instead, it was seen as a moral action necessary to preserve the cultural body's racial purity.

What might be understood as insane from a historical and moral perspective became truth under the aegis of professional authority. What mattered was not fidelity to historical ethics, but a political exigency that subtly transformed perceptions regarding life and death over those deemed genetically unfit and therefore unworthy to live. Traditional moral virtues became secondary to the professions' new construction of morality and reality.

The collaboration between public health administrators and biological science demonstrates the effect of biological theories on political power, and how willing political and professional power can be in accepting new definitions. Many conditions were determined by Nazi science to be inconsistent with racial hygiene, thereby subjecting their carriers to the possibility of sterilization: hereditary feeble-mindedness, schizophrenia, manic-depression, epilepsy, Huntington's chorea, deafness, physical malformations, and severe alcoholism. Physicians wholeheartedly supported the provision of the law which also decreed castration for homosexuals. An entire arm of the legal system, including administrative tribunals judging hereditary status, lawyers and judges trained in biology and law, were established to administer the new law premised on maintaining racial purity. The 1933 Sterilization Law also created a huge state bureaucracy including institutes, clinics for hereditary and racial care, research centers engaged in data collection, genealogical surveys, and setting up files on criminals, hereditary diseases, and non-Aryan races.

Administrative agencies functioned as collection centers for certificates of Aryan ancestry, and psychiatric and neurological research into family records. Film, radio, and popular magazines of the period demonstrated the distinction between hereditary health and disease. Physicians advised families on how to research and understand genetic inventories; instruction was given in racial health and what was required to avoid racial and blood contamination. Sanitation as a matter of public policy meant not only keeping the streets clean, but keeping the national blood clean. In Hamburg in 1939, a health passport system was instituted to register suspected genetic defectives. More than one million citizens filled out certificates testifying to ancestry and genetic fitness.

Between 1934 and 1945, at least 1 percent of the German population was sterilized. So-called inferior races were to be eliminated from occupied territories.[26] Ethnic Germans were to be screened for racial fitness and provisions were to be made to resettle them in territories cleansed of racial pollution. German bureaucrats constructed plans for what Weindling calls a "medical dystopia": "[M]idwives were to be abortionists, there were to be mass sterilizations and encouragement of high infant mortality, and all family allowances and welfare services [for the racially inferior] were to be scrapped."[27]

THE STERILIZATION LAW AND ITS IMPACT ON PROFESSIONAL PERCEPTIONS

Medicine wholeheartedly supported the Nazi Party's racial ethos. In 1936 over 42 percent of all physicians in the 31–40 age group were members of the Nazi Party (30 and under, 39 percent; 41–50, 36 percent; 51–60, 25 percent; over 60, 10 percent).[28] Over 60 percent of all physicians belonging to Berlin's Reich Physicians Chamber claimed Aryan descent. Not only were doctors highly represented in the Nazi Party, the majority of nonparty members also supported Nazi aims.

Gerhard Wagner, head of the German medical society, foresaw a great future for medicine under the Nazis. National Socialism would initiate a movement from individual medicine to medicine administering to the *Volk*. The medical press, research institutes—indeed, the entire medical culture—was absorbed into the Nazi ideology. Such respected journals as the *Deutsches Arzteblatt* and the *Münchener Medizinische Wochenschrift* compiled data on the degenerate influence of Jewish physicians on the practice of German medicine. A widely distributed medical journal, the *Medizinische Welt*, regularly published a column called "Genetics and Racial Care."

The medical profession saw an enormous increase in the number of journals linking medical with political and racial concerns. While many technical journals continued to publish freely, at least through

1939, journals connected with social issues of a more expansive public health were held to strict content guidelines. Many widely read
journals associated with the Socialist Physicians League or Jewish
doctors ceased publication altogether. *Ziel und Weg*, a bimonthly journal devoted to Nazi racial policy and associated medical issues, gained
a readership of over forty thousand by 1939. The Office of Racial Policy supported a popular magazine devoted to easily understandable
health issues called *Neues Volk*.

By the end of the 1930s, what had been considered the Jewish and
socialist influences on German medicine had been wiped out. Typical
of research in the 1930s were the following "insights" of a noted
health physician, Dr. Eügen Stahle of Stuttgart.

> In describing the various races, we must not stop with the
> external shape of the body, nor even with mental characteris-
> tics in the classical manner of [Hans F. K.] Gunther and Lud-
> wig Ferdinand Clauss. We must go beyond this, to explore
> equally important differences in the inner organs of the body,
> differences that may reflect deeper, physiological differences
> among the races. Best known in this area is "racial smell."
> Europeans find the smell not only of Negroes but of East
> Asians to be repulsive, even when they are clean; the Oriental
> himself will, of course, make similar claims.[29]

Medicine, obsessed with blood diseases traceable to the impact of
various races, particularly the *Speicherungskrankheiten* or accumulative
diseases deriving from polluted Jewish blood, expanded its research
into genetic hygiene. Stahle asked his readers to "think what it might
mean, if we could identify non-Aryans in the test tube! Then neither
deception, nor baptism, nor name change, nor citizenship, and not
even nasal surgery, could help [the Jew escape detection]. One cannot
change one's blood."[30] By the mid-1930s, blood and its constituents
became an integral part of German scientific research and popular
speculation. The universities of Berlin, Bonn, Frankfurt, Giessen,
Hamburg, Heidelberg, Jena, Konigsberg, Munich, and Wurzburg
established professorships in racial hygiene. By 1941, more than thirty-
two *Dozenten für Biologie und Rassenkunde* held important positions in
twenty-three German universities, researching the health of German

genetic strains and defending against the dangers of polluted blood. Science and politics agreed on racial policy. In the words of Dr. Hermann Boehm, head of the Doctors' Führer School at Alt-Rehse, "Experimental genetics must provide the foundations for [racial care]," themes echoed by Germany's premier racial hygienists: Eügen Fischer, Otmar von Verschuer, Wolfgang Abel, Leonardo Conti, and Hans Reiter.[31]

It is a mistake to believe these racial theories were discussed by only a small elite of German geneticists. In fact, just the opposite was true. The government established administrative centers and bureaucracies to disseminate the teachings of the medical profession. The Office of Racial Policy, staffed with more than four thousand employees, engaged in a massive effort at disseminating racial information between 1934 and 1938, organizing over sixty-four thousand meetings. Four thousand Nazi Party members participated in week-long seminars concerned with the principles of racial hygiene. The office's journal, Neues Volk, had a readership as high as three hundred thousand. The impact of the medical profession on publicizing attitudes and information about racial infection, the possibility of pollution, and the dangers to blood and heredity was quite considerable. From 1933 to the end of the decade, Jewish physicians, who had composed 13 percent of all physicians in Germany and almost 60 percent of those in Berlin, were totally purged from the profession.

In 1933 the Law for the Restoration of the Civil Service excluded all non-Germans from participation in the civil service. To maintain legal control over the implications of the racial laws, the medical definitions of health and sickness, and the integrity of Volkish blood, this purified bureaucracy established 181 genetic health courts and appellate genetic health courts. The function of these courts lay primarily in adjudicating disputes arising from the new Sterilization Law. These administrative tribunals, presided over by a lawyer and two physicians, one an expert on genetic pathology, were for the most part adjuncts to local civil courts. After 1935 and the passage of the Marriage and Blood Protection Law, the courts expanded their jurisdiction to decide who should marry whom and whether marriages might pollute the genetic pool. One of the most bureaucratically complicated provisions of the Sterilization Law required doctors to register any known case involving a genetic defect or illness.

These courts, a collaboration of legal, administrative, and medical practices, met in secret, and their proceedings never were published. The courts presided over what Dr. Verschuer called "genetic health care" and reinforced popular conceptions of the link between traditional health care and genetic health issues. As Robert Proctor puts it: "The task of medicine was thus transformed: the traditional doctor of the individual would be replaced by the genetic doctor . . . an entirely new kind of doctor: one who cared for the future of the race, one who put the good of the whole over the good of the part"—one for whom the *Kultur*-group was more important than the individual.[32]

Verschuer's journal published work by Germany's preeminent biologists, geneticists, and racial hygienists. An entirely new vocabulary appeared in the practice of medicine and legal administration: *Erbkartei* (genetic files); *Erbklinik* (genetic clinics); *Erbkrankheit* (genetic disease); *Erblehre* (genetics); *Erbrecht* (genetic law); *Erbarzt* (genetic doctor); *Erbpathologie* (genetic pathology); *Erbgesundheitsgerichte* (genetic health courts); *Erbämter* (genetic officials); *Erbkammern* (genetic changers); *Erbsünde* (genetic pollution); *Erbhöfe* (hereditary farms); *Erbpolizei* (genetic police); *Erbgut* (total genetic heritage); *Erbkranken* (genetically ill).

A few statistics give some indication of the power of the genetic health courts. In 1934, the first year of the Sterilization Law, the courts entertained more than 84,000 petitions for sterilization, 42,903 men and 41,622 women. During that period, 64,499 decisions were issued by the courts; 4,563 petitions were either withdrawn or deferred for late judgment. Of those cases that were decided, 56,244 held in favor of sterilization, 3,692 against. Nearly 4,000 people appealed their sterilization decrees, but the appellate genetic courts ruled favorably on only 377 cases. More than four hundred thousand people were sterilized in the Third Reich.

Several sectors of the population profited from the Sterilization Law: the medical profession because of demand to fulfil sterilization quotas; research and psychiatric institutes because of increased funding and resources; engineering and medical supply companies because of logistical and technological needs; medical students and medical schools because of the cultural importance attached to dissertations on purifying blood lines and improving racial stock. Sterilization, therefore, was not a procedure hidden from public view.

Supported by professional practice and major industries, the Sterilization Law was a boon to jobs, income, and prestige.

Techniques of sterilization ranged from vasectomy and tubal liga-
tion to X-raying individuals while they filled out health forms.
"[V]ictims in at least one instance were seated on chairs behind desks
or counters and told to fill out questionnaires. X-rays from equipment
installed under the chairs were then directed toward the genitals for
two to three minutes, and sterility (as well as massive burns) followed
immediately."[33] It became central to medical training that every physician develop proficiency in genetic pathology and receive extensive
training in identifying racial traits and defects. Grants were given by
the state to institutes performing such educative functions.

While the Sterilization Law did not explicitly single out Jews
(although it was most liberally applied to them), it provided a preview
for later, more drastic measures aimed at ridding the culture of its
genetic and blood deformities. In retrospect, the sterilization program
served as an early paradigm for techniques of annihilation and the public policy of sanitizing the culture against biological and genetic threat.

THE AMERICAN PERSPECTIVE

Dr. B. Gebhardt, director of the Deutsches Hygiene Museum, remarked
in a 1934 address published in the *American Journal of Public Health and
Nation's Health*: "[The] fight against sickness and unhygienic conditions
knows no territorial boundaries."[34] Consider Gebhardt's following comment about health in the context of the racial and genetic thinking of
the 1930s:

> To us the aim of education for health is: the healthy man, the
> man physically and mentally well balanced, who knows and
> perceives what is beneficial for him, who recognizes health as
> a most precious gift of life, always worthy to be striven
> for. . . . [T]o be healthy is nothing—to maintain yourself to
> work for the national welfare, that is everything.[35]

Alan M. Kraut argues in his comprehensive study of the perceptions and reality of disease in immigrants to the United States that in
this country the belief Jews were innately diseased, prone to criminal-

ity, and producers of filth enjoyed considerable popular support. In 1908, Manly H. Simons, a physician connected with the U.S. Navy, maintained that "as a type Jews are beginning to show mental and physical degradation, as evidenced by the great variability of develop-ment, great brilliancy, idiocy, moral perversity, epilepsy, physical deformity, anarchistic and lawless tendencies." Jews, in Simons's view, possessed "distorted forms and minds and constituted a high propor-tion of beggars, tramps, burglars, and other perverts who make life burdensome and fill our prisons, our asylums with insane."[36]

In March 1934, the *American Journal of Public Health* published an enthusiastic review of Germany's sterilization program: "If the objec-tive of eliminating parenthood by those unfit is actually achieved in a thorough but legally and scientifically fair way, Germany will be the first modern nation to have reached a goal toward which other nations are just looking, or approaching at a snail's pace."[37] The author, American physician W. W. Peter, commented favorably on the organization of the genetic health courts, their administrative proce-dures and legal safeguards, assuring that anyone deserving of steril-ization in fact would be sterilized. He agreed with his German colleagues that court proceedings should not be publicized, because publication would invade the privacy of those brought before the court—as if sterilization itself were not an invasion of privacy.

Peter saw much to admire in "the [German] government's racial hygiene program of which this sterilization program is but a part"[38] and concurred with the notion that "the present load of socially irre-sponsibles are liabilities which represent a great deal of waste."[39] The sterilization program supported "a philosophy of life which says in effect that human breeding is not an innate right to be exercised by all adults possessing the necessary anatomical parts, but instead, a privi-lege to benefit the individual, the family, the community, and the state."[40] He pointed to the enormous economic burden carried by the German government in caring for the "physically crippled . ... men-tally deficient, deaf and dumb, blind." And he sympathized with the reduction of public expenditure by eliminating this "internal load [of genetically unfit] the German social order is required to carry."[41] He noted that "to one who lives here for some time, such a sterilization program is a logical thing," and "the government is bending every effort to organize the 1,700 lower and 27 upper hereditary Health

Courts." He attended a racial hygiene conference attended by 498 physicians. At a similar medical conference "so many physicians enrolled that the list had to be closed," while "training schools" in race hygiene "operated all over the country with great success."[42]

In 1935, Dr. H. E. Kleinschmidt, Director of the United States National Tuberculosis Association, enthusiastically endorsed the race hygiene "health" exhibit in Berlin. He found that it "roused the people to a sense of citizen-duty in the 'new' Germany." He described his experience on first entering the exhibit: "Without being told [the visitor] 'feels' rather than learns, that what he is about to see is of vital concern to the nation—a vast group-yearning towards a high goal, and that he is a participant in it."[43] He is intrigued with a "skin-color scale" accompanied by a set of mirrors "so that one may classify his own complexion."[44] Hygienic types and subtypes were "skillfully portrayed so as to be grasped easily and quickly." He marvelled at a section of the exhibit entitled "The Carriers of Life," devoted to racial classification:

> Again the visitor is "put in tune," this time by a unique bell tower made of rough-hewn timbers and rising loftily out of a semi-enclosed area, the boundaries of which are marked off by symbolical bas-reliefs of heroic proportions. Every five minutes a huge hour glass in the lower compartment of the open tower, its sand having run out, turns over. It marks the death of seven Germans. But instantly a nursery song rings out from the set of porcelain bells in the upper tower. Cheerfully these announce the birth of nine German babies. Again and again the visitor hears the tinkle of the bells—forcefully reminding him of Germany's vital statistics.[45]

Kleinschmidt found other aspects of the race hygiene hall compelling:

> Eugenics charts and family trees abound. Sad galleries of unfortunate biological misfits—idiots, people with heritable deformities, incurable criminals—drive home the logic back of the new sterilization laws. *The anti-Semitic policy is meticulously explained.* Exhibits deploring Germany's falling birth rate betray what a sore problem it is to the new state; and, as

a corollary what Germany expects of her young matrons is made clear in no uncertain phrases. To a foreigner interested in the present psychology of the German people and in the methods of public propaganda bureaus, this hall is, of course, a treasure house and more illuminating than pages of printed matter or folios of documents.[46]

Another hall called "The Maintenance of Life" addressed itself to public health, "the sanitary and educational activities of the Nazi party."[47] Yet another exhibit detailed the immigration and land settlement "problem." Kleinschmidt enjoyed "the opportunity to press buttons, pull levers, test one's physical abilities and in general to 'play' with the exhibits." Several movie theaters showed films justifying the sterilization program and presenting the Nazi view of race classification. He found the exhibition an unqualified success "for it reached some three-quarters of a million people in six weeks, entertained and instructed them, and undoubtedly stimulated an interest in the aims of the new government."[48] And in an astounding conclusion, even more bizarre than his unabashed identification with the regime's racial aims, Kleinschmidt noted:

[The Berlin exhibit] serves also to help people discriminate between sound and unsound health advice; to distinguish between scientific medicine and quackery. Above all, it impresses upon even the most casual the "Wonder of Life." Admiration for the marvel of the human body, reverence for the mysterious thing we call life, is worth cultivating in this surfeited generation.[49]

Further, such "valuable" exhibits should be financed by foundations or donors "who have faith in the power of knowledge."[50] While these attitudes are not necessarily suggestive of a culturewide embrace of phobic racism in the United States of the 1930s, they reflect the view of a significant and influential segment of American medicine and the American public health profession in particular.

THREE

SCIENTIFIC PRACTICE AND THE ASSAULT ON THE JEWISH BODY

"Public health" from the perspective of the German administration of the ghettos meant encouraging high suicide rates and rampant disease. The chronicles of the Lodz Ghetto, established by the Germans as a slave labor camp, list hundreds of suicides.[1] The following entries are typical:

> Hedwig Kupidlarska, from the town of Horandovice in Hungary, a resident of 7 Widok Street, poisoned herself on the 8th of this month. She was taken to Hospital No. 1 in critical condition.

> On the 9th of this month, a married couple, the Fischers, a 75-year-old Ignaz "Israel" and 60-year-old Karolina "Sara," took Veronal together to poison themselves. They were taken unconscious to the hospital. The husband died after 24 hours; the wife is now in her death agony.

> On the 11th of this month, at 6 o'clock in the morning, Irma Wesela, born in 1885, a seamstress by trade and resettled here from Bohemia, hung herself in her apartment at 67 Franciszkaska Street.

On that same day, Teresa Adler, who, as the bulletin has reported, attempted suicide by taking an overdose of Veronal on May 6 of this year, died in the hospital.

Malwina Frisch, a native of Vienna who poisoned herself with Gardenal on the 7th of this month, also died on the 11th.

On the 11th of this month, Rosa Kaldor (of 25 Wolborska Street), a 63-year-old woman resettled here from Hungary, threw herself from a fifth-floor window, dying on the spot.

On May 12, at 10:30 a.m., a local resident, Maria Jakubowicz, born in Lodz in 1892, cut the arteries in her right arm. She was taken to the hospital by an ambulance. She had resided at 23 Mlynarska Street.[2]

The utter lack of regard or empathy for the suffering of the victim's body made it possible to kill without moral qualms. For example, in his extraordinary account of ordinary German policemen drawn into the killing project, Christopher R. Browning observes that the killers saw no human content in their victims.[3] Jews elicited no sense of human obligation or responsibility from their victimizers, and no shame was expressed at what was being done. Killing proceeded without any acknowledgement of the victims' humanity.

These "ordinary men," drawn primarily from local police units in Hamburg, lacked any deep ideological and programmatic anti-Semitism; indeed, many never had even thought of themselves as anti-Semites. The scope of their killing and involvement had nothing to do with a grievance suffered at the hands of Jews, a passion for revenge, a blood thirst, or rabid hate. Killing took on the status of a job, an assignment to complete, yet murdering was more than a job, since the few members of the battalion who refused to kill were simply re-assigned. Therefore, the argument that they were just following orders did not hold; nor, as Browning carefully documents, did the facts of compliance or resistance fit the defense of following orders. Although Reserve Police Battalion 101 from Hamburg had enormous difficulties with its first attempt at mass killing, it became easier and easier to do, particularly when their jobs required collecting or concentrating the victims.

Norbert Troller, a survivor of Theresienstadt and Auschwitz, noticed a similar acclimation to torturing and killing in guards assigned to the prison outside of the Theresienstadt Ghetto. "It seemed that cruelty, sadism, complete disregard of human decency could, in the name of the Führer, be taught to eager student recruits by such dedicated, pitiless teachers as our jailers and the SS [and] Gestapo."[4] He describes an example. "In 1944, new Gestapo recruits were assigned to the Little Fortress," a prison just beyond the walls of the ghetto. Fifteen young volunteers, actors from the German-speaking theaters in Bohemia and Prague, "highly trained intellectuals, not a plebeian mob," they learned their jobs quickly to avoid the prospect of being shipped to the Eastern Front. "One could read in their faces, the first two weeks, how honestly shocked they were seeing what was going on [in] their future theater of endeavors in the service of their God, Hitler." But this shock quickly dissipated. "After one month of 'training,' they were indistinguishable from their teachers and superiors."[5] The fate of the Jewish body made little difference because the Jewish body had no moral or physical status. It did not exist as human.

The Final Solution, from the perpetrators' perspective, did not *look* psychotic, but rather the opposite: it appeared a sensible, defensible precaution taken against a real public health menace. If one were a public health doctor in Warsaw, Lodz, or Kraków, one could see vivid evidence of the menace: diseased Jewish bodies dying in the streets, daily suicides, the spectral stares of individuals wasting away from this disease of being Jewish, the forlorn stares of children. All these indications of suffering only proved to the killers that their victims were sick because they carried inside themselves a poison, the deadly infection of being Jewish. Indeed, to rid the environment of these poisons became the central objective of the entire German public health services: public health meant killing the entire Jewish population.

Nazi ideology despised otherness. It could not tolerate any presence that might subvert the ideal of German culture and blood as the supreme representations of race. The Jews "formed a constitutive outside," writes Dominick LaCapra, "a phantasmatic cause of all evil and the projective carrier of the anxieties and ills of the modern world." In their status as outsiders the Jews "were also destabilizing sources of phobic anxiety and quasi-ritual contamination" and posed "both a hygienic and a ritual threat to a 'pure' Nazi identity." Out-groups disturbed this racially constructed political ideal, its images and practices, and therefore "had to be eliminated."[6] In Himmler's words, "Having exterminated a germ, we do not want, in the end, to be infected by the germ, and die of it."[7]

It would be difficult to argue that the men of Reserve Police Battalion 101 were so inculcated in the norms of the regime they had no recourse but to follow orders, automatons terrified by forceful and demanding authority.[8] In fact, their commander, a Lieutenant Trapp, demonstrated weak and uninspiring traits as a figure of authority. Lifton makes a similar point in his discussion of Nazi doctors participating in the euthanasia program and later the killing centers of the Final Solution.[9] Many had received their medical education before World War I. Few had shown the kinds of political sensibilities the SS required. Almost none had been enthusiastic anti-Semites either in medical school or in their professional careers.

With notable exceptions like Josef Mengele or Hermann Pfannmüller, director of the Eglfing-Haar Hospital who systematically starved to death disabled and mentally retarded children rather than "wasting" medicines on useless lives, the great majority of Nazi doctors, ordinary medical practitioners, Arendt's bureaucrats, were not professional torturers.[10] Yet Nazi doctors, ordinary citizens, and bureaucrats shared the group-forged recognition that Jews, gypsies, homosexuals, and the psychologically and physically unfit were "life unworthy of life." To kill, it was not necessary to acknowledge the other's being as person. The murderous practices of racial hygiene, Lifton suggests, may be likened to ancient purification rites: "Purification emphasizes human continuity, while dealing with death in its own way. Contaminants interrupt those processes and often put before one elements of the corpse, for example, as opposed to the spirit."[11]

RASSENSCHANDE: RACIAL POLLUTION

Geschlectsverkehr, or sexual trafficking, was originally written into the 1935 Blood Protection and Marriage Law to proscribe sexual intercourse between Jew and non-Jew. It was not long before the concept was extended to include any form of touching or caressing, codifying the cultural aversion to touching Jews. Considerable bureaucratic time was devoted to adjudicating disputes over whether citizens had engaged in *Geschlectsverkehr*. The phobia against touching evolved into a complex bureaucratic system, translating this psychological fear into a paranoid administrative and juristic network of political imperatives resembling the tortuous complexities of Plato's *Laws*.

In 1936, a Jewish doctor was brought to trial for having kissed his eighteen-year-old Aryan patient. Convicted of racial pollution by the court, he was sentenced to two-and-a-half years in prison. In 1942, a Nuremberg court sentenced a Jew to death for kissing an Aryan woman. Jewish men accused of violating the Blood Protection Law were guilty of assaulting German blood. German men guilty of sexual trafficking were traitors to their Aryan blood. Interestingly enough, because German mores regarded women as passive in sexual relations, women could not be found guilty of sexual transgressions. By the early 1940s, that provision of the law regarding Jewish women was, in effect, null, because all Jews were being rounded up and marked for extermination. In fact, trials were no longer necessary. Jewish men accused of violating the law were immediately sent to concentration camps. Non-Jews could be detained because they presented a health risk to the larger German population and its blood purity.

Journals such as the *Deutsches Arzteblatt* inveighed against the dangers of polluted blood and emphasized the necessity of a pure Aryan blood type untainted by marriage pollution. The Blood Protection Law received universal approbation from scientists, biologists, geneticists, and racial hygienists. Who was and was not a health risk to the general population became a matter of significant public discourse. Section 4 of the Nazi Party program insisted that " 'Volk comrades' [be] of German blood, with no hereditary taint." Both popular and scientific literature stressed the importance of pure genetic lines.

By 1936, the Reich Ministry of the Interior had established a nationwide bureaucracy concerned with the protection of German blood. Soldiers were not permitted to marry women who had been married to Jews because such women lacked the proper "racial instinct" and might themselves be infected through sexual intercourse with their former Jewish husbands. Marital counseling centers, whose primary purpose lay in genetic advice and screening for blood pollution, increased in number. Counseling bodies were attached to the

Reich Health Office and formed a central part of the German public health bureaucracy. By 1937, 742 health offices were operating, employing 2,000 full-time physicians, 4,000 part-time physicians, 3,700 nurses, 800 technical assistants, 800 health inspectors, and 2,000 clerical personnel.

In primary and secondary education, race hygiene played a prominent role in biology instruction. In one primary school class, "Nazi racial-science truths regarding the 'defective' were hammered home in a genetics experiment linking high-grade and low-grade peas with people."[12] Classroom textbooks emphasized the distinction between "national comrade," member of the *Volksgemeinschaft* or people's community, and "community-alien" or Jew, gypsy, mental defective, and so on. Graphs, charts, illustrations, and photographs depicting the Jew as nomad, outcast, and disease carrier frequently appeared in standard textbooks.

One 1938 classroom text speaks of "the '*Volk*' as a community of blood."[13] A 1938 dictionary entry describes "the essence of human existence . . . as community life, [and] common *Erbmasse* [hereditary matter] as the constant factor of a community."[14] The paranoid fear of racial infection and the strict boundaries drawn between good and bad blood constituted a phobia.

In Poland immediately after the occupation, the Germans segregated Jewish physicians. While Polish doctors continued to practice under the national health plan, Jewish doctors found themselves stripped of their right to practice medicine as Polish citizens within the Polish health care system. In the German vision of the future, Poles were to be the Reich's laborers, and strong laborers needed to be healthy. Therefore, Poles required medical care. However, the Germans did close Polish universities and medical schools, fired Polish professors, sent many of the intelligentsia to Auschwitz, and imported German doctors to supervise Polish medicine, treat Germans, and oversee the health care system. Ukrainian doctors, placed in Polish hospitals as administrators by the Germans, supervised medical practice, vigilantly pursued the race hygiene laws, and guarded against Polish doctors treating ill or wounded resistance fighters and Jews.

Medicine under Kroll and the General Government proceeded on strictly racial lines: German doctors for Germans, Polish doctors for

Poles, and Jewish doctors for Jews. Communication between Polish and Jewish doctors ceased altogether, although on occasion Poles smuggled medicines into the ghettos. Early in the occupation, questionnaires inventorying race, nationality, type of practice, and location of practice were required of all health professionals, including physicians, dentists, nurses, pharmacists, and health aides. An enormous administrative effort was undertaken in administering the questionnaire. Keeping track of who returned forms and who did not came under the supervisory functions of Polish administrators. The Polish health service accumulated huge numbers of lists delineating who was to practice where, who was Jewish, who had paid taxes. If, in the short period before ghettoization, a Pole was suspected of being treated by a Jewish doctor, penalties could be severe for these Polish patients. Jewish physicians who were caught treating Poles were summarily shot.

At what point does paranoid fear of infection become psychotic? On an individual level, this question is usually answered by some measure of severity—a dramatic difference between consensual practice and radical exaggerations of normal everyday routine. The same distinction may be applied in dealing with the *Kultur*-group. Germany's obsession with blood pollution and the strict boundaries it drew between those considered healthy and those considered infected demonstrated a phobic effort to contain the *ballasterexistenzen*, or valueless individuals, who might otherwise annihilate the healthy. This is a delusional epistemology far beyond the historical norms in avoiding and containing difference. "We see cultured and learned men hesitating at times," Benno Müller-Hill observes, "but nonetheless making steady progress, step by step, along the path to the final solution."[15]

A division of the Institute for Family Protection, Criminal Psychology, and Criminal Biology, the part of the Reich Health Office engaging in research on "half breeds" and experimental genetics, investigated Gypsy-German miscegenation. It traced the genealogical origins of all gypsies living in Germany at the time. In fact, a visitor to the institute reported on "a table several meters in length on which in tiny, millimeter-size letters and numbers the genealogical tree of all gypsies living in Germany for the last ten generations had been charted."[16] Multiply by ten thousand these efforts of one department in one government ministry, and one can begin to have some idea of the time, energy, and financial resources that went into drawing the boundaries between pure and impure blood.

In the late 1930s and early 1940s, the discussion of racial hygiene moved from the pages of medical journals into actions employing the technical talents of Germany's professions and research institutes. The Marital Health Law, the Blood Protection Act, the Sterilization Law— all required massive bureaucracies and cooperation between numerous professions and industries. German medical journals throughout this period commented on racial miscegenation as a public health hazard. Medical researchers devised racial diagnoses to identify illness. Leading public health officials enthusiastically proclaimed the inherent dangers of blood pollution and the need for sanitation.

The identification of the psychotic with the normal had a foundation in the culture's professional practices and the acceptance of these practices by the German industrial, legal, and administrative sectors. Mario Biagioli refers to this as the "loops of mutual legitimation amongst discourse, institutions, and power."[17] He emphasizes the "full interaction and mutual reinforcement between Nazi politics and German life sciences" and "the symbiosis between the discourse of racial hygiene, the medicalization of the Final Solution, the institution of the concentration camps."[18] Political acts as horrendous as the Holocaust distinguish themselves from ordinary political experiences because these practices are so extreme as to radically sever them from consensually accepted historical norms. A culture may evolve into psychotic outlawry as easily as an individual.

No standard is absolute. As Kren and Rappoport put it: "There is, indeed, no normality, for the madness or amorality of one generation or one culture may be the required norm for another."[19] Cultures often construct peculiar, bizarre, or downright horrific conceptions of the normal, appropriate, and sensible. But from the perspective of today, Nazi racial epistemology possessed logic, justifications, and rationales derived from the phobic/delusional fear of pollution; these fears went beyond and not from traditional anti-Semitic sources. For example, Otto Reche, a respected professor of racial science at the University of Leipzig, noted the debilitating biological consequences of allowing alien or enemy (*feindlich*) blood groups to subvert healthy biological specimens.

Medical philosophy had accepted the notion that the goal of science was not to demonstrate facts, but to pronounce value judgments. Leading medical journals in the late 1930s attacked the indifference (*Gleichgültigkeit*) of the Weimar Republic Jewish spirit.[20] Scientists argued that impersonal and neutral science, concerned with standards of proof and demonstration, lacked spirit, a worldview (*Weltanschauung*), a sense of purpose and commitment. Knowledge, it was argued, depends on a sense of the cultural imperative. Tied to the goals of the nation and the integrity of the racial consciousness, science could not and should not be free of values. Jewish science, according to this view, was hopelessly secular, material, and practical. In a 1935 article called "The Solution of the Jewish Problem," professor of medicine Alfred Bottcher wrote:

> The thought of the Jew is distinguished by a certain analytic or destructive character which, like his blood, derives from its chaotic or impure origins.
>
> The Jew always has the tendency to split and divide everything into its atoms, thereby making everything complicated and incomprehensible, so that the healthy man can no longer find his way in the desert of contradictory theories. . . . The healthy non-Jew, in contrast, thinks simply, organically, creatively. He unifies, builds up! He thinks in terms of wholes. Briefly put, the blood-law of the Jew demands chaos, world revolution, and death! And the blood law of the creative generic man demands an organic worldview, world peace, and life![21]

For being too abstract or too practical, too local or too international, the Jew received the blame for all that was wrong in German science, medicine, and culture. Thus, to rid the German scientific community of the Jewish presence would bring a needed spiritual renewal to the practice of German science and medicine. A Dr. Gauch writes in a book called *New Fundamental Problems of Racial Research:* "Non-Nordic Man occupies an intermediate position between Nordic Man and the animal kingdom, in particular the great apes. . . . [W]e could also call non-Nordic Man a Neanderthal; however, the term 'sub-human' is better and more appropriate."[22] It is far easier to kill sub-humans or non-humans than human beings with sentient features and ordinary passions.

EXTRAORDINARY ACTIONS BY ORDINARY MEN

In *Ordinary Men: Reserve Police Battalion 101 and the Final Solution in Poland,* Christopher Browning uses the example of a Nazi atrocity to examine psychological revulsion at mass murder. On July 13, 1942, in the village of Jožefov̆, and the surrounding forest, Police Battalion 101 murdered some 1500 women, children, infants, elderly, and sick. Male Jews, considered capable of work, were transported to a labor camp.

After the atrocity the unit experienced widespread demoralization. However, their demoralization was not the result of revulsion at the killing, but at the sight of the carnage, akin to witnessing for the first time the blood and gore of a sausage factory. The 10–20 percent of the battalion that did protest never expressed any remorse having to do with moral transgression; rather they were moved by weariness of the work, by killing women and children, by revulsion in the face of mutilated corpses. The problem that faced Lieutenant Trapp and his superiors in Lublin "was not the ethically and politically grounded opposition of a few but the broad demoralization shared both by those who shot to the end and those who had not been able to continue."[23] Sympathy for victims never entered the picture.

Browning, however, is careful to point out differences in the willingness to kill: "Many had become numbed, indifferent, and in some cases, eager killers; others limited their participation in the killing process, refraining when they could do so without great cost or inconvenience."[24] These reluctant participants may be considered to be on the fringe of the *Kultur*-group, at least in regard to the actual murdering; but they occupied the fringe not for moral reasons. It was not moral revulsion that preoccupied them, but a feeling they had let down their comrades because of a weakness of will and lack of manly fortitude. Yet, common to all participants, whether or not they took part in the shooting, was an insensitivity to the visible suffering of their victims. It was as if the nonhuman properties of the victims' embodied selves released the men from feeling any moral qualms. Not seeing or feeling the victims' suffering allowed the killers to act, and their comrades to stand by silently. Monstrous crimes were not seen to be crimes at all.[25] What was psychotic was seen to be normal.[25]

Killing thousands of Jews was just a day's work for these ordinary people, not SS savages or Ukrainian camp guards, but ordinary folk from Hamburg. It is important to note here these policemen were not soldiers fighting a war. No enemy shot back. No front lines had to be overrun. No battle stress or wartime madness unleashed the rage-filled violence. On only a few occasions did the policemen receive partisan fire.

In his effort to explain the phenomenon of ordinary citizens turning into ruthless killers, Browning relies heavily on psychological arguments that place dehumanization of the other as the primary emotional condition impelling mass murder. This is not a sufficiently complex psychological explanation. To kill as resolutely and unfeelingly as Battalion 101 required a psychological process of dissociation that made the other's body meaningless as a living, sentient entity. As a Gestapo official told a member of the Warsaw Jewish Council: "You are no human, you are no dog, you are a Jew."[26] What happened was not dehumanization as such, but de-realization: stripping the victim of his very corporeality. Once the visible reactions of the victim cease to have human significance, it is possible for the killer to act. The victims have ceased to be alive, real, and identifiable human beings.

Goldhagen puts it in the following way:

With what thoughts and emotions did each of these men [of Battalion 101] march, gazing sidelong at the form of, say, an eight- or twelve-year-old girl who, to the unideologized mind would have looked like any other girl? In these moments, each killer had a personalized, face-to-face relationship to his victim, to his little girl. Did he see a little girl, and ask himself why he was about to kill this little, delicate human being who, if seen as a little girl by him, would normally have received his compassion, protection, and nurturance? Or did he see a Jew, a young one, but a Jew nonetheless? Did he wonder incredulously what could possibly justify his blowing a vulnerable little girl's brains out? Or did he understand the reasonableness of the order, the necessity of nipping the believed-in Jewish blight in the bud? The 'Jew-child,' after all, was mother to the Jew.[27]

John Dower distinguishes between killing as a matter of state policy and the battlefield frenzy that unleashes fury against the enemy.[28]

With several notable exceptions, the Warsaw Ghetto uprising the most prominent, the Jewish population never organized itself as a resistance force. Relatively few Jews had access to weapons, much less defended themselves with armed fire. It was a culture that had almost no experience of protecting itself with violence. Therefore, the ordinary German soldiers or irregulars never confronted a hostile enemy. Further, Browning strenuously argues against the authors of *The Authoritarian Personality,* who suggest a set of characterological traits predisposing the self to brutal and sadistic actions.[29] Browning found scant evidence to support the authoritarian personality thesis. His conclusions in this respect are reinforced by Holocaust historiography, particularly Raul Hilberg, on the roles of bureaucracy and technology.

In Browning's view, the power of the group and its conforming ideals compels individuals to undertake actions they might not otherwise. He finds Stanley Milgram's experiments in obedience to authority useful in confirming the tendency of individuals to acquiesce to authoritative command.[30] Milgram in a series of experiments found that individuals, if ordered, would inflict pain on others rather than incurring the displeasure of an authority ordering the action. Volunteer subjects, as Browning describes it, were "instructed by a 'scientific authority' in an alleged learning experiment to inflict an escalating series of fake electric shocks upon an actor/victim who responded with carefully programmed 'voice feedback'—an escalating series of complaints, cries of pain, calls for help, and finally fateful silence."[31] Two-thirds of Milgram's subjects complied with the orders. Milgram found that even though his subjects knew they were inflicting pain, they were far more likely to obey authority than to resist it. Even with the many variations on the experiments in which the subjects proximity to the victim had been altered, Milgram found significant compliance ranging from two-thirds in the standard experiment, where a shield separating victim and subject prevented any visual or personal contact, to about 30 percent if the subject had to physically place his hand on the victim's and force him to touch a device administering a so-called electric shock. If the subject were placed in the position of helper or aide to an "authority" administering the shocks, obedience to these commands reached almost 100 percent. Deference to authority, then, generally took precedence over protesting actions which appeared from the perspective of the subject to be physically harmful. Browning also relies on the Stanford prison experiments suggesting that individuals tend to identify with their roles: if the group role requires sadistic and brutal action, individuals may enthusiastically embrace acts of aggression quite out of character with their ordinary lives.[32] The group's enforcement of role defines the norms governing action.

Explanations convincing to Browning merge specific social and cultural factors with psychological attitudes generated in the group. For example, Zygmunt Bauman and Ervin Staub argue that cruelty derives from group psychological perceptions and is not innate to human nature. Bauman criticizes Adorno's view of fascistic personalities or inborn characterological compulsions to kill, and argues that much of the horror of the Holocaust can be understood as a hatred fundamentally social in origin and practice, a set of attitudes turned into practice and making it possible for vast numbers of Jews to be killed.[33] Similarly, Staub suggests, "Some people become perpetrators as a result of their personality," and "evil that arises out of ordinary thinking and is committed by ordinary people is the norm, not the exception."[34]

Another way of looking at what made the men of Battalion 101 into killers lies in what George Mosse calls "camaraderie," or a sense of manliness in shared tasks. Mosse speaks of the interrelationship of the history of manliness in war in Germany and the cult of male camaraderie. Rather than peer pressure as the active agent inducing the killing, male ritual is the organizing principle working on both the group and the individual levels.[35] What coheres the group in this common project, whether within Battalion 101 or among German bureaucrats, is an enthusiasm in upholding the values the group regards as essential to the welfare of the nation.

While persuasive, it is difficult to accept these explanations as definitive. Each ignores the power of phobia in molding perception, inducing group action, and forging group identification. What, then, makes ordinary men into ruthless killers? Browning hinges his explanation on Milgram's arguments regarding the effects of peer pressure on obedience to authority and the reciprocal interaction of authority and conformity.

In Milgram's view, Nazi conformity was the product of group pressure reinforced by authoritative commands. Disobedience, because it gained no favor from the group or from authority, never materialized. Milgram concludes: "Men are led to kill with little difficulty."[36] This conclusion leads Browning to write:

> Many of Milgram's insights find graphic confirmation in the behavior and testimony of the men of Reserve Police Battalion 101.... With the division of labor and removal of the killing process to the death camps, the men felt scarcely any responsibility at all for their actions. As in Milgram's experiment, without direct surveillance many policemen did not comply with orders when not directly supervised; they mitigated their behavior when they could do so without personal risk but were unable to refuse participation in the battalion's killing operations openly.[37]

Browning rejects Milgram's argument that the kind of obedience to authority present in the atrocities of Nazi Germany required intense indoctrination. The evidence shows that SS indoctrination of Battalion 101, as with many sectors of the German population, was minimal. Racial pamphlets were rarely read, and the attitude of Reserve Police Battalion 101 never demonstrated the kind of traditional anti-Semitism pushed by such popular media as *Die Stürmer*. On this point Browning's argument is quite convincing and should dispel the belief that the mass murderers of the Third Reich were all rabid, ideological believers following the will of their Führer. In fact, members of Reserve Police Battalion 101 were remarkably nonideological.

What distinguishes the Final Solution from other historical instances of political mass murder lies in the mobilization of the scientific and professional sectors of the German population in pursuit of a culturewide phobia. It was a scientifically designated process begun long before actual combat, and with the exception of the SS and concentration camp guards, sane people ordering and carrying out the atrocities. In fact, it was the physicians, administrators, and scientists at some psychological distance from the victims who created the ideology and values of the regime. No other genocide had its major impetus in the language of science, law, and administration of the society.

EUTHANASIA AS STATE POLICY

An early foreshadowing of the murderous logic of "life unworthy of life" appeared in 1939, specifically the euthanasia program established to rid the culture of genetic taint. The committee charged with carrying out the program issued instructions to all Reich health agencies to register children born with congenital deformities, including idiocy, Mongolism, microcephaly, hydrocephaly, missing limbs, malformation of the head, spina bifida, muscular dystrophy, mental retardation, and other congenital diseases. An elaborate administrative apparatus developed to eliminate the unfit. The registration effort began in August 1939, with the help of physicians, midwives, and medical officials. Registration offices could be found in every region of the Third Reich. Public health bureaucrats formulated instructions for the identification, isolation, and ultimately killing of all such children.

Under the administrative name T-4, after the address of the project's offices in Berlin, the euthanasia program exterminated thousands of babies, children, and later adults deemed unfit to live. Children selected for elimination were sent to one of twenty institutions, including some of Germany's oldest and most prestigious hospitals. Parents were informed that transport would result in improved treatment for their children. "Treatment" included injections of morphine, cyanide gassing, the use of chemical warfare agents, and occasionally the direct injection of phenol into the heart. Families received death certificates listing the cause of death as pneumonia, typhus, meningitis, bronchitis, carbuncles, seizures, and other natural causes. Famous names in German science and medicine supported this project, including Werner Heyde, Friedrich Mauz, Paul Nitsche, Friedrich Panse, Kurt Pohlisch, Otto Reche, Carl Schneider, and W. Villinger.

Originally the euthanasia program was intended for children under the age of three, but by late 1939 it had expanded to include all children with obvious physical or mental handicaps or severe diseases. These murders proceeded under a variety of euphemisms: "special treatment," "disinfection," "cleansing," "therapy." More than five thousand children were killed between 1939 and 1941. Selection for killing took place under the most rigid "scientific" standards. Case histories were decided on by panels of physicians, administrators, lawyers, and nurses. The killing took place under the supervision of three sham administrative organizations. The Working Committee for Hospital Care oversaw operations and correspondence. The Charitable Foundation for Institutional Care took care of accounting and financial matters. And the Nonprofit Patient Transport Corporation facilitated transportation for extermination. These organizations were actually arms of the Reich Ministry of the Interior.

By the summer of 1941, when protests from the Catholic Church became publicly embarrassing to the Nazi regime, more than seventy thousand patients had been killed.[38] Beginning in 1942, the responsibility for killing or administering euthanasia shifted to individual institutions. The killing continued throughout the war, although on a much lesser scale, as the Nazi focus on mass killing shifted to the Jewish and gypsy populations. With the assumption of the T-4 program into the duties of private hospitals, popular support for the procedures continued. In several instances, parents actually wrote officials requesting their children be put to death. This also appeared to be the case in the killing of the adult mentally ill. "[B]y the end of the thirties, propaganda bodies had whipped up such fear and hatred for the mentally ill—one Bielefeld physician compared the genetic defective to a 'grenade' waiting to explode—that the elimination of these people seemed a logical or even humane measure."[39]

While Jews were seen as racial pollution, the euthanasia program saw German or Nordic "defectives" as an embarrassment to the race. Eliminating deformed children and mental patients was not so much a phobic reaction to their presence, but the result of a cultural belief that genetic deformities were a burden on the nation. An Aryan schizophrenic patient, unlike a Jew, was not disease incarnate. Rather, the patient reflected poorly on a culture that held the standards of racial and genetic purity and wholeness in such high regard. To this end, the regime encouraged "healthy" Aryan women to give birth, to create genetically pure sons and daughters for the Fatherland and the Führer.[40] Medical killing consistently received the blessings of German science and medicine. The highly prestigious Kaiser Wilhelm Institute trained SS personnel in racial theory and the identification of racial traits and diseases, and contributed research expertise to the racial surveys conducted by the Reich Ministry of the Interior. Eügen

Fischer, director of the Institute, advocated extermination of the Jewish population through work. His writings influenced engineers associated with Krupp and I. G. Farben, major contractors in the construction of gas chambers and crematoria. Fischer also counseled the SS on the prospects for "Germanizing" Aryan elements in the Russian population.

So-called pure science knew no moral bounds. Researchers at the Kaiser Wilhelm Institute of Anthropology experimented on gypsy eyes (to discern differences in color abnormalities) obtained by Josef Mengele from twins and gypsy families killed in Auschwitz. Verschuer regarded Mengele's work as fundamental, and the scientific establishment expressed no moral hesitation in using human specimens obtained through the Final Solution. Since the victims were to die anyway, so the scientific reasoning went, why not use their bodies to further the interests of research and science? Dead bodies presented no genetic threat; the dead could be harvested for the "objective" interests of science and could provide an unlimited supply of parts or "pieces" furthering the aims of research projects. Care, of course, had to be taken in handling the bodies and body parts; but scientists, trained in such measures, could avoid contamination; and the possibilities of an endless supply of live and dead subjects was a source of great enthusiasm in the scientific community. Scientists could inject live bodies with contaminated vaccine compounds; harvest fresh brain tissue; perform bone graphs, and examine organ and limb transplants on live subjects; submerge subjects in freezing and boiling water; put them into chambers testing for high altitude tolerance; burst skulls open, or mutilate and kill in countless other ways without benefit of anaesthesia, proper surgical technique, or basic principles of surgical hygiene. Bodies were utilized only to the extent they contributed to a set of scientific protocols that had utterly no moral qualms about inducing intolerable suffering in those seen as "life unworthy of life." No moral principle or empathic responsiveness guided these experiments. The physiological piece or experimental "item," detached from the dead or live human body, held importance for the scientist only as data.

The ghettos were created to contain the live Jewish vermin, protecting the surrounding population from pollution and disease. If Jews were not sealed off in ghettos, the entire population might suffer

the danger of poisoning.[41] The Lodz chronicles' description of the
fate of middle-class Jews "resettled" from Hamburg brings into question the durability of moral values like civility, decency, and compassion. It also demonstrates the starkness and brutality of the German
intent in transporting entire communities to places that could barely
sustain human life. "Some of the metamorphoses [after a few
months] could not be imagined, even in a dream . . . ghosts, skeletons
with swollen faces and extremities, ragged and impoverished . . .
stripped of their European finery . . . only the Eternal Jew was left."[42]
The chronicles continually refer to the devastating impact of continuing "resettlements," massive shifts of Jewish populations throughout
Europe to ghettos in Poland. "This constant movement of populations creates enormous uncertainty, undermines normal life, and has
a very negative effect not only on people's frame of mind (which, at
the present time, is not even taken into account!) but has a dramatic
impact on production in the workshops."[43]

Crime, according to German science, originated in genetics. University research demonstrated that the Jew possessed innate criminal
tendencies. One study argued that Jews were inclined to bankruptcy,
prostitution, pornography, drug smuggling, purse snatching, and general theft. Thus to be Jewish meant being a carrier of both disease
and criminality.

In 1941, months before the Wannsee Conference, the Reich Ministry of the Interior ordered all Jews in German hospitals to be killed
because they constituted a threat of infection to German patients.
The gassing of Jewish patients recovering in hospitals proved to be an
acceptable and popular solution to this perceived threat. By early
1942, the medical, scientific, and political communities appeared to
be in concert on what to do about the Jewish problem. The professions had embraced what the geneticist Otmar von Verschuer
described in one extensively circulated paper as the need for a "complete solution to the Jewish question." Professors Eügen Fischer and
Hans F. K. Gunther, leading scientists of racial hygiene, were the fea-
tured guests at a Spring 1941 meeting at which "radical" measures
such as extermination were discussed. In November 1942, a publication of the Reich Health Publishing House entitled "Preparatory
Measures for the Final Solution of the European Jewish Question"

was circulated among higher party officials and the medical faculties of major German universities.

Further, German physicians, scientists, and research professors had been contributing to the medical experiments carried out in the concentration camps, which had resulted in the deaths of thousands of prisoners.[44] Physicians were never compelled to participate in experiments on the bodies of prisoners and camp inmates. Those who did so saw it as a research opportunity and as a service to the nation's public health. To engage in experiments that would advance the cause of sanitizing blood and genes was a commitment to the highest ideals of the *Kultur*-group. Results of these experiments were presented at scientific meetings and conventions and published in the most respected journals. German industry, as has been well documented, benefited enormously from the experiments. Behriung-Werke, for example, a pharmaceutical company, employed concentration camp prisoners in testing new vaccines against typhus. Bayer Pharmaceutical Company entered into a contract with the administrators of Auschwitz that allowed the company to purchase Jewish female subjects for 700 Reichmarks each for experimentation.[45]

Before 1933, many German socialist physicians argued for nonviolent and nonexclusionary approaches to race, culture, and biology. By 1938, these individuals either left Germany or were silenced through imprisonment and execution. The sporadic protests against the scientific community's theories of race and blood had little effect on Nazi racial policies. Nazi imagery, obsessed with blood and purification, absorbed and defined popular culture and attitudes. Propaganda, science, and medicine all addressed themselves to issues of blood purity and purification. All supported research which had as its fundamental aim eliminating imperfection, impurity, and degeneracy from the culture's blood. Physicians, as soldiers defending the *Volk*, played a major role in defining value. Auschwitz, then, was considerably more than the victory of German romanticism. The gas chambers were the delusional outgrowth of a national phobia against blood pollution that throughout the 1930s found itself elaborated by the most powerful elements of German professional and technical life.

PSYCHOTIC PRECONDITIONS TO MASS MURDER

In normal times, children would not be systematically slaughtered; nor would thousands of human beings be shot in a single day and then shoved layer on top of layer into lime pits; nor would places like Auschwitz-Birkenau be constructed capable of "processing" twenty thousand bodies a day.[1] Even for ordinary men and women in Germany during the 1930s, the scope and methods of the Final Solution were not imaginable within a continuous history, ethical or otherwise.[2]

One SS guard, according to Kurt Gerstein, spoke with the voice of a pastor at the door of the gas chamber as men, women, and children, all naked, filed past him. "Nothing terrible is going to happen to you! . . . All you have to do is to breathe in deeply. That strengthens the lungs. Inhaling is a means of preventing infectious diseases. It's a good method of disinfection." When questioned by the doomed victims as to their future, he replied, "The men will have to work building roads and houses. But the women won't be obliged to do so. They'll do housework or help in the kitchen."[3]

Jean Améry captures something of the delusional backdrop to the German sense of the Jew as polluted matter.[4] Améry speaks as if during the period of the Holocaust he lived in a universe filled with "madmen, and was left standing around helplessly among them, a fully sane person who joined a tour through a psychiatric clinic and suddenly lost sight of the doctors and orderlies." Having no freedom, identity, or meaning in the varied universes of killing, he found himself completely at the mercy of whatever sentence was passed on him, a death threat that could "be carried out at any moment . . . totally binding."[5]

In September 1942, the Jewish Council in Lodz received an order from German authorities to give up for transport children under the age of ten and adults over sixty-five. Josef Zelkowicz, a Yiddish journalist, author, diarist, and contributor to the Lodz chronicles, described the effects of this edict:

> All hearts are icy, all hands are wrung, all eyes filled with despair. All faces are twisted, all heads bowed to the ground, all blood weeps.
>
> Tears flow by themselves. They can't be held back. . . . Our hearts writhe and struggle in these tears like fish in poisoned waters. Our hearts drown in their own tears. . . .
>
> Blood flows in the streets. Blood flows over the yards. Blood flows in the buildings. Blood flows in the apartments. Not red, healthy blood. That doesn't exist in the ghetto. . . . All the ghetto has is pus and streaming gall, that drips, flows, and gushes from the eyes, and inundates streets, yards, houses, apartments.[6]

Roundups for the death transports began:

> Woe to him who stumbles and falls. He will never stand up again. He will slip and fall again in his own blood. Woe to the child who is so terrified that all he can do is scream "Mama!" He will never get past the first syllable. A reckless gunshot will sever the word in his throat. The second syllable will tumble down into his heart like a bird shot down in mid-flight.[7]

The horror of this demand, its brutality and insanity, appears with tragic clarity in Zelkowicz's words. "All the west is bathed in blood." The pain and anguish of those who scream mattered not at all to the German soldiers, or to the administrators, lawyers, physicians, and railway officials who planned the operation far from the scene. By the thousands children and elderly rode the boxcars to gas chambers and crematoria.

> Sitting at home, casting furtive glances at your wife who has aged dozens of years in these last two days, then looking at your beautiful son, seeing his dark hollow face and the mortal fear lurking in his deep black eyes, then all the terror around you makes you fear for yourself, makes you fear for your wife, makes you fear for your trembling child.[8]

THE SHIFTING BOUNDARIES OF THE NORMAL

Milgram's and Zimbardo's experiments, Arendt's careful delineation of bureaucratic mentality, and Browning's view of group conformity are not sufficiently complex psychological explanations of the curious paradoxes of this tragedy, this cultural embrace of radical delusional logics. The break between the Final Solution, what Harold Kaplan calls "a sanitizing operation on the grand scale," and Jewish life prior to the Holocaust is so sharp that it takes on the properties of the schizophrenic break between delusion and consensual reality.[9]

For the delusional self, the schizophrenic, the body is indeed dispensable. The body in history, in time, and in society is not significant. The delusion writes the body: the body as stone, as machine, as knife, as dead, as poisonous. What the schizophrenic body is to itself is not what the body is to the doctor, family, or friends who experience the body's gestures within a consensual historical environment. To be psychotic is to be totally removed from the consensual definition of the body, its physiological functions, and what the embodied self speaks. That break is nowhere more vividly represented than in the concept of the dispensability of the body and the lack of empathy for its surfaces.

The death camps and the actions of the Order Police in Poland mark a radical break with history and with prevailing conceptions of consensuality that German society had demonstrated toward a primarily middle-class Jewish population. With the policy of extermination, the concept of Jew as person disintegrated. In its place was Jew as life unworthy of life. The languages, science, moralities, and professions making the body of the Jew dispensable, not noticing the Jewish body as a feeling, weeping, and grieving presence—that blindness to the emotions of the victims not noticed and acknowledged—allowed the authors and actions of the Final Solution to forge a psychotic text and time, a complete break with historical solutions and consensual agreement on how to treat the Jew as a culturally different embodied self.

Adolf Eichmann's plan to relocate the Jews to Madagascar is an example of the beginning of this break or disruption. Once the Jew became worthless as a form of cultural difference, separated and isolated from the rest of the culture, it was no longer necessary to acknowledge the presence, value, autonomy, or difference of the Jewish body. The embodied Jewish self ceased to exist as a human body in the eyes of the *Kultur*-group. In political terms, the mass, collective delusion played itself out in the extermination centers, places removed from the common day-to-day life of ordinary Germans. The concept of break from history, a radical discontinuity with historical time, is analogous in both the individual and group situation.

Individual Germans and their collaborators were not schizophrenic in a clinical sense. In individuals, psychotic disintegration often cripples organization and capacity. Participants in the Holocaust performed practical and theoretical tasks requiring cooperation, communication with others, coordination of complex strategies. Processes working on the individual level in provoking psychosis are not necessarily identical on the group level. What is common on both the individual and group level is delusion, or the psychotic reworking of reality. The psychotic individual generally holds this reworking inside, and whatever action happens in the delusion proceeds within the self's internal imaginative representations. There is no externalization. The delusion operates only in the imagination. In the group, however, the reworking is turned outward. Its venue is not a withdrawn imaginative internality, although that may be part of it. Rather, the psychotic group logic uses the political process to work through its most radical and damaging features.

The dynamic element lies in delusion: psychotic delusions can be well organized within the framework of their sealed logics. The logics and scripts of German racial science, its utterly absurd premises—for example, the idea that Jews innately carry the typhus germ—forged such extraordinary inversions in meaning and action that the psychotic imaginary became sane, normal politics. And in the Third Reich the implementation of psychotic logics appeared in group action.

The individual psychotic organizes his delusional universe to effect horrendous actions done in the imagination to whatever entity, group, or person has been designated as the other.[10] An analogous division occurs in the psychotic group's political actions, which appear logical, rational, and historically necessary to the group but which take actual others in the external world as their object. The *Kultur*-group constructs reality in accordance with its perceptual definitions.

This hypothesis requires a position that sees the actions of 1941–45 as a radical disruption of history. What the perpetrators saw as rational was discontinuous, profoundly irrational, and evil. As the Jewish body became more and more visible as a suffering presence to empathic witnesses, the victimizers' perception of that presence increasingly diminished. As in the psychotic delusion on the individual level, the group delusion in its projective capacity wrote reality in stark terms: good was equated with those producing violence and evil with those being exterminated. This process created a derealization of the victim's body in the eyes of the victimizer. Family, society, genes, and chemistry produce this effect on the schizophrenic individual. In the psychotic group, this derealization is caused by processes of logic and definition deriving from projection and defined through historical relationship, and which the group itself institutes and maintains. Individual members of this group appear to be ordinary.

Nazi policies of extermination created a psychotic group condition. They did not make the Jewish self psychotic, although the despair of the ghettos and camps and the knowledge of extermination may have had that effect in some individual victims. Bruno Bettelheim addresses this issue in *The Empty Fortress*.[11] The logic and science of the Final Solution made the Jewish body dispensable to the victimizer and created a group-dependent psychotic process. The German policies of extermination projected a logic whose operation in an individual would be considered psychotic and created a psychotic relationship between victimizer and victim. It defies credibility

to say that the connection between the killers and victims was a varia-
tion of normal attitudes or actions.

ACTION AND MORAL RESPONSIBILITY

As to the issue of moral and legal responsibility, the objection might
be posed: If the policies of the Final Solution created a psychotic historical action, it is then questionable whether the perpetrators can be
held responsible for what was in effect a set of insane actions. Not so.
The laws regarding culpability and the insanity defense simply do not
hold in group and political actions. When an entire society, particularly its professions, radically transforms the meanings of right and
wrong and then lives by those inverted meanings as part of normal
day-to-day events, they cannot be excused from accepting responsibility for the consequences of their actions. Further, the policies of the
Final Solution were hardly impetuous mob actions. They were rational, organized, and willed, given the logics of Nazi science and the
professions. It was not, then, a lynch mob that constructed the
machinery and technology necessary for mass murder, but a cold, scientific, and rational mentality, as both Arendt and Hilberg convinc-
ingly argue. Even though the legal foundations of right and wrong,
violent and nonviolent possessed a psychotic substructure in the
Third Reich, they embraced a set of assumptions accepted as normal
and rational by the society's governing cultural practices. Germany's
scientific establishment, particularly its medical profession, defined a
core set of cultural perceptions that the major centers of social power
in Germany accepted as true. Complicity in the killing, therefore,
became the governing historical norm, the right thing to do.

There is no evidence that the scientific and bureaucratic perpetrators of these actions were psychotic on an individual level. This is a
major theme in *Eichmann in Jerusalem*, and Arendt's thesis in this
regard is very convincing. Indeed, in clinical terms insanity immobi-
lizes selves. In the Third Reich, psychosis not only organized the
machinery of the Holocaust, but created a set of logics and justifications that very sane individuals went about implementing.

Again I distinguish between group psychosis, for which responsibility must be assigned, and individual insanity, which has a legal
defense depending on context and circumstance. Group-dependent

psychotic acts, because of intent and the power of organization, may not lay claim to a philosophical, legal, or clinical status in excusing culpability. It would be very difficult for any of those ordinary Germans who murdered innocents to argue that their individual acts of barbarism derived from an inability to see the difference between right and wrong, or that their logical and cognitive capacities were impaired. *Einsatzgruppen* squads, police forces conscripted for roundups in Poland, ordinary soldiers on the Eastern Front, chemists manufacturing Zyklon B gas, and executives of concrete companies building gas chambers could not meet clinical criteria of individual insanity. A group-authored psychosis is experienced as sane and normal by those undertaking the actions. Rational murder required organization, premeditation, and will. The mass murder was distinguished not by the pleasure of torture (although this may have been the case for some), but by the enthusiasm of preserving the *Kultur*-group from disintegration. The action of killing required adherence to a set of radically discontinuous historical standards accepted by the *Kultur*-group as immanent truth.

The collective group process embraced a psychotic text, behaviors that, as in paranoid delusional systems in individual psychosis, possessed totalizing and uncompromising properties. As Lifton argues in *The Nazi Doctors*, psychological processes such as doubling ("the division of the self into two functioning wholes, so that a part-self acts as an entire self") or "numbed habituation" demonstrate group conversion to a psychotic text, while in contexts outside of the killing environment, individuals appeared perfectly normal and sane.[12] For example, regarding the doctors at Auschwitz, Lifton writes:

> In doubling, one part of the self "disavows" another part. What is repudiated is not reality itself—the individual Nazi doctor was aware of what he was doing via the Auschwitz self—but the meaning of that reality. The Nazi doctor knew that he selected, but did not interpret selections as murder. One level of disavowal, then, was the Auschwitz self's altering of the meaning of murder; and on another, the repudiation by the original self of *anything* done by the Auschwitz self. From the moment of its formation, the Auschwitz self so violated the Nazi doctor's previous self-concept as to

require more or less permanent disavowal. Indeed, disavowal was the life blood of the Auschwitz self.[13]

The formation of the Auschwitz self was part of a collective, group-defined process that in eroding all limits and radically disrupting a historically continuous culture created a delusional organization of reality. This absolute eradication of limits enabled the Auschwitz self to commit murder with impunity, with no moral sense or any ability to judge the action with anything but a relentless logic that is insane from the outside, and with an intensity often found in the self-authored omnipotent fantasies of delusional schizophrenics.

Lifton's doubling thesis presents its own array of troubling interpretive issues, which I will return to, particularly in explaining consistency in physicians' attitudes toward murder, inhuman experimentation, and death both inside and outside the camps. Lifton holds that the Auschwitz environment was not normal for those associated with it. An increasing amount of historical evidence, however, suggests the opposite: Auschwitz was the norm for the entire society. Killing racial inferiors to protect the nation's psychological and physical integrity took on the status of right, justice, and truth.

The aims of ordinary participants, like the aims of German medicine and biology, mirrored the total erosion of limits and boundaries characteristic of psychosis, even though its individual members acted in seemingly normal ways in environments away from the killings. This is precisely what makes German science during this period so frightening: Science, biological science in particular, was used in the service of psychosis while its practitioners, far from the killing centers, partook of a so-called normal life and saw their research and policy recommendations as moral and responsible.

On the group-psychotic level the murderer participates in the engineering of destruction, yet on the individual level takes on the banal roles of parent, spouse, and friend in traditional interpersonal environments. The utter insensitivity to the suffering of Jewish victims occurred because to the victimizer's eye they possessed utterly no human properties. How could concern or decency be accorded to those who lacked any sentient presence? Jews found themselves assigned to a psychological space possessing no human status. The perpetrators could thus engage in the mechanics and logistics of mass annihilation without guilt.

PSYCHOSIS AND THE APPEARANCES OF NORMALITY: A POLITICAL QUESTION

Normal people do not murder millions of people in thirty-six months. It is not an ordinary event in the life of a culture, done with the same dispatch as obeying one's boss or maintaining train schedules. It is therefore a mistake to equate the banality of certain kinds of bureaucratic actions or character types supporting the logistics of extermination with the meaning or significance of the event of genocide itself, which was a group action. The murder of millions of innocents requires an explanatory paradigm that addresses the group dimension of behavior.

The scientific precision of Stanley Milgram's experiments, their clearly limited goals, the laboratory's artificiality, beggars comparison with the brutal quality of the actions of the Holocaust. To try to find analogous behavioral properties between the laboratory and the death camps is a dubious analytical proposition. Indeed, such an explanatory parallel is a shift of such momentous and qualitative magnitude that to make generalizations from Milgram's scientific artifice to the gas chambers ignores the radically transgressive properties of the Holocaust.

While certainly suggestive as far as they go, Milgram's scientific experiments lack credibility as a comprehensive group explanation for genocide. Equally unconvincing are Browning's comparisons with Zimbardo's make-believe prison. The men of Battalion 101 could hardly be described as sadists. Zimbardo's prison guards, however, enjoyed the torment they dished out to their prisoners; giving punishment became a source of job gratification. According to Browning's and Goldhagen's reading of the archival evidence, it appears that the men of Battalion 101 were free to withdraw from the killing. No individual in that battalion or other units was ever severely punished for refusing to kill Jews. Invariably the individual soldier was transferred, reassigned, sent to a hospital, or sent home. Similarly doctors who refused to participate in the euthanasia program or the killings in the concentration camps were transferred either to other units in the hospital or to other medical assignments in the Third Reich.

What, then, is a satisfactory explanation for mass murder? Obviously no explanation of such an event can be completely persuasive; however, consideration should be given both to the group-driven and phobic quality of this process of annihilation and murder and its psychotic properties.

It is perverse to construct an ideology that, in Peter Haidu's terms, "displays thousands of genocidally murdered victims," and then proclaims the inherent decency of these actions as self-evident. But Nazi officials never saw their actions as perverse, psychotic, or mad. Race hygiene ideology informed discourse, ethics, and action, while "endowing the individual with the possibility of social action within the institutions and normative parameters" of German society; it defined moral perspective and conscience for "agents and representatives of various kinds, including administrators and soldiers."[14] Good conscience meant being able to effectively and enthusiastically kill.

IDEOLOGIES AS INSTRUMENTS OF DEATH

In *Negation*, Freud elaborates the concept of projection. "Expressed in the language of the oldest—the oral—instinctual impulses, the judgment is: 'I should like to eat this,' or 'I should like to spit it out'; and put more generally: 'I should like to take this into myself and to keep that out.'" Boundary between self and other depends on a strict delineation between self and not-self, me and not-me. It also means attaching distinct values to me and not-me. What I want to take into myself is good; what I want to rid myself of is bad. "[T]he original pleasure-principle wants to introject into itself everything that is good and to eject from itself everything that is bad."[15] I judge an object or person based on whether I think of it as bad or good. If what is outside myself is unfamiliar, uncanny, or foreign, then it is bad, and my judgment of it is negative. "What is bad, what is alien to the ego and what is external are, to begin with, identical."[16]

Psychosis represents a drastic refusal of this negative projection, a world view remodeling historical, consensual reality. The psychotic dimension of experience is an *invented* dimension. But the inventions, because of the peculiar yet consistent logics of psychosis, make sense to those who believe them. Psychosis involves "the creation of a new reality which no longer raises the same objections as the old one that has been given up . . . it serves the desire for power of the id, which will not allow itself to be dictated to by reality."[17] Hate, in whatever form—the wish to annihilate, devour, maim, or otherwise destroy—becomes elaborated in psychosis as intricate classification systems carrying their own norms and frames of reference.

In psychosis, these norms inaugurate a significant linguistic inversion, or radical extension of meaning, logic, and causality from historical and consensual practices that over time have taken on habituated authority within the culture. Delusions may be exquisitely logical, distinguished from consensual logics by their striking deviation from historical conceptions of action and thought. "Psychosis," as Freud argued, "disavows [existing reality] and tries to replace it."[18]

It is a mistake to think of psychosis as a totally dilapidated, confused state. Well organized and consistent logics appear in paranoid delusional systems of great richness and depth. Delusions also may overtake groups and define their thinking with logic, system, identification, values, and norms that, while consistent in their causality, nonetheless radically depart from historical and consensual modes of action. In the case of Nazi Germany, this applies to the treatment of the Jewish population.

Psychosis may be organized as a logic. That logic appears as an internally consistent delusional reading of reality, and the delusional may come to be equated and identified with the normal. In political life, exclusionary legislation, attitudes toward race, the practices of medicine, law, and administration—the sciences contributing to and profiting from the Final Solution—may be understood as political actions, distinguished by delusional percepts regarding the status of Jews, their treatment, and the phobia of them.

For the Germans, expression of favorable sentiment for the Jew was regarded as crazy. In historical retrospect, it is, however, possible to name actions for what they were, to unravel and interpret the real sources of delusion. The term *delusion* here describes actions, perceptions, and beliefs that prevailing current consensual standards would regard as repugnant, beyond acceptable limits and lacking any recognizable moral context. Further, the word *delusion* need not be pejorative or exclusionary; it may be used from a contemporary viewpoint to name fantasies and actions of such viciousness as to require a transvaluation of all moral, ethical, and consensual practices, inciting disgust in any human being capable of feeling pity or compassion at the sight of the dead or the dying.

The Final Solution, as opposed to the persecution and discrimination of the past, contained within it logics and perceptions of Jews that fundamentally altered the relationship between the political regime and the Jewish population of Europe. These logics, or what Michel Foucault calls *epistèmes*, may be considered delusional.[19] Their implementation, theory, and science were all part of a complex delusional system that redefined the external world while constructing murderous scripts that followed the imperatives of what Freud called necessity—but in the Final Solution, necessity appeared as the psychotic *biological* logics of the German professions.

For Freud, psychosis, in constructing radical perceptions, produces values supportive of the newly created reality. The psychosis develops, remodeling reality over a considerable period of time. It moves through different stages in the disavowal of conventional historical practices and paradigms. In Germany in the early 1930s, the theory and practice implemented through the sterilization program, the sporadic killings, and the legal precedents suggest concrete steps on the way to this delusional implosion. Later the T-4 euthanasia program extended the boundaries of delusional logic. The ideology, theory, and denial of the Jews, then, may be thought of as a delusion that came to be accepted as a governing cultural truth—the transvaluation of values finding its apotheosis in the new vision, the new order, the new *Judenrein* world, a radically new conjunction of knowledge and power.

In this reconstruction of new scripts and percepts, the practices that accompany the group psychosis take on their own logic. Further, in Freud's analysis, psychosis derives from the implosive quality of the world of fantasy, uncontainable unconscious impulses with terribly destructive power. While unconscious fantasies feed the ego, they are only loosely attached to it, but these split-off drives exercise an enormous impact on practice and perception. Fantasy, "the storehouse from which the materials or the pattern for building the new reality are derived," projects boundary-creating and numinous imagery and may for the group provide an all-consuming world view. "[T]he new imaginary, external world of a psychosis attempts to put itself in the place of external reality." It is not only a loss of reality, but also a substitute for reality. Fantasy, coming together as a skewed system of logic and relationship, creates "a set of new external and internal constructions."[20]

Behind this construction of new images in psychosis lies an explosive emotional component. In the case of the Germans, this is hate, a grotesque variant of what Melanie Klein calls the "paranoid schizoid" position of human experience—a hate so intense that its projective components took form in a seemingly objective analysis of the Jew's inferior legal, physiological, and historical status, its blood threat, and the most efficient methods to rid the culture of the Jewish body.

DELUSION AND PUBLIC HEALTH DEFINITIONS

Nazi Germany possessed a deadly, delusional logic—the logic inherent in theories of scapegoating, racial exclusion, race purity, and cultural pollution. The Final Solution developed its own value system, moralities, frames of reference, and ethics for action, the Wannsee Conference being an example of group-psychotic reasoning. The actions implementing the Final Solution broke through historically and consensually established limits; violated any recognizable moral or consensual norms of historically derived ethical, religious, or moral systems; and established hitherto unknown logics and techniques that could only be understood from within the Nazi racial ethos.

Fred Katz speaks of Auschwitz as a "culture of cruelty" that accommodated both the sadistic impulses of twisted character types and the cold technological efficiency of the German killing machine.[21] This overt culture of cruelty was absorbed in the group-dependent projections. Cruelty, in addition to being practiced directly, took on ominous implications in the distanciation of the Jewish body and its treatment as waste.

The view of the Jews as bacilli—common to both Hitler's "reasoning" and to medical, biological, and genetic science—had profound influence on how individuals perceived Jewish flesh. When Hitler said, "I feel like Robert Koch in politics. He discovered the bacillus and led medical science into new paths. I discovered the Jew as the

bacillus and the ferment in social decomposition," he was in touch
with the public mind, especially the professions in charge of "knowledge" in the Third Reich.[22]

After a trip to the Vilna Ghetto in early November 1941, Propaganda Minister Goebbels wrote in his diaries:

> The Jews are squatting on each other, horrible figures not to
> be seen, let alone to be touched. . . . Horrible figures starve in
> the streets, whom I would not like to meet at night. The Jews
> are like the lice of civilized mankind. Somehow they must be
> exterminated, or they will invariably resume their tormentive
> and molesting role.[23]

What is resounding in this quotation is the belief that the Jews deserve
their fate, and that the German people would be rescued with their
extermination. In the words of Goebbels: "The Jews have always been
the carriers of infectious diseases. They should either be concentrated
in a ghetto and left to themselves or be liquidated, for otherwise they
will infect the populations of the civilized nations."[24] Shortly after the
Wannsee Conference in January 1942, in the company of Himmler
and Lammers, Hitler observed: "One must act radically. When one
pulls out a tooth, one does it with a single tug, and the pain quickly
goes away. The Jew must clear out of Europe. Otherwise no understanding will be possible between Europeans."[25]

The Final Solution evolved not as a specific policy, endorsed by
party and leadership, but as a series of decisions largely influenced by
the work of the *Einsatzgruppen* during Spring and Summer 1941, by the
appeal of Hitler's racism, and by the anti-Semitism of German biological science. It makes little historical sense to argue that Hitler's hatred
of the Jews constituted only a small part of popular and public opinion
in Germany. If such were the case, it would be difficult to explain the
active participation of the countless workers essential to the massive
logistical task of transport and extermination. Engineers had extensive
contact with slave labor used in the armaments industry, in chemical
and gas production, and in the construction and maintenance of rocket
research centers and aircraft factories.[26] Regarding the participation of
railway officials, Hilberg notes: "They were solid individuals, but not
mindless robots. As intelligent men they were capable of understand-

ing the tenor of their time. They could not fail to obtain an 'overview' of their situation; they could not 'bypass' their reflections. The fact is that they were part of Nazi Germany, ruthless, relentless, and Draconian practitioners in every respect."[27] The complicity of the railways added to a number of bureaucratic "multiple initiatives" that facilitated the destruction of the Jews. As an autonomous agency, a "separate power" in the bureaucratic structure engaging in "lengthy negotiations and repeated adjustments," the railways willingly complied with other agencies and departments to forge an "unfathomable will to push the Nazi regime to the limits of its destructive potential."[28]

As evidence of widespread complicity and participation in mass murder, Goldhagen documents the "ever-expanding camp world" within the Reich itself. While camps devoted exclusively to mass slaughter, the "processing" of bodies, were located in Poland (Auschwitz, Sobibor, Treblinka, Majdanek, Belzec, Chelmno), concentration and labor camps were scattered throughout the country. For example, in the state of Hesse, at least 606 camps served industrial and production needs. It would not have been possible to ignore such widespread distribution of forced labor. Berlin alone contained 645 labor camps. Jewish inmates suffered extraordinarily high death rates. The monthly death rate in Mauthausen was 100 percent. Germans staffed and maintained more than 10,000 camps across Europe, most of them in the East. In Poland alone, 5,800 camps were established.[29]

Ideology is symptomatic of belief, but it is also symptomatic of fear. Given this reading of the historical evidence, it makes no sense to think of German citizens, or ordinary citizens living in areas surrounding the camps, as a set of faceless automatons who felt nothing about the fate of Jews. The bureaucratic, or what in the historiographic literature is called the "functionalist" argument, of which Hannah Arendt clearly is one of the central proponents, tends to gloss over questions of motive and intent. Desire, fear, and phobic reactions seem not to figure into calculations having to do with the murder of millions of human beings.

Murder on the scale of the Holocaust, however, requires some measure of collective belief. Individuals serve an extermination process willingly because of belief in its legitimacy. It is this element of belief Lawrence L. Langer finds so chilling in his account of the murder of twenty Jewish children within weeks of the end of the war at Bullenhauser Damm, an auxiliary concentration camp connected with the Neuengamme concentration camp a few miles outside Hamburg. The doctors conducting medical experiments without regard for the suffering and death of their subjects saw absolutely nothing wrong with their actions. At his trial in 1959, Kurt Heissmeyer, the physician in charge, expressed no sense of moral culpability: "I did not think inmates of a camp had full value as human beings." Asked why did he not use animals or guinea pigs for his immunization experiments, he responded: "For me there was no basic difference between human beings and guinea pigs"—but in a moment amended his comment, "between Jews and guinea pigs."[30]

For both Heissmeyer and Alfred Trzebinski, the senior SS physician at Neuengamme, since the victims were only Jews, life unworthy of life, their deaths possessed no moral or ethical significance. Max Pauly, commandant of Neuengamme, where fifty thousand prisoners died, wrote from his prison cell to his son: "Always be proud of being a German, and detest with all your might those who acquiesced in this absolutely false verdict." Believing strongly in his actions and innocence, Pauly could write with utter conviction: "I am not aware of any fault of mine; I always acted in the interests of the prisoners, doing my duty to the very end."[31]

Absent evidence of coercion, the actions of killing and the legal, logistical, and medical efforts surrounding the Final Solution signified more than a banal obeying of orders. It is for this reason that the group emotions involved in the paranoid fear of infection, the impulses toward purification of the blood, and the dread of polluting the *Kultur*-group are so important. The historiography following Arendt's pathbreaking focus on bureaucracy does not pay sufficient attention to the psychodynamic components of seeing the Jewish body as bacillus. The good family policeman from Hamburg, the train engineer in Munich, the factory worker in Bremen, the chemist in Berlin, and the physician at Bullenhauser Damm had no moral qualms about killing Jews. Group identity had been molded by more than a decade of professional support of anti-Semitism in law and politics.

Himmler described the psychology of the group mind when on April 24, 1943, well into the exterminations, he declared in a speech to the SS-*Korpsführer*:

We were the first to really answer the race problem by action, by the race problem we naturally did not mean anti-Semitism. Anti-Semitism is exactly like delousing. The removal of lice is not an ideological question, but a matter of hygiene. Thus, anti-Semitism is not an ideological issue, but a matter of hygiene, which will soon be behind us. We are almost deloused, we have only some 20,000 lice left and then it will be ended in all of Germany.[32]

Because medicine, administration, social and biological sciences, and the Nazi Party so enthusiastically endorsed the concept of the Jew as infection, other professions and groups in the society were similarly affected by these images.

Moral indifference alone is not enough to explain the connection between the policies that the party proclaimed and the state initiated and the history of anti-Jewish legislation, authorized largely by German professionals, capturing the public mood and mind in the preceding decade. The evidence supports the conclusion of moral enthusiasm in the project to defend the German *Kultur*-group from its fear of contamination by Jewish flesh. The measures induced by racial phobia, segregation, concentration, and murder of those deemed unworthy of life, were motivated not by indifference, but by an enthusiastic acceptance of racial beliefs. Himmler argued that the SS should be regarded with honor and respect for "perform[ing] this task . . . the hardest ever."[33] Yet the SS were only a part of the actual exterminations—the front lines, as it were. A much more extensive and equally enthusiastic bureaucratic and professional participation extended throughout the Third Reich.

DOCUMENTARY EVIDENCE AGAINST INDIFFERENCE

By 1940, the Jewish population in Germany had withered. Those remaining had been isolated into "mysterious strangers living their lives at the edge of the village."[1] Little, if any, communication existed between Jew and non-Jew. Did the German people experience relief at the removal of the Jewish population? If so, relief hardly indicates indifference. The historical literature, at least in terms of psychological explanation, is inconclusive. Kershaw and others argue that there is little evidence pointing to popular enthusiasm in Germany for the deportation of the Jews, especially after the outbreak of war.[2]

Silence, however, need not imply passive acquiescence. It could suggest a conscious effort to conceal strong enthusiasm for the exclusion of the Jewish population. Kershaw assumes that silence indicates indifference, but apparent indifference could mask a range of emotions extending from guilt to rage. It is a mistake to take expressions of sentiment at face value. Further, some historians disagree with the indifference thesis and find strong anti-Semitism within Germany through the 1940s.[3]

It is worth repeating that while the Nazis sought to keep the existence of the death camps secret, the enormous logistical requirements to supply the camps, their function as a source of slave labor, their importance in medical experiments, and the enormous quantity of goods shipped back to the Reich made it impossible to claim that the efforts at secrecy were successful. Himmler's demand for secrecy bore no relationship to the extensive knowledge of what was happening in the extermination camps.

Contemporary political action—legislation and its consequences—is more revealing of actual sentiment of the population. Let us use as benchmark the physical extermination of the Jews as a public policy. Indifference or the assertion, "I was just not aware," seems a pale, unsatisfactory explanation for untangling the "why" of a genocide on the scale of the Holocaust.

The apparent absence of rabid anti-Semitism does not imply that it was not operational. To the contrary, the anti-Semitism is clear in the enthusiasm for public property auctions, the willingness of people to take the jobs of Jews removed from important positions, the use of slave labor, the obsession with racial hygiene at every level of the educational and professional system, and the enthusiastic coordination of many industries and professions in the setting up and maintenance of killing centers.

Between October 1941 and October 1944, the German railway system transported more than half of the German Jewish population to their deaths. "No Jew was left alive for lack of transport."[4] Further, no officials in the railway organization protested, none resigned. In the archival evidence relating to the participation of the Reichsbahn, no documents show any official asking to be transferred. As Hilberg puts it: "No hesitancy in the ranks, and no pause in the effort. . . . As always, ordinary officials performed extraordinary tasks."[5]

Support among industry was equally enthusiastic. The construction of Auschwitz required the help of Topf and Sons of Erfurt, who built the crematory ovens; W. Reidel and Son of Bielitz and Joseph Kluge of Geiwitz, which supplied reinforced concrete; the construction firm of Robert Köhler; and the Dessau Sugar and Chemical Factories and the German Pest Control Company in Frieberg, which supplied Zyklon B gas. The steel tanks used as gas chambers in the T-4 program were supplied by the Mannesmann Röhrenwerke, a manufacturer of tubes and piping. Taken to the Ludwigshafen factory of I. G. Farben, these tanks were filled with carbon monoxide gas.[6]

Further opposing the indifference argument, Wolfgang Scheffler argues, is the sheer ruthlessness with which the ghetto exterminations were carried out: "The excesses during all the ghetto liquidations throughout the General Government clearly indicate that the occurrence cannot be explained solely by the automatism of orders and obedience, as is often assumed."[7]

In Lodz, the German administration established health commissions made up of physicians and SS officers to assess the fitness of the inhabitants. These commissions cursorily examined thousands of men, women, and children in assembly-line fashion. After each "exam," a letter stamped on the chest of the subject indicated status. The elderly, children under thirteen, and "unfit" adults were generally marked unsuitable for work, meaning they faced death. Fifteen hundred ghetto inhabitants faced the commission each day, until eleven thousand had been "examined" and sent to the labor camps or to their deaths.[8]

The systemwide participation in the institutions of the Final Solution casts doubt on the monolithic character of the Nazi regime. The work of such historians as Broszat, Mommsen, Browning, and Hilberg[9] suggests there was under Hitler not a monolithic regime, but one of radical decentralization, what Saul Friedländer calls "a more or less anarchic polycracy."[10] Individual bureaucrats and officials moved in different and often opposite directions. In Summer and Fall 1941, for example, mid-level policy debate over resettlement schemes continued as high party officials and administrators made preparations for annihilation.[11]

Bureaucrats, party leaders, state administrators, medical and legal officials all engaged in decision making without the knowledge of other divisions within the administrative structure. Hitler encouraged this confusion because competitive and mutually destructive rivalry between different branches of party and state administration enhanced his position. No demonstrable order from Hitler confirms that he alone initiated the Final Solution. The planning followed a series of individual initiatives in party and bureaucracy, and the implementation of the Final Solution reflected a systemwide consensus on mass extermination as a matter of policy. The consensus was: The Jewish problem exists, how shall we solve it?

Functionalist historians give primacy to bureaucracy and technology, see Hitler staying in the background, and argue, for example, that Reinhard Heydrich intended the Wannsee Conference to leave a "fuzzy" picture of what Hitler and the party hierarchy envisioned regarding the Jewish population. The emphasis of these historians is on process, structure, impersonal events, bureaucratic decision-making, competition and rivalry between departments, ministries, agencies, and party. Saul Friedländer disagrees: "[H]undreds of thousands were aware of part of the picture, but no opposition was voiced."[12] He sides with what is called the "intentionalist" position: Hitler and the party's racist ideology propelled the Final Solution; ideas, beliefs, values, perceptions, biological and genetic theory guided policy and action decisions. Bureaucrats, technicians, and professionals followed the lead of racism and its ideological and medical imperatives. While the functionalists do not deny the importance of Hitler, the Nazi Party and race ideology, their research emphasizes structure over belief, regime and administrative in-fighting and jockeying for position over ideological fanaticism and racist attitudes.

Both sides of this historical debate contribute to an understanding of the Holocaust. Neither side is entirely wrong or right. The intentionalist position might be strengthened by a focus on group psychoanalytic and political explanations (detailed in the following chapters) and by acknowledging documentary evidence of the fear of the Jewish body as a public health menace and the destruction of the Jewish body as a project endorsed throughout the society.

EVIDENCE FOR THE "BODIES DISPENSABLE" THESIS

Is it reasonable to use the Final Solution as an indicator of a group state of mind? Or is it more plausible to suggest that what went on in the death camps was the work of a few enthusiasts on the inside, and countless numbers of faceless bureaucrats vying for position and status on the outside? Both questions can be argued either way. Given the evidence, however, the destruction of the Jews was consistent with broader anti-Semitic sentiments in German society.[13] Administrators, physicians, lawyers, suppliers, and industrialists connected with the camps were not twisted psychological perverts but apparently willing participants who for a variety of reasons upheld the racist program of the Nazi regime.

The picture of the SS as a bunch of thugs is not entirely correct; many of the officers were well educated. Benno Müller-Hill writes that "seven of the fourteen participants (excluding Heydrich) at the Wannsee conference held doctoral degrees in law." Similarly in the *Einsatzgruppen*, the notorious death squads in charge of murdering Jews in the occupied territories of the East, "six of the fifteen *Einsatzgruppenführer* . . . held doctoral degrees. At least three others . . . had studied law. . . . [S]ixteen of the sixty-nine *Einsatzkommandoführer* also held doctoral degrees."[14]

A close alliance prevailed at all levels of the regime between university-educated personnel and the apparatus of killing. Extermination required massive technical and administrative coordination, what Müller-Hill calls "interdepartmental cooperation," the mobilization of knowledge, law, and science in a concerted effort with no single agency, leader, or department claiming responsibility for the entire operation. "So we witness legal experts executing, medical experts killing by gas, and with them political scientists, sociologists, and economists analyzing, and planners restructuring" the entire landscape of the Third Reich.[15]

If racist and phobic beliefs regarding Jewish bodies were not driving dynamics behind the system/group-wide perception of the Jew, why, then, a brutal, ruthless, and totalizing genocide? Because one wishes to please one's superior or be a good bureaucrat, or the summation of "uncoordinated strategies," or the end result of historical anti-Semitism, or the belief all Jews are money lenders or lust after blond Christian women?

Hanna Lévy-Haas, a prisoner in Bergen-Belsen, describes conditions of total collapse:

General malnutrition. It is as much as we can do to move. Nobody is able to walk upright, in a normal way; they all drag themselves along, swaying from side to side. Whole families die in the space of a few days. Old mother M. died quickly; two days later it was her husband's turn, then the children's, victims of malnutrition and the lice. One of the children was a short-sighted young lad who could not cope with the lice crawling over his body. They had penetrated his skin and even got into his eyelashes, and his chest was black with thousands of them. We have never seen anything like it, and no one could have imagined such a sight. They have eaten him away, body and mind, making him look like a mental defective. He used to be a very intelligent boy, they said. Today he slowly drags his skinny, flea-ridden body from one end of the hut to the other,

moaning and whimpering. The others avoid him and his sister
and his brother are afraid to go near him. A few days ago he
spent the entire night struggling pathetically from one bunk to
the next, begging to be given a little room, but they all pushed
him away in disgust. We all lie two to a bunk but no one would
share with him, and there was no spare bunk. So, with no
place to lay his wretched body, he just died.[16]

Could the surrounding population *not* have seen the emaciated, disease-ridden bodies? "The Nazis, the SS 'supermen' took good care not
to get too close to the prisoners in the huts, because we were regarded
not as human beings."[17] If one gets too close, one may become like the
broken creatures penned inside the barbed wire; if one breathes the air
of these vermin-like objects, one may inhale or otherwise ingest or take
into the body itself terrifying destructive germs and bacilli. Lévy-Hass
speaks of inmates' brains being "paralyzed," spirits "crushed . . . injuries
inflicted on the spirit [going] so deep that it is as though one's whole
being were dead, as though one were shut off from the normal world
of the past by a massive, solid wall."[18] "Standing in a mass of filth,
refuse and excrement, we rub ourselves down with cold water. . . .
[P]eople get used to it all. Slowly they sink deeper and deeper, and
when their strength finally gives out, they die. It is the only answer."[19]

It is extraordinary the extent to which suffering is not acknowledged, much less noticed. "Life unworthy of life" possesses no claim
on empathy or care from either the guards or surrounding population. These prisoners had been completely walled off from the moral
universe of compassion. Lévy-Hass notices "new arrivals" in Belsen,
convoys of prisoners in the winter of 1944 arriving from Auschwitz.

The new arrivals are accommodated in tents. They lie on a
thin layer of straw—or, more accurately, on the damp
ground itself. They look terrible—sick, ashen, covered in sup-
purating sores. We are not able to get close to them or speak
to them. In the evenings, under the pretext of going to the
latrine, we listen to the muffled sound that rises in the darkness like a black cloud from the other side of the barbed wire,
a sound of moaning and lamenting, mixed with the crying of
children. It is impossible to pick out any words.

To listen to the groans and whimpers of these dying wretches is a shattering and terrifying experience.[20]

NUREMBERG EVIDENCE:
MEDICINE AND THE ABUSE OF THE BODY

Several features stand out in the Nuremberg reports on German medical experiments: (1) the suffering body as not there; (2) the body as object of scientific investigation; (3) the infliction of suffering as useful to science; (4) the absence of moral context to the experiments themselves; (5) the wide-ranging participation of thousands of individuals, from nurses to technicians to businessmen, in the administration of the experiments and the benefits thought to be gained from them; and (6) the disconnection between the subject's suffering and the technical operation of science itself.

Victor Brack, who conducted experiments in X-ray sterilization, wrote to Himmler in 1941:

One way to carry out these experiments in practice would be to have those people who are to be treated line up before a counter. There they would be questioned and a form would be given them to be filled out, the whole process taking 2 or 3 minutes. The official attendant who sits behind the counter can operate the apparatus in such a manner that he works a switch which will start both tubes together (as the rays have to come from both sides). With one such installation with two tubes about 150 to 200 persons could be sterilized daily, while 20 installations would take care of 3,000 to 4,000 persons daily.[21]

In June 1942, Brack again enthusiastically wrote Himmler:

Castration by X-rays . . . is not only relatively cheap but can also be performed on many thousands in the shortest time.

I think that at this time it is already irrelevant whether the people in question become aware of having been castrated after some weeks or months, once they feel the effects.[22]

Subsequently X-ray experiments in sterilization at Auschwitz received favorable attention from major scientific institutes and universities in Germany. Knowledge of experimentation was widely disseminated; articles reporting on death camp experiments continued to appear after the war. Physicians in research "protocols" conducted in the camps saw their "patients" as objects, not as human beings in pain. Screams were not treated as pain. Fevers, runny sores, mutilated and gangrenous limbs became notes in a scientific program. Torn flesh was found useful in the effort to produce more effective prosthetic devices. Execution assumed assembly-line proportions. A survivor recalls:

> The victim was ordered to sit on a stool, one hand had to be put at the back of the neck, the other behind the shoulder-blade. In such a way the chest was thrust out. Sometimes the victims were blindfolded with a towel. Driving the long needle into the 5th space between the ribs, at the left side, inside the central clavicular line, and the injection of several centimeters of phenol did not take up much time after some routine. The hangmen used to boast about their records. "Three in a minute." As a rule, not even a moan could be heard. And they did not wait until the doomed person really died. During his agony he was taken from both sides under the armpits and thrown onto a pile of corpses in another room opposite. And the next took his place on the stool.[23]

Children brought to Block 20, a barracks housing medical "experimentation," had no idea they were to die. When they discovered what was about to happen, screams echoed throughout the barracks: "The terrified outcries of the murdered children . . . 'Why are you killing me'—shall for ever remain in the memory of the witnesses of this crime."[24]

The contrast between scientific intent and its effects on victims' bodies is remarkable. Regarding experiments conducted with typhus vaccine at Buchenwald, Professor D. E. Haagen sent requests for experimental subjects to the SS routed through a colleague, a Professor Hirt of the Anatomical Institute of the Reich University in Strasbourg. He asked permission to publish a paper on his experiments with a dry typhus vaccine "which has not been made sterile by chemical agents or by heating." He argued that his research held promise in producing a "vaccine which provides not only an antitoxic immunity but also a definite anti-infection immunity which is of particularly practical significance." The proposed vaccine, however, induced "a rather long fever reaction; [therefore,] further tests are now in progress to alter the vaccine so that, without losing its antigenic property, it will produce so weak a reaction that no general indisposition will result."[25] A seemingly objective study on concentration camp inmates of the efficacy of a typhus vaccine appears to be a normal scientific experiment. In reality, however, prisoners injected with live typhus bacilli were dying gruesome deaths. Eügen Kogon, a Buchenwald inmate, testified:

Every man in the camp knew that Block 46 was a dreadful place. . . . A dreadful horror seized anyone who was brought into any kind of connection with this block. If people were selected and taken to Block 46 through the sick bay, then they knew that the affair was a fatal one. The untold horror which was attached to this block made things even worse. . . . Everyone, therefore, who went to Block 46 as an experimental person did not only have to expect death, and under certain circumstances a very long drawn out and frightful death, but also torture and the complete removal of the last remnants of personal freedom. In this mental condition these experimental persons waited in the sick bays for an unknown period of time. They waited for the day or for the night when something would be done to them; they did not know what it would be, but they guessed that it would be some frightful form of death. If they were vaccinated, then sometimes the most horrible scenes took place, because the patients were afraid the injections were lethal. . . . There were cases of raving madness, delirium, people would refuse to eat, and a large percentage of them would die. Those who experienced the disease in a milder form, perhaps because their constitutions were stronger or because the vaccine was effective were forced continuously to observe the death struggles of the others.[26]

In November 1943, Haagen wrote to a Professor Rose, Chief of
the Department of Tropical Medicine in the Robert Koch Institute,
Berlin, excited about his experiments with dehydrated typhus vaccine, and findings obtained from administering the vaccine to camp
inmates. In fact, the vaccine precipitated, in many inmates, severe
infections that resulted in agonizing deaths. The German physicians,
however, saw nothing wrong in an experimental protocol in which
vaccination lead to death.

Experiments with live typhus vaccines produced agonizing
deaths. In interrogating Professor Rose, Chief of the Department of
Tropical Medicine in the Robert Koch Institute, Berlin, the American
prosecutor was puzzled at what the German physicians called vaccination.

PROSECUTOR I am having considerable difficulty in construing the
    word "infection" to mean "vaccination."
ROSE Yes, I admit that many of these documents are written in a con-
    fusing way, but I believe that I can remember the whole matter
    adequately enough to know what the problem is. The vaccine was
    not developed enough to be used in vaccination without reaction
    and then to determine the effect. There were strong fever reac-
    tions, and the problem was how to avoid this fever reaction.
PROSECUTOR Well, why call that infection?
ROSE That is a similar condition biologically. An injection of a live, a
    virulent vaccine, from the biological point of view, is an infection.
    This expression is used often enough, but it is an infection which
    one can absolutely control.[27]

In Block 46, so-called vaccinations induced infections of such
magnitude that within a matter of hours inmates died. To call a
deadly infection leading to certain death a vaccination requires a generous leap of the scientific imagination. Evidence from the trial transcripts suggests it was commonplace to infect subjects so as to induce
death. The experimental vaccines rarely worked. Infected blood
injected into inmates was especially concentrated with typhus bacilli.
Experiments were conducted on already emaciated and fatigued bodies. At least 80 percent of those infected died. Many inoculated with
vaccine and then injected with typhus died because the vaccines were

of insufficient strength. The fantasy of gaining reputation from the experiments, the grandiosity of the science and its practitioners, completely eclipsed the suffering of the subjects.

What went on at Buchenwald typifies the "science" conducted in all camps: a literal blindness to the suffering of bodies and a delusion as to the benefits of science itself. Death mattered not at all in the implementation of the experiments. A November 13, 1944, entry in a Buchenwald medical log reads:

THERAPEUTIC EXPERIMENT
WITH TYPHUS VACCINE

By order of the senior hygienist of the Waffen SS of 12 August '44, it is to be determined whether the course of typhus can be tempered by the intravenous or intramuscular injection of typhus vaccine.

For the environment series, 20 persons were considered, of these, 10 for intravenous injection (Series A), 10 for intramuscular injection (Series B) and, in addition, 5 persons for control.

On 13 Nov. '44, the 25 experimental persons were infected by subcutaneous injection of 1/10cc. each fresh typhus-infected blood. All persons fell sick as follows: Series A—10 serious; Series B—1 medium 9 serious; Control—5 serious.

22 Dec '44

The experimental series was concluded.

2 Jan '45

Chart and case history completed.

19 deaths (9 Series A, 6 Series B, 4 Control).

DR. DING-SCHULER[28]

Physicians in these medical experiments regarded the body of the subject as matter to be worked on and destroyed. Compare the following from the prosecutor's summary regarding incendiary bomb experiments in Buchenwald:

Sturmbannfuehrer Ding-Schuler ... carried out incendiary bomb experiments in the Buchenwald concentration camp between 19 and 25 November 1943. In order to ascertain the effectiveness of the drug R 17 and echinacine ointment and liquid for the treatment of phosphorous burns, five experimental persons were deliberately burned with ignited phosphorus which was taken from an incendiary bomb. The resulting burns were very severe, the victims suffered excruciating pain and permanent injury. The drugs to be tested were manufactured at the Dr. Madaus Works in Dresden-Radebeul.[29]

These medical experiments reveal the utter blindness of Nazi medical authorities to the sufferings of "life unworthy of life"—and the complicity of powerful social and political agents in enabling such procedures to be undertaken without protest. Kogon reported the active collaboration of the "firm of Madaus and Co. at Dresden-Radebeul to carry out experiments on human beings with regard to the effect of a drug against the contents of phosphorous-caoutchouc incendiary bombs."[30] Again and again the medical reports show instances of enthusiastic collaboration between scientific institutes, industries, and camp physicians undertaking experiments. Photographers, stenographers, chemists, accountants, bankers, architects, and nurses all willingly participated in the experiments because they stood to gain from what were hoped to be medical advances.

The Nuremberg transcripts are filled with correspondence between researchers and their superiors at institutes and universities throughout Germany, and private and public agencies. Experiments including sulfanilamide, sepsis, gas gangrene, low-pressure (high-altitude), sea water, freezing, and malaria tolerance at Dachau; bone, muscle, and nerve regeneration and bone transplantation at Ravensbrueck; epidemic jaundice and mustard gas at Sachsenhausen and Natzweiler; eye, sterilization, and twin experiments in Auschwitz. Major social and professional sectors regarded scientific experimentation as central to the welfare of the Reich economy: for example, medical research; medical school instruction; firms specializing in prosthetic devices; water processing firms such as I. G. Farben; chemical research laboratories; military ordnance and aviation supply companies; X-ray and laboratory instrument firms; specialized industries connected with restorative surgeries and the containment of infectious diseases; and other biochemical and pharmaceutical firms.

Medical experiments, rather than being tangential to the interests of the citizenry, were part of daily life in the Third Reich. In Ravensbrueck, a Professor Gebhardt regularly conducted sepsis experiments to test drugs developed by the German pharmaceutical industry.[31] The Dachau sea water experiments enlisted the support of the High Command of the Navy–Medical Department and Department for Research, Inventions, and Patents; the Research Operation of the Reich Ministry for Aviation and High Command of the Luftwaffe; the Institute for Aviation Medicine; the Technical Academy of Vienna; the Medical Experimentation and Instruction Division of the Luftwaffe, Jueterborg; the Medical University Clinic in Vienna; the Chief of the Medical Service of the Luftwaffe; and the physicians and nurses in the Luftwaffe hospital in Brunswick.[32]

Yet this so-called science remained blind to the pain of its subjects. Note the following from the Nuremberg affidavit of Sofia Maczka concerning experimental operations on inmates of the Ravensbrueck concentration camp:

> The soft part of the calf of the leg was opened and the open wounds were infected with bacteria which were introduced into the wounds. . . . On the operating table, the bones of the lower part of both legs were broken into several places with a hammer, later they were joined with clips . . . or without clips. . . . A few abnormal prisoners (mentally ill) were chosen and brought to the operating table, and amputations of the whole leg (at the hip joint) were carried out . . . amputation of the whole arm (with the shoulder blade) were carried out. Afterwards the victims (if they still lived) were killed by means of evipan injections and the leg or arm was taken to Hohenlychen and served the [research] purposes known to Professor Gebhardt.[33]

Published by *Clinic and Practice*, a leading weekly journal for the practicing physician, these experiments guided German surgeons. I quote from the February 1946 issue: "During the past 10 years, 471 free autoplastic bone transplantations were carried out in Hohenlychen"—a clinic in close contact with many physicians at Ravensbrueck concentration camp.[34] The analysis of results and findings, the practical applicability of the experiments, their interpretation, and the material necessary for their implementation drew the expertise of thousands of individuals from all over Germany.[35]

Müller-Hill locates the destructiveness of Nazi science not only in the camps, but throughout the professional system. Otmar von Verschuer, a respected geneticist of his time, requested "several research grants for the Auschwitz project from the D.F.G. (Deutsche Forschungsgemeinschaft or German Research Association)."[36] His proposals described experiments in human twin studies, eye defects, tuberculosis, and specific serum proteins. Was Verschuer's use of camp inmates as scientific subjects unusual? Müller-Hill answers with a resounding no: "Other researchers had already profited from the murder of the insane. It may be recalled that some 70,000 patients of German mental institutions were killed by gas during 1940 and the first half of 1941."[37] Julius Hallervorden, assistant director at the Kaiser Wilhelm Institute for Brain Research in Berlin-Dahlem, conducted a special research project utilizing seven hundred brains of mental patients killed in the T-4 euthanasia program.

Science and scientists, Müller-Hill notes, "observe and analyze objects." But what happens when human beings assume the status of objects? "An object is a thing without rights. When a human being becomes an object, he is nothing but a slave." And what is of interest to the scientist is not the object, the object's emotions, or even the "object's own questions," but only the "questions the scientist" asks the object."[38] The scientist shows no interest in what the object's body registers as anguish, pain, or despair. Human rights possessed utterly no significance for the Jew, gypsy, and others seen as "life unworthy of life."[39]

An observer of the Luftwaffe experiments in high altitude endurance and freezing at the Dachau concentration camp recounted:

> I have personally seen through the observation window of the chamber when a prisoner inside would stand a vacuum until his lungs ruptured. Some experiments gave men such pressure in their heads that they would go mad, and pull out their hair in an effort to relieve the pressure. They would tear their heads and face with their fingers and fingernails in an attempt to maim themselves in their madness. They would beat the walls with their hands and head, and scream in an effort to relieve pressure on their eardrums. These cases of

extreme vacuums generally ended in the death of the subject. An extreme experiment was so certain to result in death that in many instances the chamber was used for routine execution purposes rather than an experiment.[40]

SLAVE LABOR AND THE DISPENSABILITY OF BODIES

The meetings of the Reich Central Planning Board describe the mechanics of conscripting hundreds of thousands of prisoners of war and concentration camp inmates to serve in basic industries located in the Reich proper. The coal industry at one time employed more than sixty-nine thousand prisoners. The notes of an April 22, 1943, meeting remark: "We subsist on foreigners who live in Germany. . . . [O]n 1 April we had in agriculture a deficit of about 600,000 laborers. It had been planned to cover it by supplying labor from the East, mainly women."[41] The bulk of conscripted labor consisted of Russians, gypsies, and Jews living in conditions as deplorable as the concentration camps—in the midst of German society.

The following extracts from the Central Planning Board indicate the extent of labor needs as of May 1944:

GABEL We must have 1,000 underground workers at once.

SAUER Definitely.

BORNITZ The Erzberg [ore mine] has furthermore a loss of from 1,400 to 1,500 men per annum due to climatic conditions. It goes up as high as 1,500 meters.

SAUR Do you give the men up systematically, and to whom?

BORNITZ Not systematically. They collapse, report sick, and the foreigners do not come back. Some escape too, as in the mountain country it is not possible to seal everything hermetically.

(Comment: A year ago the labor potential of a large concentration camp was thoroughly gone into. That possibility must not be entirely disregarded.)

GABEL Careful! Concentration camp internees are not strong enough to be able to work underground.

REICH MINISTER SPEER With regard to construction, it is important that we should not start more building than we can supply labor and equipment for. Equipment is of secondary importance. We must not continue with the mistakes we found in the air force armament industry when we took over, i.e., the beginning of no end of buildings for which, at that time, only 20 to 30 percent of the necessary labor was available.

SAUR That is the case now, unfortunately. We have at least 3 times as many buildings under construction as we have labor available.

REICH MINISTER SPEER What is the news about the Hungarian Jews?

KAMMLER They are on the way. At the end of the month the first transports will arrive for surface work on the surface bunkers.[42]

SCHMELTER Dorsch will accompany me to Greiser to try and get 20 to 30 thousand men out of him.

REICH MINISTER SPEER Kammler had his doubts about that before.

REPRESENTATIVE OF KAMMLER He didn't think the 100,000 Jews would come.

SCHMELTER To that I can add the following. Till now two transports have arrived at the SS camp Auschwitz. For fighter construction we were offered only children, women and old men with whom very little can be done. . . . Unless the next transports bring men of an age fit for work, the whole action will not have much success.[43]

SCHMELTER I have a few more points. Up till now 12,000 female concentration camp internees, Jewesses, have been demanded. The matter is now in order. The SS has agreed to deliver these Hungarian Jewesses in batches of 500. Thus, the smaller firms, too, will be in a position to employ these concentration camp Jewesses better. I request that these people should be ordered in batches of 500.

MAHNKE How many are still there?

SCHMELTER There are still enough there (43).

Slave labor contributed enormously to the war aims of the Third Reich. The Jaegerstab, a central planning board concerned with the distribution of conscripted and slave labor, particularly for the aircraft industry, sent hundreds of thousands of workers to work sites throughout the Reich. To supply industry and armaments manufacture, the Jaegerstab seized workers directly from transports coming from the occupied territories; requisitioned slave labor from the concentration and death camps; and contracted directly with the SS for camp inmates. Thus, the presence of emaciated and starved Jews at factories and transient labor camps inside the Reich became an increasingly common sight.

EXTRACT FROM INTERROGATION OF KARL OTTO SAUR ON 13 NOVEMBER 1946 CONCERNING THE USE OF CONCENTRATION CAMP PRISONERS IN JAEGERSTAB CONSTRUCTION

Were special factories built after the creation of the Jaegerstab? [44]
All building of factories above the ground was stopped, and subterranean factories were built. We divided approximately 30 factories into 700 individual workshops to avoid offering targets for attacks.

What kind of workers were used for this construction?
The construction was divided into three parts: the two Kammler parts, (a) new construction underground, and (b) expansion underground, and the Todt Organization part.

This expansion program was directed by Kammler, then? [Kammler was a leading official of the Economic Administrative Main Office of the SS, in charge of distributing and using concentration camp labor.]
Parts (a) and (b) were directed quite independently by Kammler. He had full authority from Goering as of 4 March 1944 and was then made a member of the Jaegerstab. . . . The whole affair was carried out by Kammler alone.

And the workers who were used for this purpose were concentration camp prisoners?
To my knowledge, they must have been concentration camp prisoners.[45]

FROM INTERROGATION OF FRITZ SCHMELTER
BY PRESIDING JUDGE TOMS

The Hungarian Jews, so far as I recall, were offered by the SS to be employed in armament production. At first there were 1,000 of them or 500 who were employed. Then a number of plants said that they wanted such workers, and they were then allotted by the SS to these plants and there they were obliged to work.

Then the SS, which was one branch of the German military establishment simply dealt out the Hungarian Jews to anybody who needed them? No. The Hungarian Jews, like all concentration camp inmates, were housed in camps that were either in or near the plants and which were constructed by the SS. They were then taken to work every day, and after the work they were again brought back by the SS to the camps. Also, the supervision of the work, for security reasons, was carried out by the SS. So far as the technical side of it was concerned, it was carried out by the representatives of the plant. [Thus, interaction between camp prisoners and German workers was inevitable, and in fact, happened on a regular basis.][46]

[From the direct examination by Defense Council]
The SS demanded that the [Hungarian Jewish] females should be delivered in batches of thousands only. Most factories could not use such a large number of females. Consequently, the SS was asked if it could not deliver them in smaller groups.[47]

[From cross-examination by Prosecutor Denney, quoted from an earlier deposition]
The SS once offered us a lot of [Hungarian Jewish] women. The difficulty was that, at first, at least 1,000 and later 500 were to be employed. Various firms got women after that, and I think that Heinkel, in Oranienburg, used concentration camp prisoners, not only women, but all the inmates.[48]

Frequently, concentration camp inmates, prisoners of war, foreign workers, and German nationals worked in the same environment. Max Koenig, an officer in the Wehrmacht, testified under cross-examination concerning the labor distribution of a factory in Rechlin, approximately 70 or 80 miles northwest of Berlin on Lake Mueritz.

> *You said that you had concentration camp workers—you also had foreign workers, didn't you?*
> There were about 1,000 concentration camp inmates and a certain number of foreign workers—Russians, French and Italians.
>
> *Did you have any prisoners of war?*
> Yes. We had some prisoners of war.
>
> *How many people were employed there altogether?*
> In Rechlin, prisoners of war and foreign workers, Germans, altogether there were 4–5 thousand.
>
> *Well, now we have got 1,000 concentration camp workers. So that leaves 3 to 4 thousand. How were those broken down among prisoners of war, foreign workers, and Germans?*
> Prisoners of war, roughly 500. There were about 300 foreigners, and the rest were German civilians and German military personnel.[49]

Norbert Troller comments on slave labor being brought from Auschwitz to work on a mining project near Theresienstadt. The victims

> worked in other shafts like us and on the railway tracks. Then a couple of hundred free civilian workers, Sudeten Germans, *Volksgenossen*, worked as specialists in the workshops, offices and cranes and other road machinery. Slave labor constitutes the bulk of the workforce. Slave labor was available, inexhaustible. Jews, prisoners of all occupied Slavic nations, Czechs, Poles, Russians ... About 10,000 men working ten hours per day, driven to exhaustion by the kapos, to hack, in four-man teams, nut-sized chips out of the solid rock without dynamite or drilling compressors.[50]

It appeared to be commonplace to have a mix of camp inmates, prisoners of war, foreign workers, and German nationals working in close proximity. Emaciated, sick, dying bodies, contrasted with healthy Germans, could only serve to reinforce the fear of contamination by contact with polluted flesh. Further, towns supplying the camps profited from conscripted and concentration camp labor. In a number of industries—for example, mining, transport, smelting, chemical, pharmaceutical, and armaments—conscripted labor constituted a significant percentage of the total labor force; it contributed 40 percent of the armament industry labor needs. Russian prisoners of war made up over 88 percent of the labor force required to construct Germany's most advanced airplane engine.[51]

Six to seven million "foreign" workers, hundreds of thousands drawn from "inferior," "mongolized," and subjugated races, resided in Germany during the war. From the Nuremberg transcript:

> It was sought to disguise the harsh realities of the German foreign labor policy by the use of specious legal and economic terms, and to make such policy appear as the exercise of conventional labor relations and labor law. The fiction of a "labor contract" was frequently resorted to, especially in the operations of the Todt organization, which implied that foreign workers were given a free choice to work or not to work for German military industry. This, of course, was purely fictitious, as is shown by the fact that thousands of these "contract workers" jumped from the trains transporting them to Germany and fled into the woods. Does anyone believe that the vast hordes of Slavic Jews who labored in Germany's war industries were accorded the rights of contracting parties? They were slaves, nothing less—kidnapped, regimented, herded under armed guards, and worked until they died from disease, hunger, and exhaustion. The idea of any Jew being a party to a contract with Germans was unthinkable to the National Socialists. Jews were considered as outcasts and were completely at the mercy of their oppressors. Exploitation was merely a convenient and profitable means of extermination, to the end that "when this war ends, there will be no more Jews in Europe."[52]

INFERENCES AND CONCLUSIONS

What inferences can be drawn from these data? The claims of "not knowing" or "being insulated" or "having no idea" of the camps or conditions in them hold little weight because of the widespread dispersal of slave and concentration camp labor in Germany. As the testimony above indicates, the SS received frequent requests for batches of concentration camp labor. It would be naïve to suggest that such forced labor use in the construction of factories, armaments, and bunkers, and the production of agricultural goods, mining, and manufacture could be completely separated from the surrounding culture. German workers, suppliers, and political officials all came into contact with foreign workers and slave labor.

Sectors of the German population vital for the prosecution of the war prospered from the collaboration; it stretches credibility, given what the population saw in these bodies—particularly in light of the fact that well over four million slave workers were conscripted by the Germans—to claim that ordinary citizens, particularly the professionals who maintained control over knowledge and distributed its insights, either had little idea of what was going on or were indifferent.

The Nuremberg evidence shows the intimate involvement of the medical profession in the project of mass murder. Lifton explains this phenomenon by elaborating the concept of "doubling": two selves occupying the same person. The Auschwitz self, for example, becomes accustomed to the killing, while the self outside the camp might be horrified at a dog run over by a car.[53] Doubling enables the Auschwitz self to undertake actions it might not otherwise initiate outside the camp environment.

To an extent, this explanation holds. What it does not explain, however, is the ease with which Nazi doctors moved from environment to environment, without feeling any guilt or remorse, or even questioning their actions. For example, in Johann Paul Kremer's diary, entries recorded outside the camp show a self remarkably similar to the one at Auschwitz: no conflict over the killing, no ambivalence, no bad dreams or murky conscience.

May 24, 1943
Today conference in District Building with Dr. Grässner, not on
the subject of the Driburg case, as I had supposed, but because
they wanted my cooperation as lecturer in the District propaganda machine (population policy, race hygiene). He made the
proposal I should first attend a course dealing with such essential
problems and taking place in Berlin-Babelsberg. I accepted this
proposal with joy, if only to look for some beetles in Berlin. [Kre-
mer was an enthusiastic beetle collector.][54]

A few weeks later he attended the Reich School of the Race Policy Office in Potsdam-Babelsberg. "Room and board are good ...
most of the time is spent in recreation and conversation without constraint."[55] On one of his free afternoons he wanders about the town
looking for beetles for his scientific experiments.

Whatever the merits of Lifton's interpretation of "doubling," it
was also the case that Kremer, and people like him, had utterly no
qualms about what happened to Jews, inside or outside the killing
centers. It was a state of mind that, rather than suggesting a complex
psychological defensive operation, appeared to reflect a general attitude toward human beings who, if they were seen at all, looked as if
they were the living incarnation of horrifying disease. And if one
were in the public health profession, or concerned with national
hygiene, as all the professions were, healing the nation meant killing.

The moral problem with the doubling thesis is that it tends to
diminish individual responsibility. Adaptability to Auschwitz as a public health facility does not require another self, but does indicate a
continuation of an already operating ideological system. As Berel
Lang puts it: "It is more plausible to infer a single moral agent—one
that granted greater conviction to evil than to good—than two independent moral domains that were constantly being traversed."[56]
Adapting to the physically gruesome sight of bodies being gassed and
burned requires a certain amount of acclimation. But these are two
different issues: Ordering the death of "life unworthy of life" involves
willed belief, and not necessarily an alternative Auschwitz self.
Watching thousands of bodies burning in crematoria or open pits,
which even Himmler had trouble stomaching, might involve psychological operations like numbing or distancing. Yet these operations on

perception do not imply the creation of a complete self. It is important to distinguish between psychological defensive operations and the construction of an entirely new self.

Physicians and scientists inside and outside Auschwitz subscribed to racial and hygienic principles driving the policies of the political regime. In light of identification with an ideological and moral vision, the doubling explanation seems forced; numbing oneself to the stench and horror of burning flesh need not imply the elaboration of something as complex as an alternative self. With very few exceptions, what these doctors undertook in Auschwitz, they would have done in their offices in Berlin, Hamburg, or Munich. Making selections on the receiving ramps of Auschwitz constituted part of one's public health service. It just took time to adapt to the rather grueling conditions of a death camp.

Lifton's contributions to understanding the role of medicine in the Third Reich are enormous. The range of his research and analysis marks a major contribution to understanding the Holocaust and is central to the argument of this book. The doubling thesis, however, detracts from his larger point: the participation of the professions in the killing and the fundamental medical core of the Nazi ideological program. The Nuremberg evidence reveals, in fact, how much the Auschwitz self seemed to reflect the will and intent of a systemwide *Kultur* of killing.

THE PHOBIC GROUP AND THE CONSTRUCTED ENE-MY

If one sees the Final Solution as the work of a group of petit-bour-geois thugs, then what Hitler and his henchmen said can be dis-counted. But if one regards the Nazi Party as an integral part of German society, representing the *Kultur*-group and its will, then what leaders said and did figures prominently into an accounting of motive behind the Final Solution. As late as April 1945, Martin Bormann referred in a conversation with Hitler to the need for the nation to free itself from the "Jewish poison." The regime that accomplished this would "earn eternal gratitude for exterminating the Jews in Ger-many and Central Europe."[1]

Raul Hilberg notes that the *Volkssturm*, the Austrian reserves who in February 1945 killed over 80 percent of Russian prisoners of war escaping the Mauthausen concentration camp, were "considered the laughing stock of the German armed forces, [consisting] of older men scratched together and sometimes armed with French rifles."[2] The *Volkssturm* was another example of ordinary men who without hesitation killed thousands of Jews—in their case, Hungarian Jews being marched through the mountains surrounding Mauthausen. Is this passive acquiescence to orders? Physicians who before 1938 had led relatively normal lives claimed the right to make selections on the ramps at the killing camps; photographs from the period show busy, well dressed industrialists and German officers smiling, making plans, chatting in the midst of grotesque suffering and squalor. These industrious businessmen were not forced to comply with orders from the SS.

It was not, then, only a bureaucratic, organizational, and technological machine that drove the Holocaust. Faith, belief, commitment, choice, and will motivated a significant dimension of the killing project. In a speech given in Kraków, August 2, 1943, Hans Frank described the success of his work in Operation Reinhard, the plan to exterminate all Jews in central Poland: "We started here with three and a half million Jews, and what remains of them—a few working companies only."[3]

Throughout Eastern Europe host populations welcomed the collaboration between Nazi death squads and local officials in seeking out and killing Jews and Communist functionaries. The following selections from reports filed by *Einsatzgruppen* commanders show considerable enthusiasm for the numbers of Jews killed.

> The territory, with the exception of the Hungarian-occupied area around Svanzia, was cleared of Jews. The Rumanians had driven thousands of selected persons unfit for labor, such as invalids and children, from Bessarabia and Bucovina into the German sphere. In the vicinity of Svanzia-Mogilev-Podolski-Yampol, a total of approximately 27,500 Jews were driven back to Rumanian territory, and 1,265, partly younger ones, were shot. 3,105 more Jews and 34 Communists were liquidated in Chernovtsy in the course of search actions east of the Dniester. No terror and sabotage groups were discovered.
>
> August 29, 1941[4]

> Einsatzkommando 9 found 149 Jews of Yanovichi to be NKGB informers and political functionaries who were handled accordingly. Some of these Jews sabotaged German projects. They stayed in hiding in order not to be drafted to gather the harvest, and for road and aerodrome construction work.
>
> After three German soldiers were killed in the vicinity of Vitebsk, a German Army pacification-action was carried out. On this occasion we seized 19 Jews and Jewesses wandering around in the forest where the murder had been committed.

They were executed on the strong suspicion of having taken part in the attack and committing arson in Vitebsk.

The Vorkommando Moscow was forced to execute another 46 persons, among them 38 intellectual Jews who had tried to create unrest and discontent in the newly established ghetto of Smolensk.

September 4, 1941[5]

Executions of Jews are understood everywhere and accepted favorably.

September 12, 1941[6]

Repeated complaints had been voiced [by the local population] alleging that the Jews in Monastirshchina and Khoslavichi had shown an impudent and provocative attitude. A Kommando of the Vorkommando caused all Jews in these villages to be marked [identified with a yellow Jewish star], transferred into a ghetto, forced to work and registered by name. It also shot the existing Jewish council and another 20 Jews.

Sonderkommando 7 arrested 21 Jewish economic saboteurs and looters and subjected them to special treatment. . . . The major accused the Jews especially of continually sabotaging his measures. . . . A large-scale anti-Jewish action was carried out in the village of Lahoysk. In the course of this action, 920 Jews were executed with the support of a unit of the SS Division "Reich." The village may now be described as "free of Jews."

September 23, 1941[7]

Such groups were not acting in an ideological vacuum. Many of their officers held advanced degrees, and the soldiers of these squads came from a cross-section of German society. *Einsatzgruppen* reports were distributed in as many as forty-eight copies. The number of people reading these could not have been minimal. Soldiers, suppliers, logistical support units returning from the Russian front brought with them stories and accounts of the mass killings as well.

In addition, conditions in the ghettos created a self-fulfilling prophecy. Martin Broszat writes:

> There now existed a concrete picture of an inferior race which had to be eradicated.... the discriminated against, crowded, tormented and frightened Jews in the East finally looked the way they were caricatured in the anti-Semitic periodicals. Epidemics in the ghettos made them a threat to the health of the general population.[8]

Horwitz describes the disgusted and frightened reactions of townspeople on witnessing the emaciated bodies and hollow stares of the Hungarian Jews in their forced march through Mauthausen-Gusen, Ebensee, and Gunskirchen. One observer recounts the scene:

> I saw those of shaved heads with faces altogether sunken. Others with eyes framed deep and black. That is, a procession of ghosts, a batch of persons who walked along the edge of the road. And on the road lay corpses that were covered with coats or rags. The inmates were driven on . . . they staggered, shuffled along . . . their looks apathetic, downcast.[9]

No acts of sympathy came from onlookers.

The horrified inaction of masses of herded, dehumanized Jews is tragically understandable given their ostracism. One wonders about the motives provoking the following incident (April 21, 1941) described in the Lodz chronicles.

> At two o'clock in the afternoon, Cwajga Blum, 41, a resident of 21 Limanowski Street, was shot to death next to the barbed wire at the end of Brzezinska Street. The victim was suffering from mental illness and had recently been released from the mental institution on Wesola Street. According to witnesses, the unfortunate woman had walked up to the barbed wire several times and requested that the sentries shoot her. The Order Service [the Jewish police] had already pulled her safely away from the barbed wire a couple of times. On the fateful day, the [German] sentry had asked the mentally ill woman to dance in front of the barbed wire. After she had performed a little dance, the sentry shot her dead at nearly point-blank range.[10]

How far can the human spirit be driven before it begs for release from its misery? Had she lost her children? Had they been transported? Had her husband been selected for "resettlement" to a death camp? Had her parents been shot in front of her eyes? "Mental illness" may not be the right term in explaining the wish of Cwajga Blum.

It runs against human nature not to want to find some reason to events unparalleled in human history. If someone is driving me insane, are not their actions also insane? As Müller-Hill puts it: "Hitler came to power because he made it possible for German citizens to think of their dreams of destruction as a science with a biological basis."[11] When the psychotic becomes normal, politics becomes terrifying—but only for those who find themselves the victims. For the perpetrators and their sympathizers, engaging in what Müller-Hill calls the "blood sacrifices of innocents,"[12] or Lifton "purification rituals,"[13] the psychotic/normal evolved into an accepted part of cultural practice. Mass murder became the right thing, supported by everyday science, politics, and industry. Even the language of killing and murder took on a bizarre technical normality. Euphemisms for disposing of Jewish bodies include *Umsiedlung* ("resettlement"); *Aussiedlung* ("evacuation"); *Sonderbehandlung* ("special treatment"); *entsprechend behandelt* ("treated appropriately"); *Auflockerung* ("thinning out"—for example, periodic transports from the ghetto to the death camps); *Befriedungsaktion* ("special pacification"); *Ausschaltung* ("removal"); *Abwanderung* ("having been migrated"); *Säuberung* ("cleansing"); *Sicherheitspolizeilich durchgearbeitet* ("worked through or directed in a Security Police manner").[14] Jean Amery speaks of the Jew being "shut out from German reality and therefore also from the German language"; the population internalizing metaphors of sickness, disease, and health had utterly no interest in the fact that the new language of death negated the Jewish body's humanity, its essential being. "[T]he Jew who infuses Near Eastern poison into the German national body" became a metaphor consistent with the imagery of corruption, threat, and disposal.[15] It was, however, not a metaphor at all consistent with the *Jewish* experience. Note the following description, by an Auschwitz midwife and survivor, of a woman whose newborn was about to be killed. Newborns in Auschwitz were immediately drowned in barrels of cold water.

She wrapped the infant in a dirty piece of paper and pressed it to her breast. Her lips moved without a sound, evidently she wanted to sing a song for her baby, as was often done by mothers there, who hummed various lullabies, thus trying to make their babies forget the cold, hunger and misery. The Vilna woman had no strength and could not utter a sound, only tears were falling down from her eyes onto the doomed baby's small head. It is difficult to say what was more tragic: this simultaneous death of two human beings closest to each other, or living through the death of an infant, dying under her mother's eyes, or the death of the mother, being aware of the fact that she was leaving her child at the mercy of fate.[16]

According to this report, of the thousands of babies born in Auschwitz, only thirty survived.

German scientists of the period such as Rudolf Ramm, Kurt Blome, Gerhard Wagner, and Walter Gross all believed absolutely in their ideology, theory, and linguistic paradigms. None of these men, in their personal lives, could in any way be considered insane; yet their language, practices, and theories fulfill major psychodynamic criteria for psychosis. The practices of the Final Solution broke all historical boundaries and transvalued historical and consensual meanings attached to the words *justice, tolerance,* and *right*. It is in this sense that group action can be psychotic, and the individual not. Psychosis can also be distinguished by the unwillingness to grieve or to feel any empathy for the victims slaughtered in delusional imagination. Similarly, the major sectors of German society showed no guilt, no expression of grief, no feeling of having done anything wrong. It is a state of mind that has lingered long beyond 1945.

THE ENTHUSIASM OF BELIEF

For Freud, delusion consists of "a patch over the place where originally a rent had appeared in the ego's relation to the external world."[17] Yet he understates delusion's power in absorbing the ego and in redefining its limits, contents, and parameters. Delusion as a "patch" is not an accurate metaphor; rather, delusion is an entirely new skin growing over the old one. In Germany the cultural superego implemented knowledge and practices that a decade or two earlier would have been considered ludicrous. It would have been unthinkable in 1928 to have instituted a project of physically eliminating the entire Jewish presence in Europe—many party members did not take Hitler seriously on this point as late as 1935–36.

The Final Solution was developed during a period of German prosperity and the belief that victory and a thousand-year Reich lay within reach. German armies had conquered most of Europe, the Russian campaign was proceeding successfully, the economy enjoyed its highest employment levels in decades, and the German people seemed to be supremely self-confident—a much different collective state of mind than the period following Versailles.

Given these facts, it would be difficult to attribute the impulses behind the Final Solution to economic or historical factors. The state of thinking in Germany in late 1941 was far more unified, idealized, and hopeful than it had been during the Weimar period or even the mid- to late 1930s. It is then a terrible mistake to suggest the Final Solution derived from the same disastrous economic conditions or anti-Semitism that brought Hitler and the National Socialists to power in 1933. What put the Final Solution into practice was a delusion, a widespread belief in the scientific definition of the Jew as poison, and the ordinary person's willingness to accept, internalize, and act on this delusion.

Dr. Friedrich Mennecke wrote to his wife in April 1941 regarding euthanasia exterminations at Sachsenhausen: "Our work is very, very interesting. ... Thanks to it, I am getting the benefit of many new experiences."[18] In the laboratory, concentration camp, and extermination center, Mennecke's letters show a consistency in his belief that certain bodies should be killed, that killing would benefit the nation, that mongrel races, like Russians and Jews, "the most primitive, stubborn and shabby heap of humanity that we have in Europe," should be eliminated. Mennecke is not the odd, perverse scientist, but representative of a species scattered throughout influential institutes, administrative agencies, and concentration camps. Mennecke's letters mix the banal with the grotesque—wonderful meals, lovely sunsets, good fellowship with comrades and scientists, pathbreaking work in the labs, terrific brain specimens, disgust at Polish and Jewish bodies—without once expressing doubt. The following observation is typical:

I got away from the clinic at seven . . . and was able to buy a
bouquet (carnations) before the storm really hit. At work,
from four to five there was another phenomenal lecture on
medical psychology; afterwards, we . . . took a look at the
seven brains that had come from Eichberg today [a hospital
killing site supplying brains and body parts to research facili-
ties]. I heard a lot of nice, gratifying things.[19]

It is not a "doubling" self that speaks here, but an integrated, total-
ized self, thoroughly aware of what he is doing and the nature of his
biases and preferences, who expresses personal and professional gratification in the experimentation and extermination projects. Mennecke reflects about himself: "You see that I remain consistent."[20] On
April 20, 1943, on a train to Kielce, he speaks of the "first impression
of the day . . . begging, starving Polish children who descended in
hordes from the nearby city . . . with miserable faces, they begged:
'Bread, please!' They've already learned how to say that. I threw two
slices to them. As I said, the night was good again; I slept well and feel
very good and cheerful."[21] In the same passage, he writes of his mar-
velous dinner of fish, beef, and bread, and the fantastic price he paid
for it.

A similar enthusiasm characterized the engineering profession in
its support of Nazi goals. The participation of the engineering profession in the aims of the Third Reich had little to do with what was
seen as the vulgar materialism of Western civilization. Technological
progress served the interests of *Volksgemeinschaft*. And, as with scientists and physicians, cooperation could not be construed as a case of
indifference. Eügen Diesel, an engineer and son of the inventor of
the diesel engine, referred to the dangers to "our blood and essence"
as early as 1926. Technology, if harnessed to the right ends, could create a "nobler race . . . of stronger life instincts."[22] Peter Schwerber, a
leading technology theorist of the 1930s, spoke of "the Jewish materialist suffocating embrace [*Umklammerung*] of our life elements" and
saw National Socialism as embodying a "primal life instinct."[23] In 1943
the engineering periodical *Deutsche Technik* referred to the Jews as the
"filth of civilization," and to the "American Jewish destruction of German nature."[24] Jewish materialism threatened *Lebensphilosophie*. The
blood heritage and *Volkish* spirit of the German people found itself

under siege by the Jewish pollution of technological method. To restore the German soul required drastic action.

The spirit impelling Auschwitz emerged through the construction of racial logics to be implemented as efficiently as possible. Delusion may produce consistent, rational, but radically skewed logics. The complex bureaucracies, legal systems, and structures created to adjudicate the nature and content of genes and blood, the participation of Germany's preeminent scientists, the logics impelling theories of racial hygiene, the history of German law, medicine, industry, education, and engineering in the 1930s—all suggest a society proceeding quite rationally and systematically with the project of ridding the culture of infection. There seems to be little romanticizing of nature in the murderous action of Auschwitz. The cold, rational logics of public health officials and policy planners seem more persuasive than seeing Auschwitz as the culmination of mob feeling.

Jeffrey Herf, a historian of the engineering profession in the Third Reich, emphasizes the importance of technocracy in mobilizing action against the Jews, but he also sees the values surrounding the use of technology as primarily an outgrowth of German romanticism. While Herf's thesis of reactionary modernism and the worship of nature, soul, and the nonrational describe faith in the Reich and the Aryan race, it is still the case that rational engineers and other professionals undertook tasks with a frightening detachment. If by "reason" Herf means tolerance, limits, historical continuity, and the belief in an ethical tradition prizing limitation and difference, then, indeed, there was not enough reason. But by seeing German society as irrational, Herf misses the most terrifying aspect of Nazi political life: its elevation of racial hygiene into the rational pursuit of the normal, "normal" understood as the killing of impure life.

While Herf rightly criticizes the indifference argument, he locates the impetus for the destruction of the Jews in an irrational, emotion-laden set of actions, the outcome of a conservative romantic tradition going back to the early modern period and its idealization of spirit. Yet he places too much emphasis on the romantic in explaining motive behind the annihilation of Jews. German society was an eminently rational culture in its professions and use of method and artifact. Auschwitz proceeded after deliberate planning. The Final Solution was not the outgrowth of nostalgic romantics calling for an orgy of death.

By 1943, the notion of Nordic will, *lebensphilosophie*, the romanticism of the past, had been eclipsed by the phobia of coming in contact with Jewish blood. Some historians see this as indicative of the fact that popular opinion simply did not think of the Jews at all.[25] But the focus on the *Kultur*-group's apparent indifference misses very real actions, undertaken by Germans, in all walks of life, to isolate and annihilate the Jewish people. Rather than a product of reactionary modernism, this phobia of Jewish flesh, obvious in the utter lack of regard for Jewish suffering in labor, concentration, and death camps, grew into a vital national component of public sanitation. Ordinary German citizens were not fixated on the glories of the Volkish past. Kershaw notes that "the war seems to have encouraged a 'retreat into the private sphere' as regards political opinion in general and the Jewish issue in particular. . . . '[T]he Jew' was now a completely depersonalized image"—but certainly not a forgotten image.[26]

The Jew became "life unworthy of life" not because the ordinary German bureaucrat fantasized about past Aryan glories or Jewish materialism or the Aryan nation; rather, in the post-Wannsee period, the Jew, in both professional and popular literature, took on the status of an imminent and major blood threat. It was this deep, unconscious fear that the Jew might provoke the disintegration of German flesh, that contact with Jews could literally destroy one's family, that pushed German professional culture into creating the apparatus of mass death, removing forever this infection. As Moishe Postone put it, rather than the Nazi seizure of power in 1933, "Auschwitz was the real German Revolution."[27]

It is critical not to underestimate the power of phobia in driving the perception of the Jew as bacillus translated into the public policy of sanitation and infection. Certainly stories filtering back to Germany about the conditions in the ghettos—the extent of disease, the deadly environment—added to the prevailing scientific view of the Jew as bad blood.

A similar attitude prevailed regarding homosexuality. In 1938, Reich Legal Director Hans Frank, who later became head of the General Government in occupied Poland, wrote that homosexuality "is clearly expressive of a disposition opposed to the normal national community. Homosexual activity means the negation of the community as it must be constituted if the race is not to perish. That is why homosexual behavior, in particular, merits no mercy." In his diary Goebbels called homosexuality a "cancerous disease."[28]

DEGENERATION AND BLOOD: PHOBIA AS POLITICAL ACTION

Werner Sombart, a leading anti-Jewish theorist of post–World War I Germany, believed the Jews were "born representatives of the liberal world view of the 'abstract citizen'" grasping at the world with reason rather than with the passion of blood identification.[29] He characterized Jewish collective psychology: "Paper stands against blood. Reason against instinct. Concept against perception. Abstraction against sensuousness." Sombart's thinking was horrendous enough, but a set of beliefs about Jewish intelligence, reason, and love for abstraction is insufficient to produce a reaction as horrendous as Auschwitz. Identifying and propagandizing a group's collective traits and seeing them as so threatening they warrant annihilation through gassing and burning are two radically different projects. To explain the Jewish genocide requires more than the belief that the Jew is too rational. To explain Auschwitz as the logical result of seeing the Jews as materialistic, sexually degenerate, or exemplary of the modernist rational spirit ignores the utter finality of a genocide and the massive collective paranoia impelling it. There is, then, a difference between despising a given group, encircling its presence, separating its flesh from the host *Kultur*, and killing every single member of that group. Certainly, a conservative ideology romanticizing the *Volk* was part of it but by no means the whole story.

One comes closer to the truth in examining the psychological distance between victim and victimizer, and the role of technology in facilitating the mechanics of mass death. Auschwitz is not a case of passion or passionate killing; Auschwitz is processing. But what kind of psychological dynamic is behind the most grotesque processing of bodies in history? The psychotic had absorbed the normal. The anti-Semitism of the past was very much a part of German culture, although it fails to explain the assimilated German Jew and the fact that anti-Semitic violence occurred infrequently in Germany before the National Socialist takeover. The Jewish caricature, popularized, for example, by magazines like *Die Stürmer*, is primarily a depiction of foreign Jews, since so much of German Jewish society, its middle-class properties and activities, were distinctly German in habit and identification.[30]

George Mosse refers to "The Beautiful Nose, or Justice Triumphs," an 1878 play by Peter Sturn, as typical of culturewide German anti-Semitism that lasted well into the twentieth century.[31] In this play, a greedy Jew, consumed by materialist lust, auctions his nose to a bidder willing to pay a very high price. He soon regrets his decision and buys his nose back at a price far above the auction price. These images and other physical stereotypes—for example, Jew-masks for actors, characterized by "dark skin, sharply marked facial lines, thick eyebrows, bent nose"[32]—saturated the culture. Yet to argue that these culture stereotypes accounted for Auschwitz assumes a continuity in the processes of exclusion. It is a long way from the German theater of the 1920s, to the anti-Jewish legislation of 1933 aimed primarily at Jewish professionals, to the crematoria of Auschwitz.[33] Between 1933 and 1939, the Nazis initiated more than four hundred anti-Jewish laws.[34] The apparatus responsible for the Final Solution had little to do with cultural stereotypes, but a great deal to do with medical science and professional practice. Mosse's analysis of culture is correct as far as it goes; it does not, however, give adequate weight to the role of science in forging professional percepts (what Foucault calls *epistèmes*) critical to understanding the Holocaust. Watching a play about crooked Jewish noses and swarthy figures lurking near the school grounds does not lead to thousands of killings a day at Auschwitz or Treblinka.[35] Cultural stereotypes may lead to legislative discrimination and sporadic pogroms, but they do not lead to death camps. Historians, for the most part, give enormous weight to the role of cultural stereotypes in leading to the Auschwitz mentality, but fail to examine the psychology motivating mass, industrialized killing. It is more psychologically accurate and therefore more helpful in finding "reasons" to recognize that the Auschwitz mentality originated in the political alliance of science, technology, and the professions, impelled by the phobia against touching, rather than in the spiritualist or mystical worshipping of the *Volk* or the popular Jewish stereotypes. The Jew in German society took on the properties of what Julia Kristeva calls abjection, a radical transvaluation of what Jewish flesh psychologically signified for the German *Kultur*-group.[36]

ABJECTION AND THE CONSTRUCTION OF DELUSIONAL PERCEPTS

The concept of abjection was embodied in the horror of touching Jewish skin, a phobia of pollution. Through its hallucinatory power, abjection breaks limits, erodes boundaries, and forges violent and destructive definitions of reality. Abjection creates new codes and ways of thinking and it constructs phobic prohibitions. It turns all social judgment, rules, and moralities aside. It is a murderous state of mind, harboring the most vicious of impulses. Abjection mobilizes killing in the service of an ideal. It revels in death.

Abjection thrives on "exclusion or taboo," undertaking "various means of purifying" through the destruction of the impure.[37] Because it incites repugnance and disgust, abjection "pulverizes the subject."[38] It refuses to "respect borders, positions, rules"; it disturbs existing order while creating its own system of order. It appears in "the criminal with a good conscience . . . the killer who claims he is a savior . . . a terror that dissembles, a hatred that smiles . . . shattering violence of a convulsion."[39] Its consequences are to be seen "in the dark halls of the museum that is now what remains of Auschwitz . . . a heap of children's shoes . . . the breaking down of a world that has erased its borders."[40] If one imagines the thousands of bodies piling up in the ghettos and work camps, "the corpse, seen without God . . . is the utmost of abjection. It is death infecting life."[41]

Abjection also serves to demarcate in an ethical and moral sense the "Pure and Impure, Prohibition and Sin, Morality and Immorality."[42] I do not see my actions towards the other as violent, as an assault on a human body, because the other possesses no human properties. I am attacking matter, dangerous matter; therefore I will protect myself from this other's abjection, poison, and corrosion. I kill the other because I fear being polluted or defiled by him. This kind of thinking produces massive distortions of the other's actual threatening capacity. It is not my own insides which threaten me, but my fear projected onto the other. So I say to myself: I am threatened by the other. The other is poisoning me. So I turn my aggression onto him and make historical and scientific fact out of my phobia of infection. I invent a complex scientific machine to eliminate the object of my phobia.

The Germans' construction of the phobic object evolved into a horrifying spectacle of annihilation as a series of public health measures. Phobias represent the failure of the self to contain and regulate its overwhelming fear. The group saves itself and its own equilibrium by turning that failure into a qualified success: forcing the other to serve as object of the *Kultur*'s violent phobic reactions. Death lurked in the Jewish skin, in its potential to carry infection. The Jew-as-death was psychically enforced by convincing the *Volk* that to touch Jewish flesh, even to have friendly contact with it, was to risk self-destruction because of its power to infect the individual and thus the entire cultural group.[43]

Phobia rewrites reality. Through the 1920s and early 1930s, Germans engaged in business and personal relationships with Jews without the fear of being poisoned. But the phobic hallucination, while lacking any substance in reality, has power precisely because the projector is filling the hallucination with meanings that hitherto had never existed. The Jewish skin became a hallucinated presence endowed with psychic valences possessing a novel relation to historical reality. Seeing poison in the Jewish skin and therefore destroying it represents a phobic compromise, an effort to deal with this fear by populating it with images and actions that create a dreaded possibility. The fear of the Jew is explained by removing the noxious presence and thereby making the *Kultur* safe.

With the poisoned Jewish flesh eliminated, the *Kultur*-group experienced its own psychological boundaries as more secure. To burn Jewish flesh, therefore, not only gratified the wish to kill the hated object, it also satisfied the need to reinforce the boundaries between the good and the abject, the pure and the dirty, and the Aryan race and its biological enemy, the Jew.

SEVEN

THE UNIQUENESS OF THE HOLOCAUST

Auschwitz, Treblinka, and Babi-Yar did not just happen. The *Kultur*-group initiated massive blood sacrifices to biological purity. The systematic genocide of the Holocaust was more than an unusual action. It was a hallucinatory reality more horrifying than anything imaginable in normal day-to-day existence. Yankel Wiernik, a survivor of the death camp Treblinka, describes the fate of children:

> All through that winter small children, stark naked and barefooted, had to stand out in the open for hours on end, awaiting their turn in the increasingly busy gas chambers. The soles of their feet froze and stuck to the icy ground. They stood and cried; some of them froze to death. In the meantime, Germans and Ukrainians walked up and down the ranks, beating and kicking the victims.
>
> One of the Germans, a man named Sepp, was a vile and savage beast, who took special delight in torturing children. When he pushed women around and they begged him to stop because they had children with them, he would frequently snatch a child from the woman's arms and either tear the child in half or grab it by the legs, smash its head against a wall and throw the body away. Such incidents were by no means isolated. Tragic scenes of this kind occurred all the time.[1]

In such a universe of death, hopelessness invades the imagination. No one, in Charlotte Delbo's description of Auschwitz, is "sure [of] what we see."

> Standing, wrapped in a blanket, a child, a little boy. A tiny shaven head, a face in which the jaws and the brow ridge stand out. Barefoot, he jumps up and down without stopping, with a frenzied movement that makes one think of that of savages dancing. He wants to wave his arms too to keep warm. The blanket slips open. It is a woman. A skeleton of a woman. She is naked. One can see her ribs and hip bones. She pulls the blanket up on her shoulders and continues to dance. A mechanical dance. A dancing skeleton of a woman. Her feet are small, thin and bare in the snow. There are living, dancing skeletons.[2]

FOREIGNNESS AND ANNIHILATION

Paranoia and hate, significant psychological forces in the Holocaust, derive from an internally conflicted self. The self experiences part of itself as strange or abject. Instead of confronting this painful side, the self externalizes the rage and places it on others. Vamik Volkan argues that this need for enemies (and allies) arises from primitive psycho-developmental structures, generated in childhood, coalescing as an internal perceptual and emotional system and constructing concrete enemies and identifiable allies.[3] The process begins early in human development; for Volkan, the concept of enemy is a vital and—most importantly—a *natural* psychological developmental structure. Its appearance in perception and play is part of what it means to be human, a phenomenon central to the psychological underpinning of human values. One could not be human, he argues, unless one posited enemies—from a very early age.

The real enemy, however, lies in the disowned part of ourselves emotionally composed in large measure of hate and fear. In political terms, because of the intolerability of holding this rage within the self, it is projected into a designated other—the scapegoat race or religion that becomes the hated enemy. A projection commonly shared across a culture possesses the power to unite a hitherto disparate population as a focal group. The identity of this focal cultural group finds itself embodied, articulated, and elaborated through an ideology justifying why the other should be hated, ostracized, and ultimately annihilated.

Projection, however, disguises the real cause of our hate and fear, the foreigner that lives within us.[4] If we could acknowledge this presence in ourselves and face it directly, we might be spared the phenomenon of dumping unwanted or despised self-objects into an other invested with properties of abjection. But of course we do not. We refuse to own the paranoia and demystify its power. We isolate the foreigner as other. We transform this presence into an alien double of ourselves. Herein lies the root of prejudice, discrimination, racial violence, and murder.

The politically frightening development appears when this narcissistic self becomes defensive, frightened, anxious, and projects out of itself a destructive urge (in the form of ideology) it cannot contain. That destructiveness, composed of basic negative attributions, finds its place in an other who becomes the epitome of evil and destruction. The other threatens my being; therefore I must destroy the other before I am destroyed. Violence is inevitable. Oppression and discrimination define political life, and the projected destructiveness—now residing in the scapegoat—directs how identity is seen and experienced. Fear, hate, and conflict frame not only individual identity but also group and national identity. The state of mind of the focal cultural group legitimizes destruction of the other and constructs a new set of meanings attached to political language, morality, and action. What emerges as a national or group identity are the values, perceptions, and practices of persecution and domination.

THE FUNCTIONING OF
THE UNCANNY IN THE GROUP

It might be useful to spell out the functioning of this potentially psychotic dimension of the group-self, the emotions of hate, the boundary-disintegrating capacities of anxiety and fear—all part of what Freud calls the uncanny—by looking at the concept of the unconscious fantasy, specifically how unconscious fantasies drive the group.

The concept of the unconscious fantasy has its origins in Freud and later Melanie Klein. In *The Interpretation of Dreams*, Freud posited that the "general basis of psychical life" lies in the unconscious and may be thought of as "the larger sphere, which includes within it the smaller sphere of the conscious." Unconscious determinants motivate what is experienced as consciousness, including symptom-formation and defense. The ego, or consciousness, possesses what Freud calls "an unconscious preliminary stage." To search for what is true about the self—what provokes emotional pain and dislocation—requires an interrogation of the "unconscious [which] is the true psychical reality."[5]

This interrogation lies at the heart of Melanie Klein's project, but her mapping is far more intricate (some argue, metaphoric) than Freud's. For Klein, psychical reality is the only reality that counts in assessing delusion and symptom formations accompanying psychotic states. Psychical reality is made up of complex fantasies, largely unconscious, that impel the different kinds of identifications and values accompanying passions such as hate, fear, and envy. "[T]he child's earliest reality is wholly phantastic; he is surrounded with objects of anxiety."[6] Further, psychosis in adults indicates the presence of "extremely complex" unconscious fantasies. "[F]or the psychotic, the world—and that in practice means objects—is valued at the original level; that is to say, that for the psychotic the world is still a belly peopled with dangerous objects."[7] If this is the case for the individual, it may certainly be true for adult *groups* which populate the world with dangerous objects and then develop radical reasons to annihilate those objects. The psychotic itself becomes the reason driving so-called normal actions—for example, the public policy of sanitation understood as the annihilation of Jewish bodies.

Klein accepts the Freudian hypothesis that fantasy impels consciousness. Fantasy formation begins during infancy, forged through continuous interaction with the outer world, and thought itself emerges from the persistent impact of imaginary constructions on external reality.[8] Fantasy absorbs reality, remodels it, and structures it according to the dynamics of unconscious identification. That structuring may contain bizarre logics, totally inverting historically legitimated practices of exclusion and introducing radical practices such as genocide. Fantasy (the Kleinian fantasy of paranoia as was the case in Germany) *becomes* reality and constructs entirely novel logics and frames of reference. Fantasy is politically significant when it impels group action. The group does not say to itself: "I wish to annihilate the other." Instead the group constructs elaborate defenses against acknowledging this wish and projects the wish outward, away from itself. It is this projection of fantasies unconsciously disowned by the group that concerns us in looking for reasons behind mass murder.

The unconscious fantasy emerges in specific social and political practices, and in the case of the Third Reich, in the practices of the professions. The fantasy penetrates action, defines value, and molds perceptions. It may be thought of as spirit (*Geist*), but not spirit in the strictly Hegelian sense of outside of self. Rather, it is spirit inside, embedded in the unconscious of the collective self. It exists inside as fear and rage, and outside as ideology and professional practice. The strength of the phobia lies directly in the psychological properties framing that fantasy. It is a kind of mass delusional wish mistaken for reality. The fantasy invades the body's nervous circuitry, causing one to feel the danger the other holds for the integrity of the group, for the resiliency of the boundaries separating the clean from the unclean. The phobia conditions the workings of consciousness, guiding action and framing external reality and the objects on which the phobia may be projected. Such is the power of these largely unconscious structuring influences in both the self and the group.

In Nazi Germany, science acted as the legitimating methodology for the group ego, and the technologies of science acted as defense for the unconscious fantasies of phobic hatred and the wish to annihilate. Science in the Third Reich sanitized paranoia, disguising hatred of the Jew in the language and practice of a biological-medical argument premised on identifying the Jew with infection. This view of reality wrapped itself around the unconscious wish to destroy bodies. Scientific practice and justification assured the perpetrators-practitioners that what they were doing was in the highest political interest not only of science but of their cultural ideals.

THE OBLITERATION OF CONSCIENCE

If the Nazis' persecution of the Jews consisted only of *Kristallnacht* and similar pogroms, Zygmunt Bauman observes, "it would hardly add anything but an extra paragraph, a chapter at best, to the multivolume chronicle of emotions running amok, of lynching mobs, of soldier[s] looting and raping their way through the conquered

towns." But such was not the case. The Holocaust occupied a different level of murder. Its uniqueness lay in its bureaucratic and technical scope and the fact that "one could neither conceive of, nor make,
mass murder on the Holocaust scale of no matter how many *Kristall-
nächte*."[9] Yet Bauman's reading is psychologically limited precisely
because he refuses to see rationality and its scientific practices as
defense for a deeper reservoir of paranoia that took shape in the perception of the Jewish body as infection.

Political power like that of the Nazis annihilates conscience. It
conceives of human beings as matter to be processed and constructs
technologies based on those perceptions. Nothing analogous to a
superego exists to restrain power that has dissociated itself from traditional moral viewpoints, resulting in actions that would have been
incomprehensible scarcely a generation before.[10]

Power, rather than reinforcing superego constraints and conscience, moves to eliminate them entirely. Any resistance to the Holocaust bureaucracy came not from group ethics, but from individuals.
Superego or conscience had been destroyed through an alliance of
scientific objectivity, bureaucratic functionalism, and the moral blindness of technology. In placing mass murder on the same level as
industrial processing or public health clean-ups, the Nazi regime
removed any moral context to acts of murder.

However, a technological and sociological account focusing only
on mechanics misses the deeper psychological forces contributing to
the crime. The historian Hans Mommsen writes that the Holocaust
demonstrated a "cumulative radicalization of Jewish persecution . . . a
consequence of a combination of uncoordinated strategies . . . [by]
party radicals and the state administrations, [and a] widespread moral
indifference."[11] Annihilation, he argues, may be seen as the outcome
of an often conflicted collaboration of radical party leaders, state
administrators, and policy planners, undertaken as a series of uncoordinated strategies leading to massive organized extermination. No
hint of any unconscious group process appears in this kind of historical interpretation; murder followed the accommodation between
competing bureaucratic and technocratic interests. It is then an
incomplete explanation that places responsibility exclusively on the
technicism and functionalism of the machinery, technology, science,
and popular opinion.

The Nuremberg laws of 1935 produced an entirely new normative code for the culture. Legislative fiat eliminated guilt as the foundation of civilized social law and therefore initiated a transvaluation of logics governing action and meaning. Transforming logics, inventing radically new moral precepts, constructing novel historical narratives and practices are properties of psychotic thinking. Psychotic persons build very special dramas, filled with the imagery of implacable goods and absolute evils, battling in a constructed universe where the very salvation of mankind is the outcome. Groups can produce psychotic political actions while individuals composing the group may not exhibit any psychotic properties. The psychotic part of the self is embodied or acted out in the actions of the group, and the group acts out for the individual. The Nazi conception of "the concentration camps' slavery as a unique and wonderful opportunity to conduct medical research for the advancement of scholarship and—of course—of mankind" is psychotic.[12] If one were to walk into an Auschwitz today, it would appear insane. The camps may be understood as instances where boundaries between the inner sense of security and external catastrophe broke down altogether.

No shame or guilt or moral positioning integral to ethics entered into the legal scientific legitimation of the death camps. Jews had been absolutely excluded from any historical set of moral provisions. Their isolation and murder occurred in a moral vacuum that today would be considered utter madness. Yet this guiltless biological morality bred an industry of scientific research, encouraged the proliferation of research institutes, provided funds and opportunities for collaboration with the regime, and laid the foundation for a radical solution for coping with a group perceived as a public health menace.

Civilization did not have the moral strength to protect individuals from the technology it created and the power of that technology to turn life into death. But how could it? Political interest lay not in protecting a morality of empathy, care, and restraint, but in facilitating the free flow of violence generated by the cooperation of science, technology, the professions, political action, and fantasies driving the practices of death.

Mommsen observes: "In the eyes of the liquidators, but also of those who accidentally witnessed the selections at the Auschwitz ramp or similar events, the Jews had already lost the character of human beings. . . . [N]ot even the quasi-moral mechanisms of human reaction were operating any longer."[13] On the level of group action, this blindness to death and suffering, and its justification as a sanitation problem, suggests the ascendancy of a delusional organization of reality.

THE MORAL POSITION OF RESISTANCE

Given the power of delusion to elaborate itself as moral organization, extraordinary will is required to resist the logics and beliefs inherent in a *gestalt* the social consensus accepts as truth. To resist that explanatory *epistème* meant contradicting a dominant perceptual code. Such a code written into the canons of professional practice takes on an even greater power because of its authority as representing the *Kultur* ideal. As Martin Heidegger in 1933 defined the moral content of the group, "The Führer himself is the only present embodiment and future embodiment of German nation and its law. . . . To oppose him would be treason against Being."[14]

The resistor, then, becomes an enemy to the socially constructed moral code. In Bauman's reading of this phenomenon, the resistor— in this case, those who publicly denounced the Nazis, hid Jews or helped them escape—protected civilization's traditional moral interests. Insubordination, or action "openly defying social solidarity and consensus," manifested the heart of a traditional ethics.[15] Kren and Rappoport would agree that the modern state erodes traditional moral concepts. "There is no moral-ethical limit which the state cannot transcend if it wishes to do so, because there is no moral-ethical power higher than the state."[16] The will of the state rewrites moral rules. The Holocaust shows that no moral rule is sacrosanct. Even the most traditional moral canon falls before the presence of unlimited Power. "What the Holocaust forces upon us, therefore, is recognition of nothing less than a moral equivalent of the Copernican revolution."[17] No ethical center remains to restrain social and political forces seeking radically transgressive ends, especially when they are tied to "enterprises of applied science," in this case, the technology of mass killing.[18]

What Hannah Arendt saw as the "animal pity by which all normal men are affected in the presence of physical suffering" failed to appear in relation to the Jews.[19] Rousseau argued that the first passion of nature and the most rudimentary human emotion is pity, a sense of sympathy or empathy for the dead or the dying.[20] But in Germany, there was no sympathy for Jews.

Bauman sees the Holocaust as a distinctively modern form of mass murder distinguished from previous actions against the Jew by its system, organization, and distance from the victim. For the regime to accomplish murder, therefore, required not the mobilization of sentiment against the Jews, but rather the *neutralization* of sentiment— what might be understood as the expulsion of guilt. Pogroms, like hatreds, are from the technological point of view inefficient and wasteful of energy and resources. Pogroms had been, for the most part, unpopular with German citizenry. The bureaucratic planners of the Holocaust had no use for thugs, sadists, and degenerates. To facilitate the technological operation of annihilation, then, it was essential for the individual German not to waste his energy on active anti-Semitism, but to see Jews as refuse and let the Reich sweep them away.

Nothing in the historical pattern of prejudice in Germany predicted the radical response to the Jewish presence that was the Holocaust. Even Hitler's 1933 pronouncement of his aim of ridding Europe of the Jews was taken by the party as propaganda. Until the early 1940s, very little evidence suggested anyone in the Nazi Party or the state bureaucracy advocated genocide. Yet, throughout the 1930s, Jews found themselves increasingly separated from the surrounding culture. Bauman concludes:

> The point that cannot be overemphasized is that all these negative reactions to the open display of anti-Jewish violence coincided, without any visible contradiction, with a massive and deep approval of the anti-Jewish legislation—with its redefinition of the Jew, eviction of the Jew from the German *Volk* and the ever-thickening layer of legal restrictions and prohibitions.[21]

I differ with Bauman and Mommsen in interpreting this neutralization or absence of sentiment. By making the Jew invisible, Bauman suggests, the Germans transformed the real Jew into an abstract set of metaphysical images. The Jew as a person, a colleague, a friend, a neighbor, was absorbed into the category of Jew as other—a set of properties created because the Jew was nowhere to be seen. With the

Jew isolated as a biological outcast, primitive moral drives—Arendt's animal pity at the sight of suffering—did not figure into calculations. Such drives, in the context of the mechanics of murder, became irrelevant and, in relation to the Jews, evaporated in the group action creating technological murder. The Jew "had been removed from the horizon of German daily life, cut off from the network of personal intercourse, transformed in practice into exemplars of a category, of a stereotype—into the abstract concept of the *metaphysical Jew*."[22]

True, technology forges indifference and neutralization of sentiment. True, modern civilization is powerless, morally and otherwise, against a technology tied to the ends of ideology. True, there is a radical difference between traditional pogroms and the genocide of the Holocaust. Yet nothing in Bauman's explanatory scheme looks at the power of the group to construct psychological and physical boundaries in order to protect itself from a fantasized danger to its boundaries. Raul Hilberg writes of the 1935 Law for the Protection of German Blood and Honor: "The courts ruled that sexual intercourse did not have to be consummated to trigger the criminal provisions of the law . . . touching or even looking might be enough."[23] The abject Jew, with disease-ridden body, horrified the *Kultur*-group obsessed with the purity of its blood and the integrity of its boundaries. Indifference and neutralization reveal very little about what this phobia of Jewish flesh signified.

Bauman's examination of the difference in historical anti-Semitism and the Final Solution captures the uniqueness of the historical anomaly, its unimaginable quality. This gulf, however, rather than a product of indifference, was a product of fear of infection—the fruits of years of scientific and legal theorizing about the nature of the Jewish biological threat. Indifference belied a more crippling anxiety. Isolation, segregation, concentration, and finally elimination of millions of people signified a rational response to a deep-seated psychotic fear. Reason and bureaucratic rationality served as a defense of a group consciousness fed for years on the so-called scientific facts of blood pollution. The metaphysical Jew and the social production of indifference are not enough to explain the horror of the unique properties of the Holocaust. A metaphysical picture does not kill the sentient beings. Enthusiasm for killing derives from a visceral reaction to flesh and blood and its application into practice.

The assaults against the Jewish body consisted of a war not against a metaphysical presence produced by the literal absence of the Jew as community, as body, but a war against real live human beings, whose flesh terrified both conscious and unconscious perceptions in the large group, in addition to professional sub-groups charged with implementing the culture's epistemological frameworks. Evicting the Jew from society required the enthusiastic support of an entire culture of practitioners and workers, and was not a product of indifference.

A 1942 Ministry of Transport memo regarding Operation Reinhard, the transportation of Jews from central Poland to Sobibor, Treblinka, and Belzec, gives some indication of the extraordinary effort, scheduling, and participation involved in the killing project.

EVACUATION OF THE POLISH JEWS

Urgent transports as proposed by the Chief of the Security Policy and the SD:

> 2 trains daily from the Warsaw district to Treblinka
> 1 train daily from the Radom district to Treblinka
> 1 train daily from the Cracow district to Belzec
> 1 train daily from the Lvov district to Belzec

These transports will be carried out with the 200 freight cars already made available for this purpose by order of the Directorate of the German railways in Cracow, as far as this is possible.

Upon completion of the repair of the Lublin-Chelm line, about November 1942, the other urgent transports will also be carried out. These are:

> 1 train daily from the North Lublin district to Belzec
> 1 train daily from the Central Lublin district to Sobibor,

insofar as this is practicable and the required number of freight cars are available. With the reduction of the transport of potatoes, it is expected that it will be possible for the spe-

cial train service to be able to place at the disposal of the
Directorate of the German railway in Cracow the necessary
freight cars. Thus the train transportation required will be
available in accordance with the above proposals and the plan
completed this year.[24]

No reciprocal sets of moral obligation existed after the segregation of Jew from German: no emotional communication remained;
life processes of German and Jew did not touch each other; the vic-
timized group's suffering had no significance for the larger *Kultur*-
group. By isolating the Jew, the society made it easier for its
professional, political, and administrative components and their
alliances to undertake a series of actions which, in terms of scope and
prosecution, demonstrate a dramatic enthusiasm for the techniques
and plans of extermination. Distance, rather than creating indifference, intensified a group-authored perception that the Final Solution
was essential to the health of the *Kultur*-body.

Delusions destroy conventional moral notions, values, and percepts. This process is equally striking in individual psychosis and in
group-dependent psychosis, where traditional forms of moral behavior cease to function in relation to the scapegoat group. Bauman
insists the "silencing of the moral urge and the suspension of moral
inhibitions" derived from distance and indifference, thereby paving
the way for the rational-technical or autonomous technology in producing mass death.[25] Yet, if the "targets of action" are not visible to
the surrounding population, what kind of moral object do they
become? Not accessible to moral judgment, the acts generated by
autonomous technology occur in a kind of free fire zone, constrained
only by the limitations of technical inventiveness. Combined with
what Bauman calls a "bureaucratic division of labor," the action of
the weapons and their mechanical components become the overrid-
ing concern: the victim, as person, ceased to exist. Replacing the relationship between victim and perpetrator was a set of rational
bureaucratic imperatives defined by bureaucratic actor and technical
instrument.

Weapons, however, do not act by themselves. Technologies are
autonomous only to the extent that their functions are determined by
mechanical logics. Someone operates the machines. Someone pours

the gas into the chambers. Someone administers, makes legal decisions, constructs gas chambers, performs medical experiments, interprets their results, arranges for transport.

The societal consensus on the necessity of the Final Solution required enthusiastic, willful participation. Indifference does not explain the apparatus of mass murder and the staggering logistical and technical effort to accomplish the extermination. Bauman, Arendt, and Mommsen never address this group-dependent psychotic nature of the action itself and its foundations in a globalized fantasy.

Hilberg writes: "In 1941 the Holocaust was not expected and that is the very reason for our subsequent anxieties. We no longer dare to exclude the unimaginable."[26] But the unimaginable becoming real, the transvaluation of reality, history, and consensual norms, is demonstrative of a psychotic process absorbing the normal itself. The unimaginable in historical fact turned into normality; delusion defined the normal way of proceeding with life *and* death.

The Jewish body *made* a difference; it was the object of the group's fear. The *Kultur*-group first shunned this body through legislation and then destroyed it in the crematoria. The *Kultur*-group demonstrated considerable enthusiasm for safeguarding its racially pure and genetically unimpaired self by legitimizing the Holocaust. That enthusiasm, phobia elaborated as delusion, is yet another piece of the puzzle in trying to understand how millions of people were killed with utterly no moral concern and no expression of guilt or remorse. The German ideology of sanitation created a universe of horror beyond comprehension. In the words of Paul Celan's "Todesfuge" (Death's Fugue):

> Black milk of daybreak we drink it at sundown
> We drink it at noon in the morning we drink it at night
> We drink and we drink it
> We dig a grave in the breezes, there one lies unconfined.[27]

EIGHT

TABOO, BLOOD, AND PURIFICATION RITUAL

As objects of the *Kultur*-group's phobia, the Jews found themselves invested with images of contamination. Reading this process on a political level, the phobia coalesced as a new historically constructed taboo, the theme of defilement and abjection taking on a powerful medical and cultural authority and replacing older, cruder anti-Semitic imagery. A new language of public morality and historical explanation emerged. The taboos on touching Jewish flesh reinforced the sense of boundary between good and evil. Fear of defilement, generating increasing vigilance, became essential to the *Kultur*-group's sense of its own health and purity. "It is as if the skin, a fragile container," Julia Kristeva writes, "no longer guaranteed integrity of one's 'own pure and clean self.'"[1] Therefore, from a group psychological perspective, more aggressive actions had to be undertaken to protect the culture's boundaries from attack, containing and killing potential contaminants of the culture.

The psychoanalyst Thomas Ogden makes a similar point. In paranoid situations of perceived or experienced threat, the individual may experience "his surface (which in a sense is all there is of him) as a hard crust or armor that protects him against unspeakable dangers."[2] If the fear is unnameable, it will soon enough acquire names; it may even come to be represented by a set of ideological injunctions that various groups in the culture (such as the professions) believe to be true and binding.

In Germany this generalized fear or threat provoked the defensive reaction of armoring and named the threat as Jew. In other times and places, the threat was perceived as black, Indian, Kulak, Muslim. The group deposits its own filth and dejection in a phobic object. Consciousness, to preserve itself and prevent its severance from wishes or fantasies of unity, intensifies its aggressiveness against the phobic object. The group requires this action to maintain coherence in the face of impending psychological disintegration. As Freud argued in *Totem and Taboo*, transgression of a taboo brings on disastrous consequences; to be taboo is to be unclean and threatening to the welfare of the group.[3]

RITUALS OF PURIFICATION:
THE EFFORT TO CLEANSE THE SELF

Purification rituals enhance the group's power and identity. The phobia of defilement allows the group to condone actions such as ghettoization, purging, and killing, which assure the integrity of the boundaries between pure and impure. By engaging in these rituals, individuals and groups attain a sharper sense of the boundaries between their healthy and integral self and the dirty or infected other. The fantasy of cleanliness, therefore, impels the culturally sanctioned rituals of purification, and killing preserves group boundaries, a phenomenon Kaplan calls "redemptive violence."[4] As a cleansing medium for unwanted but unconscious thoughts, desires, or traits, rituals may take on violent, explosive properties.

The group defines its identity through this process of exclusion. The purification rite takes the object of filth and radically removes it from the secular universe. Also jettisoned from the group and its symbolic system of explanation and language are underlying anxieties regarding defilement and disintegration. By locating these anxieties in the other, the symbolic system preserves its own logics, no matter how crazy these logics seem in historical perspective. Exclusion, and naming the outcast as the defiling presence, maintains the radically skewed and insane explanatory system, which to the participants is logical, necessary, sane, and verified by scientific fact, a whole new classification system. To kill Jews is ethical and therapeutic. To allow Jews to live is unethical and dangerous for the health of the national body.

No matter how skewed or radically disconnected it was from historical methods of resolution or exclusion, the set of practices and logics internal to the Final Solution appeared to the participants, the *Kultur*-group, to be sensible, rational, and justifiable. Phobia became institutionalized in a set of psychotic practices and laws that appeared normal, sane, and sensible.

Exclusion and purification rituals indicate a broad set of practices supporting numerous divisions between clean and unclean. In addition, the killing rituals in the Third Reich constructed specific languages and economies with practices and norms which were accepted as historically necessary and part of everyday thinking and action. The *Kultur*-group sanctioned the new practices and gave them legal authority. Death became the "twin god, death as companion, as weapon, as agent of mercy and salvation." The decadent, poisonous, infected Jew invoked "redemptive themes of purging and purification [which] led relentlessly to massive destruction. . . . With the death's head their sign, the Nazis were the high priests of death, the first modern people who returned to human sacrifice."[5]

Rituals of purification intensified and localized hatred, allowing it to be enacted in the death and concentration camps. Further, the intensity of the experience of pollution was proportional to the totemic power of the prohibition impelling it. Images, caricatures, stories, and myths about Jewish corruption strengthened the boundaries between the clean and the polluted. Filth is not a property inherent in the other; it allows for the construction of a boundary between the pure self and the dirty other. Through ghettoization, the Jew was jettisoned beyond that boundary and placed psychologically and physically outside the culture, its practices and values, its social and political institutions and living spaces.

The identification of contaminant with the Jewish body worked because social and cultural authority redefined the body as a public health menace. The political and professional agents of the culture asserted their right to annihilate the impure, and to remove from impure matter any human properties. Distinguishing the Jewish body as poison enhanced the larger culture's sense of itself as clean and pure, strengthening the *Kultur*-group's skin ego. This distinction created a resilient and powerful sense of collective mastery, a group identity that thrived on maintaining the border between clean and unclean. The more extensive the sanitizing murder, the more intensely the *Kultur*-group felt the protective properties of purity. Peter Haidu speaks of the ethos of race hygiene and its utter lack of empathy for Jews as representing "the absolutistic hypostasis of tribal blood identity." The impact of this identity appears in "the ideological *sine qua non* for the extermination of the Jews."[6]

The *Kultur*-group defined itself in part by the physical characteristics distinguishing the Aryan from the Jew. Given this, it is indeed possible that the German victimizer came to see the Jewish body in the terms with which Kristeva describes the perception of the abject: "A decaying body, lifeless, completely turned into dejection, blurred between the inanimate and the inorganic. . . . The corpse represents fundamental pollution. A body without soul, a non-body, disquieting matter, it is to be excluded from God's *territory* as it is from his *speech*."[7] Further: "[T]he corpse is waste, transitional matter, mixture, . . . the opposite of the spiritual, of the symbolic, and of divine law. . . . The human corpse is a fount of impurity and must not be touched."[8] The German destroyers of Jewish flesh saw their actions in much the same terms, bestowing themselves with absolute right and the Jews with the status of the walking dead. The Jews rounded up for slaughter in places like Auschwitz were seen as decaying bodies that could not be touched because of the danger of pollution and abomination. Death happened because the murderers hated and feared the Jewish body.[9]

EVIL AND ITS CULTURAL FACE

Jean Améry's ordeal in Auschwitz leads him to take a dim view of Hannah Arendt's concept of banality. He speaks of looking into the faces of his torturers, the men from the Gestapo and the SS. He saw "plain, ordinary faces"—banal, in Arendt's sense—but faces containing a malevolence that "overlays and exceeds banality," and one not entirely exclusive to death camp sadists. Arendt, he argues, in never encountering these faces, "knew the enemy of mankind only from hearsay, saw him only through the glass cage" of the dock.[10] Améry refuses to dismiss Arendt's thesis outright. Instead he argues that she diminishes the importance of remembering how human, and therefore how vicious and hateful, evil can be. Further, he refuses to distinguish the guilt of the Nazis from the guilt of the German people as a whole. It is a bitter testament, but one he refuses to relinquish. "I could and can say that the crimes of the regime entered my consciousness as collective deeds of the people."[11] He continues:

> The far-too-many were not SS men, but rather laborers, file clerks, technicians, typists—and only a minority among them wore the party badge. What was taking place around them and with us, they knew exactly. For they perceived the burnt smell from the nearby extermination camps as we did, and some wore clothes that only the day before had been taken on the selection ramps from the arriving victims.[12]

A German laborer "once proudly presented himself to me in a winter coat, a 'Jew coat,' as he said, that his skill had enabled him to procure." Hatred and denial of the Jew spread across the culture, regardless of class. "Workers, petty bourgeois, academics, Bavarians, Saarlanders, Saxons: there was no difference."[13] It was, then, "not only radical Nazis, officially certified by the party, who denied that we were worthy of being loved and thereby worthy of life. All of Germany—but what am I saying!—the whole world nodded its head in approval of the undertaking, even if here and there with a certain superficial regret."[14] Sensitivity to suffering had no place in his treatment by camp guards, in the German national interest, or in the complicity of ordinary German citizens and their collaborators.

When the victim is perceived as an abomination, a radical and qualitative historical change occurs. Previously unthinkable logics, rule systems, and legislation coalesce as deep epistemic structures in the culture. The view of bodies as abject constructs a persecuting machine or bureaucracy, and the drive to kill evolves into an accepted and enthusiastically embraced cultural logic. The abject threatens the *Kultur*-group with the possibility of defilement. The group reacts with rage and paranoia; its skin ego assumes the shape of a persecutory machine.

A useful psychoanalytic approach to these issues may be found in Didier Anzieu's formulation of the skin ego and its properties.[15] The development of a skin ego insures a continuous sense of fundamental well-being. This psychological "covering" helps to turn one's fantasy of destruction outwards; rather than destroying one's own body, one creates a sense of boundary and continuity. To maintain one's own skin, one flays the skin of the other. By destroying the other, the group preserves its own sense of being, that is, its own skin.

On an individual level, mutilating one's skin is a pathological effort at maintaining boundaries. By carving into the flesh, and thereby communicating a message, the self affirms its identity. At the most primitive level, the self knows it exists through the experience of pain.[16] This is particularly true if integrity is threatened by massive infusions of hate and fear unsettling ego percepts. The group, however, rather than mutilating itself, finds an emotional substitute in the other's skin. Biologically, a break in the surface of the skin means that the body is open to infection. Analogously, a psychological skin requires a certain strength to ward off perceptual and affective assaults. The skin ego, therefore, functions as a psychological shield; and a leaking skin ego endangers the self's integrity, its boundaries.

By not touching the other I make myself invulnerable. As a group member, I construct a fantasy that has the effect of draping me and the group in a common skin. The group supports this fantasy; it gives me identification. My belief in what ideology and science define as truth attaches me to others who share these assumptions and percepts. I idealize and maintain my ideology by attacking the surfaces of those who threaten its cohering content—in the case of the Third Reich, the Jewish body.

The skin ego possesses knowledge and thus plays a vital role in gathering, transmitting, and storing information. The group's skin ego absorbs the ego's particularity, elaborates a common set of identifications, and imparts to individual consciousness strong fears and perceptions which may coalesce into a group ideology. This absorption of individual perception and elaboration of a group will or fantasy was central to the psychological functions of race ideology in the Third Reich. Fear of touching Jewish flesh enveloped the group and defined a common threat. Racial and biological theory was a kind of cultural or societal frame of reference that provided adhesion for the group and its ego functions, while forging a radically new historical identity.[17]

In summary, the skin ego protects the group, holding it together, protecting it from the world, and signifying the boundary between health and disease. Like the skin enveloping the physical body, the skin ego encloses the psychical apparatus. Besides containing drives, instincts, and perversions, the skin ego also regulates the drives, particularly those of hate and fear, and is the agent of projection and protection. In political terms, the skin ego appears as an ideology defining allies and enemies.

Strengthening the cultural skin ego requires a simultaneous denial of the other's surfaces and the repair of one's own psychic vulnerability. If repair drains the resources of the individual skin ego—if anxiety, fear, uncertainty, or frustration break through the skin—the individual may draw from the group's psychical resources through identification. One's own group identity, and therefore the collective skin ego, becomes stronger through denial and hatred of the other's surfaces, specifically the other's skin and the emotions registered on it.

RESISTANCE TO ALIEN BLOOD

The skin acts as a gatekeeper, protecting the body from foreign invaders. Similarly, in its political function as group identity, the skin ego acts like the membrane surrounding organic cells, guarding the integrity of the cell by identifying foreign bodies and keeping them out. The skin ego enforces the me/not-me exclusion. Its emotional message is not "I feel the Jew's suffering," but "I feel my own suffering at having to live with the Jew; I therefore will kill that infection, and in so doing, make myself strong, clean, and continuous with my culture."

The unconscious fantasy does not say: "I acknowledge this horror in myself, this horrifying guilt, these wounds." It instead dissembles, plays tricks on consciousness: "I keep these wounds, my own ugliness, from myself. By projecting them onto the other, I keep from lacerating my own skin. I destroy the other's skin to maintain the illusion of my own clean and continuous being." If I am to acknowledge my own imperfections and the hatefulness of my own projections, I must first see myself, experience my skin ego with holes and thereby in myself sustain a level of persecutory anxiety (and vulnerability) which does not force me to externalize it. But if I project this hate, this internal division, onto the other, I do not acknowledge the source of this rage in myself. I run from this potentially explosive knowledge and invent theories to take the pressure off myself. To escape feelings of persecution, even fragmentation, I and my group consciousness mutilate the skin of the other, chosen unconsciously as the repository of all evil. If I begin to sense the "imaginary skin which covers the Ego . . . a poisoned tunic, suffocating, burning, disintegrating . . . toxic," I may choose to burn the skin of the other.[18] I inscribe the poisoned tunic on the other's skin, and to rid the world and myself of that poison, I attack that tunic.

On the group level a similar phenomenon took place in Nazi culture, if the group be understood as a common commitment to shared cultural ends and to the biomedical ideology defining the Jew as bacillus. It might be useful to think of this ideology as a grandiose group-self, defending against primitive images of fragmentation and boundary disintegration, with psychological functions analogous to grandiosity in individual pathology. Group images of grandiosity in the Third Reich–ideology, racial theory, scientific demonstration, medical practice—may be thought of as a group skin ego defining itself through shared beliefs.[19]

Groups, like individuals, fear disintegration. If the Tavistock model of group dynamics demonstrates anything, it is how threatening feelings of fragmentation, disintegration, and lack of boundary are to the maintenance of group identity and group cohesion.[20] It is not unusual to find groups increasing their adhesive identifications precisely because of the unbearable anxiety at losing boundaries, disappearing, or falling into fractious conflict which threatens projecting group identity into shapeless, unbounded space. Rather than endure such intolerable psychological processes, the group rigidifies its skin surface, its skin ego, by persecuting the hated but boundary-defining surfaces of the denied and despised other.

The skin ego of German culture found itself thickened through the protective functions of an ideology that resisted, because of its radical exclusivity, any possibility of a narcissistic wound, any sense of insecurity regarding the culture's racial ethos. This covering provided by science and the professions offered an illusion of certainty and justice. It may have been the case that the radical medical ideology of the German cultural group did provide security, what Anzieu calls "invulnerability and immortality," a "double walled" organization of the skin ego. If that is true, then indeed popular perceptions of Jewish threat received considerable, if not determining, legitimacy from the German professions.

CONSTRUCTION OF THE GROUP SKIN EGO

The German public health profession became the ideological tunic of the group skin ego, a belief system draping the group in meaning, context, and value. This drape of the public health sciences in Nazi Germany, including medicine and genetics, relying on experiment, justification, and logic, enforced a series of prohibitions that maintained the *Kultur*-group's security. Every prohibition draws a rigid line separating two opposed versions of psychical space, each of which contains different psychical properties associated with their bodily surfaces: the dark, dirty Jew versus the pure, white Aryan. The public health profession was largely responsible for constructing these boundaries.

The prohibition of touching, the dynamic behind phobias, and the constitution of phobic objects separate what we know as familiar and safe from the strange and uncanny, which carry troubling and dangerous images: the Jew as poisoner of Christian babies, carrier of typhus, and threat to genetic purity. Further, the psychological structure of taboo has deep roots in the self's prehistory, and prohibitions on touching are consistently inscribed on the psyche from the beginning of life. Parents teach children what to touch and what not to touch. But touch and surface end up so intertwined that the self comes to see the *surface* as that which harms, particularly the surfaces of strange and foreign bodies thought to have the power to infect. Cultural stereotypes, drawn from childhood and prevailing moral beliefs, forge powerful taboos whose fantasizing can be externalized in any number of directions and used to construct differing readings of reality. The construction of psychical space, whether in the group or the individual, depends on how the fantasy defines good touch and bad touch, and the sociocultural agents designated as the guardians of boundaries and touch.

The effect of touch on character development is enormous, continually reverberating through psychical space. Tactile communication has a significant role in the organization of psychological space. Other sensory and motor functions follow the lead of touch and those imaginary surfaces the self constructs in its own defense. The phobic object symbolizes a whole series of aversions, counter-desires, and compromises. But the sense of the other as poisonous to the touch suggests a return of the repressed, a reappearance in different form of primitive tactile memories, original psychical communications impelled by dread and fear, and pre-Oedipal anxieties repressed in unconscious fantasies.

If the skin ego is relatively paranoid-free; if it is flexible and responsive, its moral sense may project respect, tolerance, appreciation of difference, and acknowledgement of rights. Strong but flexible ego ideals make for tolerant democracies protective of human rights and mutual respect. Not so if the envelope in relation to the hated other is defined by coldness. Emotional stoniness defines the moral sense that the psychical group ego displays toward others' efforts at contact, and has as its goal the constitution of a stronger protective envelope. Such a hermetic psychical envelope not only keeps designated others at a distance but also has the power to freeze the other, to turn the other's body into stone, an object without human properties, which is a denial and assault on surfaces, on the body as a representation of a presence which incites paranoia and hatred. As Thomas Ogden describes it: "As experience is increasingly generated in paranoid-schizoid and depressive modes, words like 'armor,' 'shell,' 'crust,' 'danger,' 'attack,' 'separateness,' 'otherness,' 'invasion,' 'rigidity,' 'impenetrability,' and 'repulsion' are attached to the quality of sensory impressions" of threatening objects.[21] The psychical envelope projected outward leads to death and annihilation; it makes the boundary between group-self and hated other rigid, armored, and impenetrable; it allows the group to act on the other without compassion or empathy; it blocks any reciprocal flow of concern or care. The group-self, in this case the German *Kultur*-group self, full of hate and fear, reinforced the rigidity of its own boundaries through action; the most extreme examples of these actions appeared in the stark reality of the gas showers and crematoria.

NINE

MURDEROUS GROUPS AS NORMAL GROUPS

It is often remarked how odd it was so few people in Germany felt outraged by what everyone knew was happening to the Jews. It was far more safe psychologically to defuse fragmentation anxiety by containing it in the science of biological and heredity genetics than in confronting the paranoia at the core of the *Kultur*-group's unconscious fantasy.

Perhaps what Anzieu describes as the cohering action of the group-in-process illuminates at least part of what was involved in Germany's systematic genocide of the Jews: "A group is born when a number of individuals bound together by, and anxious over, the omnipresent image of the dismembered body, manage to overcome this anxiety." The forces of common belief contain the equally powerful forces of anxiety, restlessness, and disintegration. Members of the group discover a certain commonness, both conscious and unconscious, that helps them "to reassure themselves and see and feel themselves as human beings, to feel pleasant, common, positive feelings." It is as if the members of the group attach themselves to attributes allowing each individual to forge an identification beyond specific self-interest and economic position. "These feelings may then give rise to concerted actions and thoughts, enabling [the group members] to describe the changes that have overcome them." At this point, the aggregation of members experience themselves as a unit, members of

a common race or party. The *Kultur*-group takes on the status of
being "superior to each individual," but each individual has a part.
When these parts find themselves united by common belief, practices, functions, or ideologies, "then the group is born, like a living
'body.'"[1]

"Who am I?" Groups continually ask themselves this question. It
is an ongoing struggle to find and maintain identity. However, when
identity appears in the cohesive properties of the Nazi biomedical
vision, the answer to the question diminishes, if not altogether
represses, the underlying fragmentation anxiety of each individual
member of the group. Rather than the group destroying its own
body, it destroys Jewish and gypsy bodies. It is, in Anzieu's words, a
"phantasmatic and therefore fragile" resolution, but in the Third
Reich it worked.

THE POLICY SCIENCES:
DEFENSE AGAINST DISINTEGRATION AND RAGE

What are some of the concrete historical representations of the
group's defenses against its own fragmentation anxiety, and how did
these defenses appear in the operation of the killing machine in the
Third Reich? It cannot be overemphasized how different were the
Jewish and German concepts of sanitation. In his account of life in
the Theresienstadt Ghetto, Norbert Troller describes the Jewish
approach to public health: "The [ghetto-run] department of pest control closed one house after the other and fumigated them thoroughly.
Thus, we got rid of lice, fleas and bedbugs." The Jewish-run health
department, concerned about the town's welfare and the physical
health of those imprisoned inside its walls, developed public health
stratagems for dealing with "the great threat of a typhus epidemic
[that] lurked into the foreseeable future." For the Germans, however,
the typhus epidemics helped to cleanse the ghettos of its unwanted
inhabitants, what Troller calls "we invisible persons."[2]

Jewish deaths, therefore, contributed to what the Germans saw as
Kultur sanitation. The more deadly the conditions inside the ghetto,
the greater the benefits to the health of the German *Volk*. The Lodz
chronicles, for example, continually remark on the grave conditions
of public health.

As we have learned from Dr. Wiktor Miller, head of the [*Judenrat*] Department of Health, the causes of the typhoid epidemic are to be sought in the following abuses: fecal matter contaminating the well water; insufficient means of transportation for removing excrement; and the devastating effect that the shortage of adequate housing is also having; the low level of sanitary conditions; the filth in apartments; the impossibility of combatting typhoid because no compulsory hospitalization exists. No precise statistics are available since many people do not summon physicians. . . . It is expected that the onset of cold weather will put an end to the infestation of flies, and it is also feared that convalescents will then be highly susceptible to pulmonary diseases. At present, tuberculosis and hunger edema are the main causes of death.[3]

The connection, in practice, between the raging, hating group self and the rational, scientific group self lay not only in the killing technology, but also in the practices and debates embodied in arguments over public health, ghettoization, and elimination of Jews in the occupied territories. The link between the group and its collective killing actions lay in the public health and policy actions of bureaucratic planners. Whatever the objective—the control of disease, economic production in the ghettos, the concentration of the Jews for transport—the technical approach to implementing the Final Solution derived from an engineering efficiency and bureaucratic apparatus inextricably bound to the fear of racial pollution.

In the Lodz and Warsaw ghettos, an often intense struggle developed between German administrators who saw the Jew as source of cheap labor and those who believed the Final Solution could be hastened by starving ghetto inhabitants to death. Food distribution became central to the politics of the ghetto and the imposition of deadly power by the Germans. And the Germans used starvation systematically. In the Lodz Ghetto, for instance, workers were paid with food coupons.

In occupied Poland, those favoring production and the economics of slave labor sought to set the ghetto up as an economically self-sustaining entity. Those who believed in the desirability of eliminating the Jewish population wished to kill as many Jews as possible through diminishing food rations, overpopulating the ghetto districts, with-holding medical supplies, and turning off vital public services. But even those favoring production, with their vision of full employment in the ghettos and dreams of enormous profits, notably Hans Biebow, head of the Lodz Ghetto, could shift gears depending on directives and policy from Berlin.

When the Final Solution took shape in early 1942, the German managers of the ghettos quickly turned their administrative skills to liquidation. It was not technically or emotionally difficult for these administrators to shift priorities from production to annihilation. In both cases the Jew-as-person could be distinguished from the task. Whether the task was production or destruction, the Jewish body remained poison.

Such shifts were common throughout the administrative struc-ture of the Third Reich. At one point, prior to the decisions of the Final Solution, those favoring production had some influence in Poland. The starvation policy fell out of favor, and those supporting it were sidelined in the hierarchy of the SS. Rather than being starved and subjected to continuing deprivation, the ghettoes were to be transformed into workshops producing for the war effort. This occurred simultaneously with training camps specifically established for the *Einsatzgruppen* and their preparation for the imminent murder of Russian Jews.

The German policy debate concerned the use of Jewish bodies. Those insisting on exploiting Jewish labor were not concerned with suffering bodies but with efficiently utilizing masses of bodies and easing the demands placed on the Reich's resources. Oscar Schindler, as a producer of goods, a supplier of bribes, and an employer of Kraków Ghetto Jews, was quite useful, at least initially, to the occupa-tion. If the ghettos and labor camps could become self-sufficient, it would not be necessary to divert funds and food from the army, the home population, or the ethnic Germans living in the occupied areas.

The economic argument had nothing to do with the welfare of the ghetto or labor camp inhabitants. The utilitarians were motivated by a desire not to save lives but to perform organizational tasks well while seeing the Jew as the carrier of infection. Lodz was transformed into "the most industrialized ghetto in all of Eastern Europe."[4] By the spring of 1943, well into the Final Solution, the entire ghetto population of almost eighty thousand was involved in textile manufacture. By the time the focus shifted to mass murder a few ghettos had developed the foundations for successful economic organization. The ghetto managers saw their economic experiments meeting and even in some cases exceeding production goals. Enthusiasm regarding this exploitation of labor had spread through the administration ranks. Yet, even with demonstrably effective production, ideology and the politics of public health reasserted themselves in defining goals and the attitudes of administrators toward Jewish bodies and the proper use of them.

When the policy of production was overturned in favor of the Final Solution, no mass resignations resulted, no organized protests were heard. Any resulting disappointment in the ranks of the General Government had nothing to do with worry over the fate of Jewish bodies. The bureaucratic battle over production had been lost. Administration had to be turned to the prodigious task of organizing the genocide, beginning with Operation Reinhard. The apparently smooth transformation of German managers from producers to mass murderers involved the successful interplay of centralized political decision making (the chancelleries in Berlin) and the ability of those in the field to accommodate themselves to shifts in ideological objectives. That receptivity derived from the construction of a group identity assaulting the Jewish body as if it were a body that did not suffer, a body of worthless life.

The perpetrators, acting within a framework that appeared normal, believed their actions contributed to the Germans' biological future and therefore supported the scientific ideals of public health. Sanitation policy spearheaded this movement into the future. Actions that led to annihilation could not be seen as criminal, immoral, or barbarous by the perpetrators. The crime, in their judgment, lay in the sanitation threat of the Jew. Elimination of the Jew and his genetic and blood deformation was seen as justice. Heinz Höhne writes:

> The system and the rhythm of mass extermination were directed not by sadists ... [but by] worthy family men brought up in the belief that anti-semitism was a form of pest control, harnessed into an impersonal mechanical system working with the precision of militarised industry and relieving the individual of any sense of personal responsibility.[5]

The power of the group ego ideal to so disguise the unconscious fantasy of destruction, the hatred of the foreigner within, and the fear of a terrifying disunity, contributed to practices whereby thousands of ordinary people engaging in the policy, analysis, and practice of mass murder justified a savagery that other moral positions would condemn as monstrous transgression. Yet the willingness to engage in these actions suggests a hatred and rage that cannot be denied and for which the perpetrators must accept responsibility. Blindness to crime does not mean that crimes did not occur or that responsibility for these crimes should be displaced onto superiors. The technocracy and science of the Final Solution demonstrated a hideous unconscious project: to protect the group identity from fragmentation by dismembering an other designated as life unworthy of life.

The following speech by a physician involved in the "public health" of the Warsaw ghetto gives some indication of this macabre interweaving of science and hate. These remarks are addressed to a professional audience of physicians convening at a local health resort.

> [S]hooting will be employed when one comes across a Jew outside the ghetto without special permission. One must, I can say it quite openly in this circle, be clear about it. There are only two ways. We sentence the Jews in the ghetto to death by hunger, or we shoot them. Even if the end result is the same, the latter is more intimidating. We cannot do otherwise, even if we want to. We have one and only one responsibility, that the German people are not infected and endangered by these parasites. For that any means must be right.[6]

The audience enthusiastically applauded this address.

It was fitting to the delusional aspect of this logic of racism that the policy created the very epidemic it was supposed to prevent. Because of the hunger, overcrowding, and filth imposed by the German administration, the Jews found themselves suffering from the very diseases the Germans used in order to justify imprisonment behind ghetto walls. Therefore, the decision having been made to respond to the Jewish body as a repository of deadly bacilli rather than a human being in unmitigated suffering, physicians and administrators in the public health system accepted as truth a psychological position explicit in Hitler and Himmler's ranting about racial pollution. Public health officials in the German administration of occupied Poland had in fact, through their identification of the Jew as carrier of infection, justified a public policy of mass murder.

Immediately after the occupation of Warsaw, the Germans forbade Jews to participate in communal prayer because of the danger of spreading infections. Jews likewise could not ride trains because of the close proximity of bodies. Public health officials insisted German manufacturers not send goods to be processed in the ghettos for war production because of contamination. Groups of Jews often were murdered as a means of "quarantining" typhus. At a work camp at Osowa, located near the village of Chelm, fifty Jews had agreed to volunteer for labor. Typhus broke out; the SS forced them to dig their own graves and shot the entire group.

In a space of less than 1,000 acres the Germans enclosed over 30 percent of Warsaw's prewar population, approximately 400,000–500,000 Jews. The decision was made by a number of administrative sectors, including public health officials who believed the walls would keep typhus out of the surrounding Polish population. However, according to Charles G. Roland, who has extensively studied the disease process inside the Warsaw ghetto, "There is little evidence that such epidemics existed to any serious degree before the ghetto was created and no evidence that Jews were any more likely to suffer from or to transmit typhus than any other group."[7]

In setting up the ghetto, the Germans created a self-fulfilling prophecy. In provoking disease environments through overcrowding, starvation, the lack of water and sewage systems, and limited medical supplies, the Germans constructed the conditions that led to a serious epidemic of typhus in late Spring 1941. In the words of a Warsaw Ghetto physician, "Until the sealing off of the Ghetto, hunger and exanthematic typhus did not particularly affect the Jewish populations."[8]

Felix Landau, an SS soldier who had volunteered for one of the *Einsatzgruppen* task forces operating in the Soviet Union, described in his diary a series of killings in which Jews were placed at the edge of graves and shot. He wrote in an entry dated July 12, 1941, "Curiously, absolutely nothing disturbed me. No pity, nothing."[9] No empathy or sorrow for the victims moved this man; not the weeping or the silent courage of those about to be killed, not the tragedy, not entire families being slaughtered. Given the ferocity of disease and illness in ghettos established across Poland, Landau's observation appears to capture the mood of German public health officials.

The *Kultur*-group, and such agents as public health officials and administrative managers, conceptualized their efforts as heroic action necessary to protect racial purity of ethnic Germans living in the occupied territories. That is why so many of the explanations of German complicity—obeying orders, fear of reprisal, terror—were inadequate. Ordinary men and women, including public health officers, most of whom had been raised in conventional moral environments before Hitler's ascent to power, were not coerced into pursuing ghettoization and starvation. Germans recruited or volunteering for sanitation management engaged in mass murder without moral qualms. But the real effect of the actions of these public health officials can be seen in the following observation of a physician working in one of the run-down and ill-equipped ghetto hospitals. A young boy, "practically eaten alive by lice, [he] looked more like a corpse than a human being. I didn't even find out if he had typhus. He died before being moved to the ward."[10]

Hilberg notes "the uprooting and annihilation of European Jewry was a multi-pronged operation of a highly decentralized apparatus. . . . [T]his congeries of bureaucratic agencies, these people drawn from every area of expertise, operating without a basic plan, uncoordinated in any central office, nevertheless displayed order, balance, and economy throughout the destruction process."[11] Bookkeepers, railway officials, municipal authorities, police, public health officers—ordinary folk—enthusiastically pursued their jobs, sending in reports, tallying up accounts, deciding who was responsible for what payment and who should pay whom. "Jews became a sub-heading . . . Wages—Jews, Rations—Jews, Taxes—Jews, Production—Jews."[12]

Actions so horrendous, so unprecedented in their ferocity, and so well organized and backed by scientific legitimation and practice suggest a radical transformation of perception. The rational means employed by German technocrats and physicians to annihilate the Jewish population of Europe disguised an evil whose origins lay in unconscious perceptions populating the emotional environment with hated scapegoats. Systemic genocide, accomplished through the scientization of hatred, became an activity in the service of the *Kultur*-group's psychological welfare. Racism, and widespread enthusiasm for its epistemological premises, drove the project. The Final Solution, a policy carried out in spite of its economic irrationality, killed Jews because the *Kultur*-group identified the Jew as an absolute genetic and biological threat.

The process to mass murder was incremental. It resulted not from a sudden move into the unimaginable; instead the participants all made choices, implemented decisions, and demonstrated a willingness to embrace ever more radical measures to deal with the racial and hygienic problems posed by the presence of Jewish bodies and their concentration in ghettos.[13] No policy suddenly proclaimed: "It is time for mass murder." The interplay between ideology, racial theory, conditions in the ghettos, an evolving sense of bureaucratic mission, the cues taken from higher authority, the warnings of public health officials—all contributed to the realization of the Final Solution. Yet in defining functions, the bureaucratic mentality consistently accommodated and internalized the image of the Jew as a polluting disease. Extermination brought into play a grotesque mixture of moral justification, willing enthusiasm, the energetic embracing of personal responsibility, and finally the justification of the death camps.

Karl Brandt, Hitler's personal physician, in testimony regarding euthanasia at Nuremberg, commented:

Each doctor took personal responsibility for what he had to do within the framework of these measures [to deal with the socially unfit], which culminated finally in euthanasia. The individual doctor took full responsibility for his judgments as assessor, as the surveyor did in his. Doctors at both the observation and the euthanasia centers also assumed full responsibility for their actions. In no circumstances is it to be understood that any doctor serving under this scheme was ever obliged to perform euthanasia in a case where he himself had not decided it was necessary. On the contrary, it was his duty, if he did not agree with any such decision, to decline altogether to perform the operation.[14]

Rarely did physicians, including public health physicians, decline. As Gallagher puts it: "What is interesting *and* important about the killing program is not the mad-dog killers, but rather the careful, orderly, and quite methodical manner by which the full German medical and scientific establishment proceeded to kill its patients over a period of years."[15]

THE MASKING OF MURDER AS CULTURE CLEANSING

Even the administration of death in the T-4 euthanasia program, an early harbinger of the Final Solution, possessed a professional, scientific component. The distribution of pharmaceutical poisons used to kill the socially undesirable was under the control of the Forensic Institute of the Reich Criminal Investigation Office, which delivered poison directly to a number of mental institutions: Uchtspringe, Stuttgart North Children's Hospital, Görden, Ansbach, Eichberg, Gross-Schweidnitz, Tiegenhof, Kalmenhof-Idstein, to name a few. In addition, the Forensic Institute, contracting with a number of pharmaceutical firms, supplied poisons to other central administrative agencies entrusted with the Reich's public health. Through couriers, these agencies supplied lethal drugs to asylums under their jurisdiction. Local pharmacists also willingly contributed killing agents to resident physicians in hospitals, a practice commonly followed, for example, at Hadamar.[16]

It is extraordinary how early in the process of mass death the public health apparatus of the Third Reich defined itself in the language of elimination. Killing socially undesirables, the mentally ill, Jews, racial inferiors, misfits of different types, cleansed the fatherland of polluted flesh, blood, and genes, and set the boundaries for public health policy. The execution of patients became a routine part of medical life. The extermination process itself received little interest from ordinary citizens; killing the genetically deformed occurred within a moral environment in which such actions were seen as vital to the health of the nation. The language of public health created a vocabulary utilized to justify annihilation. Not to kill valueless life was considered immoral and evil. In this bizarre moral inversion, thousands perished. In the view of Götz Aly, "It is in fact a singular accomplishment of the German intelligentsia that the crematoriums could be promoted as a solution for social ills."[17]

Old-age homes, sanitariums, orphanages, workhouses, and geri-
atric wings of general hospitals emptied their patients and residents
into the extermination centers of the Reich. Thousands of people died
through this so-called emergency medical planning. Bed space was
needed for war casualties, so these asylums became something akin to
concentration camps. Aly notes: "The directors, along with the physicians and chief physicians serving under them, turned into white-uni-
formed combinations of camp commandant and executioner."[18] Scores
of such "camps" existed within the Reich. Many executed, gassed, and
burned their mental and socially undesirable patients. Aly concludes:
"Organized administrative murder of the unproductive and infirm
must have become so natural that it was no longer an issue after
1945. . . . [A]ll levels of German administration, as well as the German
people in general, were willing to accept such a procedure."[19]

The psychotic had indeed become normal. With resistance rare,
the significance of the T-4 program, in addition to its technological
connection to the later mass murder of European Jewry, lay in its
extensive political acceptance, in the enthusiasm shown for murdering
defenseless, marginalized, and physically impaired persons, and in the
willing participation of physicians, nurses, administrators, and other
professionals. In Aly's view, it is hardly surprising "that the national
leadership drew the obvious conclusions, continuing its extermination
policy and trusting that Germans would silently consent to this policy."[20] Aly's interpretation of silence, however, points away from the
indifference thesis. "If people did not protest even when their own rel-
atives were murdered, they could hardly be expected to object to the
murder of Jews, Gypsies, Russians, and Poles."[21]

In 1941, Carl Schneider, a professor of Psychiatry and Neurology
at Heidelberg and a consultant with the T-4 program, wrote a report
for the sixth annual meeting of the Society of German Neurologists
and Psychiatrists in Wurzburg. While the war forced the meeting's
cancellation, his remarks dealing with the treatment of psychosis
demonstrate the German obsession with the health of the nation, the
Kultur. For Schneider, therapy for the nation "exorcised" the poisonous influence of genetic corruption. Physicians had been designated
by medical science and the culture as agents who would stand vigilant guard over the nation's biological and genetic health.[22] It was,
Schneider argued, "both humane and economically expedient to use

intensive treatment [killing] as far as possible to prevent both chronic mental illness and the need to institutionalize numerous patients suffering from endogenous psychoses." Schneider addressed the need to "relieve economic pressure on our people resulting from expenditures for useless institutional inmates, and all eugenic measures in the broadest sense, are long-term measures." *Treatment* was a code word for the murder of patients. The true patient was not the individual suffering from illness, but the nation, the *Volksgemeinschaft*. Therapy to the national community meant excising the ill, the degenerate, the infirm, and the racial pollutants. In Schneider's words, "treatment" achieved "the goal of relieving the nation of the burden of incurable psychoses in every conceivable way."[23]

Euthanasia, then, assured national health. Attentiveness to the dangers of genetic and physiological contamination, Schneider maintained, should elicit "moral recognition" for those physicians, including psychiatrists, who worked for the "good of the entire nation," who protected the "biology of the [national] psyche" from "dangers slumbering within."[24] Protecting the nation's biology required vigilant and unrelenting research into the anatomical lesions of social undesirables. Extermination hospitals scattered throughout Germany delivered the raw material, bodies. Research institutes provided the environment for dissection and morphological analysis. Schneider reported on dissection in Wiesloch, an institute associated with the Heidelberg University Psychiatric Clinic, in a request to the Reich Committee for Mental Hospitals, the political and administrative agency supervising extermination hospitals.

> In the anatomical department, the majority of the brains sent us from the Eichberg institution were examined. New and surprising findings constantly emerged, as well as disturbances which have never before been described. Only the continuation of these investigations can ensure further information; thus we urgently request a greater number of brains of idiots and severely feeble-minded patients.[25]

Killing children to attain anatomical material for research constituted a central part of the program. One Professor Nitsche, a psychiatrist associated with T-4, wrote that doctors should initiate a thorough investigation of "available cases of congenital feeble-mindedness and epilepsy [in children] before disinfection [killing]." Systematic extermination created an immediate research environment, a "linkage between anatomical data and clinical conditions." Schneider saw the "rapid anatomical . . . clarifications" attendant on dissection as critical in solving "the most important and practical problems affecting public health."[26] Research institutes throughout Germany, Aly notes, turned "the planned death of a child into nothing more than an intermediate step on the road to scientific knowledge."[27] The following is a partial list of the reciprocal relationship between scientific institutes and extermination centers for the socially unfit.

EXTERMINATION CENTER	INSTITUTE
Berlin-Wittenau	Rudolf Virchow Hospital
	University Pediatrics Clinic of the Charité Hospital
Leipzig-Dösen	University Pediatric Clinic, Leipzig
	Kaiser-Wilhelm Institute for Brain Research, Berlin-Buch
Brandenburg-Gorden	Kaiser-Wilhelm Institute for Brain Research, Berlin-Buch
	Reich Training Asylum for Juvenile Euthanasia
Munich-Haar	University Pediatrics Clinic, Munich
	Kaiser Wilhelm Institute, Munich
	German Institute for Psychiatric Research
Ansbach and Kaufbeuren	German Institute for Psychiatric Research
Am Steinhof (Vienna)	Vienna Chair in Pediatrics (Franz Hamburger)
Eichberg, Kalmenhof, and Wiesloch	University Pediatrics Clinic, Heidelberg
	Psychiatric Clinic, Heidelberg

Eichberg	I. G. Farben Pharmaceutical Research Department, Höchst
Loben (Lubliniec)	Professor von Weizsäcker Neurological Research Institute, Breslau[28]

Julius Hallervorden, a pathologist active with the Kaiser Wilhelm Institute for Brain Research and head of the Department of Brain Histopathology in Buch, noted concerning his collaboration with an extermination center:

> I heard they were going to do that and so I went up to them and told them, "Look here now, boys, if you are going to kill all these people, at least take the brains out so that the material could be utilized." They asked me: "How many can you examine?" and so I told them an unlimited number—"the more the better.". . . There was wonderful material among these brains, beautiful mental defectives, malformations, and early infantile disease. I accepted these brains, of course. Where they came from and how they came to me was really none of my business.[29]

In 1944 Hallervorden wrote with great excitement to Nitsche: "I have received a total of 697 brains, including those which I myself removed in Brandenburg. This includes the ones from Dosen. Many of them have already been examined, but it remains to be seen whether I will make more exact histological examinations on all of them."[30] Public health officials, physicians, scientific researchers greeted the Holocaust with considerable excitement; it provided them unlimited opportunity to put into effect racial theories, to demonstrate hypotheses regarding racial sanitation, to conduct experiments with an unlimited supply of bodies and body parts, and to enact technologies of destruction, that in their belief system, would assure the survival of the Aryan race.[31]

TEN

PSYCHOSIS AND THE MORAL POSITION OF ENTHUSIASM

Compelling historical evidence suggests a group psychological dimension exercising a powerful dynamic in constructing the ideological percepts that allowed the Final Solution to happen. Evil, rather than being banal, exhibited hideous, rage-filled properties impelled by a vicious phobia and sacrificial fantasy demanding the extinction of millions. As Kaplan puts it: "[T]he Jews were the recipients of a hatred that would accept nothing less than murder for gratification."[1] Arendt's argument does not minimize the horror of the regime, but by shifting the focus away from ideology, belief, and value, it threatens to water down the evil of the Final Solution and see it as a technology employed by passionless, functional bureaucrats. Friedländer criticizes the bureaucratic/functionalist interpretation for refusing to examine "an independent psychological residue.... The psychological dimension, whenever recognized, is usually reduced to a vague reference to the 'banality of evil.'"[2] Friedländer raises an important issue: Too much emphasis is placed on the "how" of the Final Solution; more needs to be given to the "why," including consideration of moral and psychological questions raised by mass murder and genocide.

Friedländer argues: "[T]he exterminations perpetrated by the Nazis . . . represent an amorality beyond all categories of evil. Human beings are no longer instruments; they have entirely lost their humanness."[3] Jews had taken from them social, economic, political, and moral utility. Explanations focusing on instrumental rationality and bureaucratic functionalism fail to explore *why* human beings may be reduced to the status of infected matter. Questions of motive, psychology, the moral environment in which evil practices, Friedländer suggests, may shed some light on the sinister and incomprehensible actions of faceless bureaucrats and ordinary citizens doing their jobs. Group-dependent motives, moral environments, the context of practices, the psychological dynamic of paranoia, the delusional inversion of consensual historical percepts—all help to disentangle forces behind the "why." It would not be sufficient to hinge the group mind only on ideological proclamations of Hitler and Himmler. Historians such as Kershaw argue the radical anti-Semitism of the party raced ahead of the masses. This is true only to an extent. By mid-1942 hatred of the Jews not only appeared in strident speeches by Hitler and party leaders, it also had been legislated into existence and practiced for several years in a number of different sectors of the population.

If the explanation of the Holocaust rests on theories of instrumental rationality, on bureaucratic processing or functionalism, it is difficult to see the instrumental properties in gas chambers and crematoria. Rationality and economic concerns may describe some of the motives behind medical experiments and the use by German industry of slave labor. But the death of those who perished in gas chambers possessed no functional utility; no economic gains or rational self-interest could be ascribed to the genocide. Annihilation of Jews contributed nothing to the war effort; in fact, great resources, particularly railway stock, was diverted from both fronts to transport Jews to the killing centers. Bodies that could have been instrumental to the war effort, for example those involved in production in the ghettos, were gassed and incinerated. It makes no sense, Friedländer maintains, to attribute a rational component to these kinds of "special actions."

If Auschwitz as exemplar of the Final Solution is possible anywhere at any time, its peculiar horror is diminished. The uncanny and utterly incomprehensible quality of Auschwitz indicates an essential difference from what human beings are by nature. Its uniqueness distinguishes its presence in history, and its unyielding commitment to killing places it in a moral latitude without any recognizable coordinates.[4] Therefore, Friedländer refuses to see Auschwitz as the consequence of a rational or rationalizing process. Arendt's thesis suggests we share common propensities that might lead to mass criminality or to the support of a criminal regime. But mass murder, Friedländer argues, for no reason, no purpose, no end, is not part of what it means to be human.[5] Nor is it part of normal day-to-day human activity or politics to enlist a society's thinkers, industry, and professions in the elimination of an entire race of human beings. Genocide is not a hidden piece of human psychology; the murdering during the Holocaust shows a "horror and uncanniness . . . a fundamental dissonance [and] explicit commitment to breaking the most fundamental of human taboos, i.e., wiping from the face of the earth each and every member of a specific human group."[6] It was not Nazi policy to transport homosexuals and mental defectives from the occupied territories. Only Jews found themselves herded into boxcars by the millions. That kind of violence is not resident in all human kind.

Friedländer's quarrel with Arendt and the functionalists is not disagreement over historiographic method. It goes to the core of understanding the human context of the Holocaust, rather than subsuming its horror under the rubric of banality or bureaucracy or, in Mommsen's terms, "uncoordinated strategies."[7] The purpose of the Holocaust was the extermination of Jews, murder as desirable cultural and moral commitment. It was indeed an uncanny phenomenon, defying comprehension. It is impossible to imagine Auschwitz, or what it was like to live in a culture where national policy dedicated itself to eliminating everyone of a specific racial group. No one in their right mind could say such action was comprehensible.

How the incomprehensible was put into practice may be ascertained in the Nazis' own view of their project. In a speech given in Posen on October 4, 1943, Himmler described what the ideology demanded of its adherents:

> Most of you know what it means when 100 corpses are lying side by side, when 500 lie there or 1,000. Having borne that and nevertheless—some exceptional human weaknesses aside—having remained decent . . . has hardened us. . . . All in all, we may say that we have accomplished the most difficult task out of love for our people. And we have not sus-

tained any damage to our inner self, our soul and our character. . . . This is the most glorious page in our history, one not
written and which shall never be written.[8]

Friedländer sees Himmler's remarks in the context of "the mass
extermination actions of the various perpetrators and particularly of
the higher bureaucracy of death," and wonders why ordinary people
could be capable of such extraordinary actions. "We cannot but
admit, on the one hand, the human ordinariness of the perpetrators
and notice, on the other hand, the 'mechanical,' nonhuman aspect of
their actions."[9] The incomprehensible, or what Freud called the
uncanny, appears not as "automata approaching the semblance of
life," but with ordinary people "approaching the state of automata"—
in relation to the "special treatment" given to the Jews.[10] Normal
bureaucrats processed death as if shoveling coals into a furnace.

Expunged from group consciousness were "any feelings of
humaneness and of moral sense in relation to groups other than their
own."[11] The bureaucrats indeed treated the Jewish body indifferently,
as if it were not there, but these same bureaucrats were not indifferent to their task as it affected the *Kultur*-group. The killing project, in
defense of German blood, distinguished itself with great enthusiasm.
The group defended its skin ego by projecting onto the other its horror of disintegration and then killing the other to foreclose the possibility of the group's death. This it did with great ingenuity,
enthusiasm, and will.

This transformation of bureaucratic processors into animate
actors appeared in the energy and proficiency with which individual
bureaucrats tackled their jobs in their rapidly growing logistical
demands. As the Final Solution intensified, greater challenges faced
all levels of the bureaucracy. This enthusiasm, echoed in Himmler's
Posen speech, is the opposite of banality: killing afforded the faceless
bureaucrats an opportunity for group identification through work, a
vitalization of emotion and passion, an awakening from the state of
bureaucratic routine which had served as the historical norm.

The prospect of killing increasing numbers of people, Himmler's
vision in the Posen speech, fed a professional joyfulness, a gratification response to the emptiness of administrative and technological
function. The grandiosity of the project; the individual identification

with the group's ideological vision; the paranoid fear of being poisoned by sick and diseased flesh; and the elation at being able to solve impossible logistical problems relating to transport, elimination, and organization of supplies and bodies heightened the awareness of the "historic" mission entrusted to the agents of the Third Reich.

As the Final Solution gained momentum in 1943–44, Nazi officials "do not appear anymore as bureaucratic automata, but rather as beings seized by a compelling lust for killing on an immense scale, driven by some kind of extraordinary elation in repeating the killing of ever more huge masses of people (notwithstanding Himmler's words about the difficulty of this duty)."[12] A good day's work meant a good day's killing for the *Kultur*-group.

Friedländer points to the pride in numbers that appears in the *Einsatzgruppen* reports, in Rudolf Hoess's autobiography, in Eichmann's proclamation that "he would jump with glee into his grave knowing that over five million Jews had been exterminated."[13] One finds a similar pride in the actions of Reserve Police Battalion 101, in diaries and letters home written by physicians at Auschwitz and other death camps, in the work of medical commissions in the ghettos, in the research of social scientists, statisticians, and "resettlement" experts, in the detail and effort given by engineers to the construction of gas chambers and crematoria, in the careful attention given by policy planners to the slave labor needs of German industry, in the excitement of scientists and other interested observers in the concentration camp medical experiments, and in the prodigious efforts of Reichsbahn employees and accountants to assure sufficient rolling stock for transport to the camps. It is an elation felt in relation to the *Kultur*-group at preserving the German body and the boundaries of the nation.

Toward the Jewish body these bureaucrats acted like automata. This is the distinction Arendt did not see: bureaucratic enthusiasm at protecting the *Kultur*-body as opposed to the indifference felt toward bodies sanitized through gassing and burning. Thus, elation is experienced not so much in the physical annihilation of the Jews, but in preserving the *Kultur*-group identity .

Friedländer's thesis offers vital psychological insights. The phobic underpinnings of what he calls "elation" should be emphasized. It is true, elation and gratification may have been the case for those performing their jobs well, whether in or outside the camps; for those benefiting from the property and positions made available because of Jewish exclusion and separation; and for the tens of thousands of bureaucrats and citizens directly and indirectly involved with the extermination. Other evidence of overt pleasure at removal of the Jews or elation at doing one's job may be more difficult to identify in the landscape of the Third Reich. Kershaw and others have made this point, and of course it is central to Arendt's argument in *Eichmann in Jerusalem*.

While Friedländer's argument makes a great deal of sense, it is not enough to explain the reduction of the Jewish body to the status of a public health menace. The motive behind the murdering may also have involved the unconscious fear of being killed, poisoned, and destroyed, a phobia against touching, universal to human experience—elaborated in the Germany of the Third Reich as a normalized political doctrine justifying the physical elimination of polluted flesh. In conjunction, then, with the enthusiasm that Friedländer identified was the role of phobia in inducing horror and the psychotic rituals of purification.

It is difficult to mark the exact moment when phobia transforms into delusion, but with many phobics the logic that organizes, defines, and populates the phobic object takes on a delusional content accompanied by severe anxiety. It is this delusional dimension of experience acting on and absorbing the normal that marked the outcome of the phobia of touching the Jewish body—a psychological identification instilled, promulgated, and stimulated for years through scientific reasoning, political legislation, and the dramatic transformation of the culture's moral evaluations. Friedländer's identification of the transformation of the bureaucrat into killer illuminates the tragic dimension of the Holocaust, but in explaining the systemwide participation in exterminating inanimate objects his thesis requires additional psychological analysis.

THE MORAL PLACE OF THE HOLOCAUST

Friedländer argues that the tragic and moral dimension of the Final Solution will be lost in historical interpretation that looks only at the functional, technical, and bureaucratic dimensions of the killing. His position touches on what the Holocaust demonstrates as failure of moral will. What the Holocaust teaches modern society is therefore problematic. Given its moral opaqueness, its lack of a definable identity and a specific historical relevance, the Holocaust cannot be used to explain other instances of mass murder. Instruction in Auschwitz is not a guide for historical understanding.

"[T]he 'Final Solution' as a result of its apparent historical exceptionality, could well be inaccessible to all attempts at a significant representation and interpretation" as opposed to an understanding of the bureaucratic and legislative events leading to it. "It could remain fundamentally irrelevant for the history of humanity and the understanding of the 'human condition.'"[14] If Friedländer's reading is correct, and the moral character of the uncanny were to be subsumed under technical historical considerations and its horrifying moral issues lost to ever more specialized studies of the Holocaust, then the scope of this tragedy will be radically diminished, at least in moral terms. One cannot attempt to find significance in the deaths of millions of people; Auschwitz had no significance for its victims.[15] They died for nothing.

But one can attempt to understand the process. The Final Solution cannot be allowed to remain opaque. To study the Holocaust is to keep in mind the power of delusional readings of reality and to caution against the potential affinity of psychosis and the seductive influence of brutalizing power in attracting the participation of society's major professional groups. It is also witness to the transformation of human bodies into objects and the foreclosure forever of their place in the human community.

It is a mistake to describe the evil of the Holocaust as banal. Evil may appear to be banal; people like Eichmann may look ordinary. But they and others in the *Kultur*-group found themselves acting out unconscious drives with tools and percepts creating unspeakable havoc for millions of human beings.

Perhaps this is one of the moral lessons to be derived from an event as unimaginable as the Holocaust: When delusion defines a culture's reality, and the psychotic-normal becomes equated with the real, political life degenerates into an unimaginable terror. It is not that we are all capable of mass slaughtering; the political issue appears in the extent to which we transform humanity into "life unworthy of life," seeing the other not as human, but as polluted flesh ready for disposal.

Transforming murder into a public health issue involves monumental psychological transformations in self and group. It makes little psychological sense to argue that we can slip into this state of mind like a new shirt or a new job. Breaking with the past and embracing a radically new *gestalt* requires the massive participation and power of the professions, the holders of moral and practical knowledge, to define perception, public value, and bureaucratic action. It requires a close alliance of politics, science, ideology, and administration.

It is doubtful that the potential for mass violence exists in all human beings as a matter of nature. It does, however, exist in political regimes that project ideological formations representing collective phobias, fantasies of regeneration, purification, and blood sacrifice. Human nature, hate, vengeance, or prejudice alone did not produce the Holocaust. The sublimation of these traits into an autonomous technology, coupled with a deadly set of phobic identifications, enabled the extermination of the Jews.

It is vital to distinguish the action of the Holocaust from the notion that human beings, no matter what the context, are capable of the slaughter of millions of innocents. It is essential to distinguish the history of human aggression from this scientization of fear and power, and to acknowledge the unique cultural alliance of public, political, scientific, and professional interests in the annihilation of an entire race of human beings.

MORALITY AND THE POSITION OF SANITY

Of course, individual acts of courage stood out in the midst of the unsympathetic culture. Hiding Jews, aiding or joining resistance groups, collective national resistance in Denmark and Bulgaria, the refusal of Italians to cooperate in the segregation of their Jewish population all suggested alternative moral positions. In the context of the Final Solution, to resist constituted a kind of sanity in the midst of limitless violence. Sanity in these circumstances was a repugnance at senseless death, an intuitive pity at the sight of the dead or dying, and a willingness to resist outrageous actions against the victims of the

Holocaust. When the psychotic absorbs the normal, sanity—understood as a world of limits, tolerance, and rights—disappears. In a continent transformed into a charnel house, moral positions maintaining a respect for human bodies and dignity fell victim like individual bodies.

The moral position of sanity emerges in the courage of resistance: the willingness to acknowledge outrage at the transgression of limits and values, at the massive inversion of concepts of human and humanity. That some were able to so act implied that sanity still prevailed somewhere, no matter how ineffective against the technology of destruction. But it was indeed the rare individual who acted against the group percept of mass murder.

While racist delusions and group psychotic perceptions defined the political policy of German culture, they had not eclipsed all other moral positions. Other individuals and countries could remind themselves of the insanity of the German project. Danish officials refused to cooperate with German requests for deportations; the Bulgarian Church and national leadership denied most Nazi demands for Jews. Raul Wallenberg singlehandedly rescued thousands of Jews in Budapest; Oscar Schindler saved hundreds; and a German police official in Kraków managed to save scores at the cost of his own life. Unfortunately, alternative moral positions had little effect against the vast onslaught of German and collaborationist participation in the murdering.

Consensual standards had been so thoroughly inverted that resistance to mass murdering was seen as crazy—a theme, for example, in Horwitz's account of townspeople's attitude toward Jews and Russian prisoners of war at the Mauthausen concentration camp.[16] Normal ethics now demanded the death of millions of human beings. The psychotic-normal absorbed the group mind, defining right and wrong and offering explanations for preserving the purity of culture and self.

The truly sane position, however, respected the integrity of bodies and refused to see an entire racial group as poisonous. Sanity manifested itself in a place like Auschwitz through little acts of resistance, efforts to retain dignity, to keep clean, to help others. The survivor himself is resistor because, as Terrence Des Pres sees it, the self refuses to cooperate in killing while at the same time retaining some measure of human dignity and integrity.[17]

Troller, himself a survivor, develops a more cynical view. Unlike Des Pres, he finds little to admire in the survivor's means of coping. "[H]uman beings cling to life, and fighting against death seems to be a law of nature, to do anything and everything for as long as possible to assure oneself of another sunrise." It is not a sanguine picture of human motive. "History teaches us that man never was very choosy when it came to methods [and] means [of survival]."[18] Yet he refuses to countenance moral judgment of survivor strategies. "Who could blame us, condemned to ghettos and other concentration camps, if ethical maxims were slowly displaced by the instinct for self-preservation." Traditional moral concerns evaporated in the face of such suffering. "[We] all became corrupted in the desperate flight toward 'protection.'. . . Our ship is sinking; it is each man for himself. Let the others drown; jump into the lifeboat, try to reach land."[19] Extremity creates heroic actors and heroic resignation; it also produces the desperate self-preservation that Troller describes.

ELEVEN

THE POLITICS
AND PROCESS
OF HATE

Auschwitz is a symbol of decimated boundaries, annihilated respect, institutionalized hate, and the disappearance of identity. The Holocaust assaulted physical boundaries and historical identity, breaking them down and decimating civil forms of exchange—for example, the respect for the body; the belief that we will sleep unmolested; the knowledge that if we suffer, individuals or social institutions will respond with care and concern; the security of knowing our families will be there when we need them. These certainties, which make life endurable, disappear when a majority group violates the identity-creating boundaries of a minority group. Without a firm commitment that the majority will respect boundaries, minority groups may suffer fragmentation, disintegration, and, as in the case of Jews, gypsies, and the genetically unfit in Nazi Germany, extermination.

There is no more compelling testimony to the fragility of psychological and political boundaries than the diaries written in the ghettos during the Holocaust. It is a point also powerfully made in recorded Holocaust testimonies. Many Jews went to their deaths not believing that culture, science, and politics wanted them dead simply because they existed. If societies fail to construct barriers inhibiting the pursuit of savagery, the lust for killing finds willing partners with modern technologies and belief systems. The record of the twentieth century gives little comfort. Power tramples civility; and civility and respect for difference fall victim to the repressive dynamics of violence and domination.

Annihilating power transvalues established meanings. Its cultural agents invent whole new categories of interpretation and action. An extreme example of this is the German notion of "compassion" in Auschwitz. Newborns could not live in Auschwitz; any birth discovered in Auschwitz automatically meant death for the mother. Nazi doctors, in a perverse use of the term compassion, argued that to send mothers with their newborns to the gas chambers showed mercy, since it would be wrong to separate mother and child. Killing, in this twisted argument, becomes equated with "compassion." Sara Nomberg-Przytyk, a survivor, recounts Josef Mengele's rationale for the murder of babies.

> Orli had told me once how Mengele explained to her why he killed Jewish women together with their children. "When a Jewish child is born, or when a woman comes to the camp with a child already," he had explained, "I don't know what to do with the child. I can't set the child free because there are no longer any Jews who live in freedom. I can't let the child stay in the camp because there are no facilities in the camp that would enable the child to develop normally. It would not be humanitarian to send a child to the ovens without permitting the mother to be there to witness the child's death. That is why I send the mother and the child to the gas ovens together."[1]

In Auschwitz, a new universe emerged. The past died, old values abruptly vanished. Death and the disposal of what science and politics had agreed was polluted flesh defined Auschwitz's purpose. On another occasion Mengele had 150 women rounded up and taken to what was euphemistically called the "infirmary" for what the women believed would be physical examinations. The group silently waited outside, while the women were taken individually to a room inside. Each was given an injection of phenol into the heart and killed instantly. The bodies were piled in an adjacent room. Those remaining outside noticed that no one came out. Panic set in. The guards herded the rest of the prisoners into the building where they were murdered en masse.

Environments like these lay outside the interpretive province of contemporary ethics. Such things, we believe, cannot happen. The elemental principles of compassion guarantee against such transgressions. Yet the respect for rights presumes sophisticated mechanisms governing the political process and the willed belief that these processes protect cherished ethical commitments and elemental human kindness. Nothing guarantees such mechanisms. Even material prosperity may not be effective in diminishing the psychological power of racism and ideologies demanding genocide.

Auschwitz, for example, emerged not from dire economic conditions. The Wannsee Conference and the plans for the Final Solution took place during a time of rising economic productivity when it appeared Germany could win the war. The eclipse of civility came not from economic depression, but from public policy decisions made in prosperous times by individuals accepting and acting on racist biological theory.

A faith in the essential decency of human life and the willingness of institutions to protect that decency lies at the heart of a culture respecting difference. But how strong is that faith? The boundaries between civility and barbarism are protected by human institutions. If social agents find themselves overtaken by belief structures with exclusionary ways of thinking—with, as in the case of Nazi Germany, a medical ethos that defined certain groups as "life unworthy of life"—no natural law or belief in the innate decency of humankind will save scapegoats.

The defense against Auschwitz is as good as the political institutions and ideology governing a given territory. Nazi Germany rewrote moral norms and rules. Jewish and gypsy children, for example, found themselves living in the environment of death. Corpses in the ghettos established by the Third Reich became as commonplace as cobblestones and human refuse. Emmanuel Ringelblum, who maintained a meticulous diary of conditions in the Warsaw Ghetto, wrote: "[D]eath lies in every street. The children are no longer afraid of death. In one courtyard, the children played a game tickling a corpse."[2] Children dreamt about transports; suffered nightmares about tortured and mutilated parents, imprisonment, deportation, and death by wires, ropes, drowning, gassing, and burning. In Auschwitz, a group of Greek Jewish children played games of simu-

lated beatings, doctors at the ramp selecting for death, guards impos-
ing punishments, parents collapsing in the snow. Games, no matter
how macabre, played out terrifying fantasies of annihilation and
dread.

German culture lost sight of the belief in the sanctity of boundary as defined by an ethics that would regard mass racist murder as
abhorrent. The boundaries between self and other, between groups
and competing ideologies, between racist science and benevolent science all fell away. Laws in democratic regimes respecting human
rights ideally protect divisions between hostile and mutually exclusive
belief systems.

The historic effort of politic to deal with negative, hateful, and
debilitating passions places an extraordinary strain on institutions.
This was especially true of the Weimar Republic. While political
groups committed to liberty and rejecting racism possessed powerful
tools for acceptance, tolerance, and legitimacy, they could not prevent
hateful radical transgressions of body and self. A Hungarian inmate
of Auschwitz observed: "The concentration camps have created a civilization within a civilization. And in this new civilization the truth
and laws whose validity we believed in for centuries have been turned
upside down."[3] Hate turned the inmates' world upside down; hate
came to be understood as normal politics.

TURNING VALUES UPSIDE DOWN:
GHETTO AS DEATH

In Warsaw, Lodz, Kraków, Lvov, Vilna and hundreds of places like
them, the civilizing values of respect, tolerance, and rights eroded
away in a matter of weeks. It is impossible to imagine the suffering of
children herded into pits, and systematically annihilated. Yet the failure of imagination should not keep us from looking at the ghettos'
reality. Values present in environments not defined by murdering in
the pursuit of a racist ideal stopped functioning. How could an ethics
with an empathic sense for the suffering of others continue amidst
the horrifying spectacles of round-ups, destruction of traditional
homes, and confinement in unfamiliar, cramped surroundings with
entire families occupying a single room?

Ghettoization ripped people from family and friends. Children felt the deprivation of their bleak new surroundings. Genia Silkies, a teacher in the Warsaw Ghetto, remembers:

> One little girl, she was dying, told her sister she would like to see a leaf, to hold something green. Her sister went out, under the wall. The children would pick away bricks and go under the wall. If there was a kind Jewish policeman, they would bring in food. This little girl went on the Aryan side, to a park, and picked a little leaf. That was all. She came back through the hole and put it in a glass by her sister's bed. The other little girl lay there sucking her thumb, smiling. And then she died.[4]

Reliance on the protection of law and the normal restraint of human civilization were taken from the Jewish population. One moment families lived a normal life, the next were ordered to give up their possessions, marched to loading squares, shoved into boxcars, and shipped like cattle to ghettos, sometimes thousands of miles from their homes. The Lodz chronicles describe the effects of dislocation and the impact of "resettlement" on Jews from Hamburg. The entry for May 7, 1942, begins: "Barely half a year has passed since they arrived in the ghetto. At that time they arrived here in long lines, festively attired people whose appearance contrasted so sharply with our native squalor. You couldn't tell there was a war on from the way those people looked."

The transformation in geography confuses and disorients the new arrivals. The overcrowded and unsanitary conditions produce panic, indignation, and impatience. Losing confidence in the present, the group's self-control disintegrates. People fight, children wonder if they have any future. No one in the ghetto offers reassurance. The Hamburg Jews face a world far more horrifying than they could have imagined: soup kitchens with barely edible food, starvation, rampant illness, rundown accommodations, terror, suspicion, brutality, and random death. The word *future* possesses no meaning in these conditions.

Deceived by the Germans, who elicited cooperation from the victims by offering hope through lies, they had been told their destination was an "industrial center where each of them would find suitable employment. . . . Some of them even asked if they might not reside in a hotel of some sort." (Similarly, the SS officer at the doors of the gas chamber in Treblinka calmly reassured victims that after showering men would be given suitable work and women could take care of home and children.)

Many ghetto inhabitants traded clothes for food. For the Hamburg Jews, money quickly disappeared. "Events outpaced time, people changed visibly, at first outwardly, then physically, and finally, if they had not vanished altogether, they moved through the ghetto like ghosts." Begging replaced arrogance and will. "Once it had been others, but then it was they who prowled the 'city' with a cup or canteen on a chain to [beg] a little soup." With resources depleted, "a soup kitchen meal became a luxury . . . [as] they sold off the last of their possessions to secure themselves food of any sort." Six months later: "[T]he metamorphoses could not be imagined, even in a dream. . . . Ghosts, skeletons with swollen faces and extremities, ragged and impoverished, they now left for a further journey on which they were not even allowed to take a knapsack."[5] Almost no one escaped the gas chambers.

The fate of the Hamburg Jews and millions like them in Europe shows how quickly power breaks down limits; how the operation of cruelty within a matter of months produces emaciated bodies and annihilated spirits. None of this seemed to matter to most Germans, who persistently trampled the thin veneer separating group sadism from the sanctity of and respect for the individual body.

Powerlessness of the kind experienced in the ghetto demoralizes and drains spirits. Take the fate of children in Lodz when the Germans demanded the ghetto administration turn over all children under ten and all adults over sixty-five. Chaim Rumkowski, head of the *Judenrat*, publicly argued for the proposal, maintaining that while the choice was horrible, it might save several thousand lives.

> I have to cut off the limbs in order to save the body! I have to take children, because otherwise—God forbid—others will be taken. . . . I have come like a thief to take your dearest possession from your hearts. . . . I did succeed in one thing—saving all children past the age of ten. . . . You see before you a broken man. Don't envy me. This is the most difficult order

that I have ever had to carry out. Give into my hands the victims, thereby to ensure against further victims, thereby to protect a community of a hundred thousand Jews.[6]

Power operated unrestrained. German hatred for the Jew knew no limits. Resources and participants mobilized for these operations lacked empathy or compassion. The Germans killed children and infants because, given the ideological dynamic, Jewish children constituted a biological and blood threat to the future. Besides, Himmler argued, children might avenge their parents. As a matter of public health, it became necessary to kill every last Jew.

This promise to kill as a matter of national therapy, its racist epistemology, lies beyond the protective boundaries of a world view that has at its core the respect for human life and boundaries protecting cultural and political difference. In regards to the Jewish population, the culturewide phobia of touching Jewish flesh reinforced the boundary between the good and bad. The culture's belief system insisted the Jews be segregated, quarantined, and eventually annihilated precisely because they threatened the integrity of what the victimizers had constructed as psychological boundaries around the group.

In his diary, Joseph Zelkowitz described the initial reaction to the selection of children:

People don't talk to one another, as though everyone had left his tongue at home or had forgotten how to speak. Acquaintances don't greet each other, as though they feel ashamed. Everyone is rigid in motion, rigid standing in the long lines at the distribution places and rigid in the enormous lines at the vegetable places. A dead silence dominates the ghetto. . . . People run through the ghetto streets like transmigrant spirits, perhaps like sinful souls wandering through the world of chaos. With that same stubborn silence on their clenched lips, with that same dread in their eyes—that's the way those spirits must look. . . . Rigidity, terror, collapse, fear, dread—there is no word to describe all the feelings that swell and grow in these petrified hearts that can't even weep, can't even scream. There is no ear that can catch the silent scream that deafens with its rigidity and that rigidifies with its deafening silence.[7]

The will to live disappeared. Fathers castigated themselves for weakness. Mothers wandered the streets, muttering, weeping.

What cruelty more horrifying than being forced to turn over children to murderers? On the day of the roundup:

> People scream. And their screams are terrible and fearful and senseless, as terrible and fearful and senseless as the actions causing them. The ghetto is no longer rigid; it is now writhing in convulsions. The whole ghetto is one enormous spasm. The whole ghetto jumps out of its own skin and plunges back within its own barbed wires. . . . Everyone is ready to die. . . . You sit at home and constantly hear yet another scream from a neighbor who, in his great despair over the children who were seized from him, tries to end his broken existence with a knife or by leaping from a high window.[8]

In this assault on physical and psychological identity, human beings dissociated from life itself. With the annihilation of will and spirit comes the death of meaning and purpose. The murder of one's children is accompanied by the death of one's being. Death camp literature refers to "musselmen," inmates who aimlessly wander the camps, speechless, shuffling about, not responding to any stimuli, whether a simple conversation or a savage beating from a guard.[9] Withdrawn, non-communicative, indifferent to even the barest essentials of survival, the musselmen soon died.

The wish for death, common in the ghettos, suggested a despair beyond the capacity of modern understanding. The self died, withered, and disappeared. Ghettoization, its logic of slow starvation, illness, and deprivation, annihilated the will to live, drenched consciousness in sorrow and bitterness. It was only a matter of time before the worn and starving body died. If ghetto inhabitants escaped starvation, illness, and exposure, the death camps ultimately claimed them. Either way, the only exit from the ghetto was death.

Ghetto diaries refer to orphaned children, alone or in gangs, wandering the grim streets, begging for food or shelter. Scores died each day. Lawrence L. Langer writes: "They [the Germans] buried people twice, once before their death, and once after, and this is perhaps the most vicious of their many crimes." We try to imagine, he continues, what it must have been like for parents "to save the 'many' [by giving up] the 'few.'. . . Those of us who are parents or grandparents ourselves can't imagine it." Langer quotes the "anguished words of a father who was there, words preserved in a Yiddish fragment written on the back of four pages of a ghetto soup kitchen record":

Wednesday, September 8, 1942
Yesterday I lost Mookha, my sweet little daughter. I lost her through my own fault, cowardice, stupidity and passivity. I gave her up, defenseless. I deserted her, I left the 5-year-old child, did not save her, and I could have done it so easily. I killed her myself because I didn't have the least bit of courage. . . . I, her father, did not protect her, I deserted her because I feared for my own life—I killed. . . . I am broken, I feel guilty, I am a murderer and I must atone, because I won't find peace. I killed my child with my own hands, I killed Mookha, I am a killer, because how can it be that a father deserts his own child and runs away? How can he run away and not save his own child?[10]

What do we make of what Langer calls these "choiceless choices?" It is not a question of when the father is to die, but how long he endures his own death beginning with compliance with the German demand. Destruction of human spirit and dignity through brutalizing power tramples moral understanding. One may be tempted to judge the anguish of this man, but condemnation ignores the uncanny properties of the "choice." How do we place ourselves in a situation where choice lies between giving up ourselves or our children?

It is not choice, surely not in any moral sense of choosing between viable alternatives. The terror felt by those parents lies beyond historical forms of moral comprehension or judgment. Therefore, to judge these actions would imply you or I may have acted differently in circumstances reflecting the absolute collapse of civility. Given the conditions in the ghetto, the slow and persistent starvation, the impediments to human dignity, and the omnipresent terror, judgment of these "choiceless choices" presumes an emotional knowledge of horror we cannot possess. I cannot envision willingly giving up my children to murderers.

Is traditional ethics prepared to protect against such choiceless choices? Hardly: a moral epistemology respecting limits and boundaries operates within historical contexts governed by what its theorists call civility. But Lodz and places like it, past and present, constitute radical attacks on civility and demonstrate the powerlessness of an ethics of tolerance against brutality couched as rational public administration.

No ethics grounded in an elementary respect for difference can predict or contain the unimaginable. Hate driven by a racist politics overcomes any ethics of restraint or limitation and ends up legitimizing the death camps. Racist ideologies projected as political truth merge with the cultural superego. Belief, morality, and justice derive from what the group phobia defines as limits guarding the safe, healthy, and clean from the defiled and dangerous. We are fortunate in living in a political and moral environment recognizing the essential humanity of theories of liberty. But to protect difference and its *boundaries* requires more than a rational agreement on civil behavior, the acknowledgement of constitutional utility, and acceptance of moral conditions governing justice. To resist what the Germans called "special treatment" may demand more than a belief in the validity and humanity of moral sentiments. The true humanist died quickly in the concentration camp, the victim of a too generous, uncomprehending, and sensitive conscience.

It is important to remember in this respect that the Final Solution emerged in governmental ministries, research institutes, universities, and medical faculties, because these institutions fundamentally agreed on racist, cultural, psychological, and political assumptions. Eminent researchers and professors prepared intellectual and scientific defenses for the Final Solution long before the first crematoria were built.

Ghettoization, construction of death camps, and the implementation of extermination policy drew in countless sectors of German society. And the genocide of Jews and gypsies evolved into the major centerpiece of German political policy during a time of considerable national optimism, production, and cooperation. The strength of boundaries between groups depends on the mutuality of respect: the tolerance of the other's body; acknowledgement of the other's liberty and utility; a willingness to rely on institutions, and not violence or force, for the resolution of difference. It is extraordinary how easily racism destroys these principles and the mutuality they encourage.

GAG RULES AND CULTURAL CONSENSUS

Germans respected authority, law, and procedure; the moral premises supporting authority, law, and procedure rested on racial ideology. It was right to murder the racially inferior; it was wrong to protect such persons. Nothing of what we, today, would consider normal constitutional restraint—minimally, the unwillingness to commit mass murder in the name of some political ideal—protected, in Germany, groups whose psychological and physical reality had been wrapped in abjection. The social consensus for group restraint possessed no moral significance in their application to Jews.

Take, for example, Stephen Holmes's notion of what he calls the gag rule.[11] Depending on circumstance, groups refuse to act on desires having divisive consequences. The gag rule encourages negotiation and compromise. Groups exercise self-restraint and, even when it is not in their interest to do so, censor the public pursuit of desire. Groups consciously decide what claims to pursue and what to relinquish. But gag rules require a universal acceptance of the rules. Groups violating these rules question the very operating assumptions of the system.

Group theorists from Wilfred Bion[12] to Fred Alford[13] have demonstrated time and again not only that groups persistently violate gag rules accepting boundaries but also that unconscious drives impel groups to transgress limits and subvert gag rules. Some of these drives suggest quite powerful impulses in the group, dynamics that appear to unite all members in a common purpose or project. Bion for example speaks of the power of the fight/flight impulse, a consciously shared set of emotions in the group that pushes it into action. Whether the group collectively decides to fight or flee derives not from deliberate rationality (Bion draws data from primarily group experience), but from unconsciously felt, collective associations providing group identity through action. Unconscious desire, appearing as a group perception, defines how the group acts. The process is unconscious, like the Nazi phobia of touching Jews.

Not only do groups persistently violate gag rules, but as Bion and history demonstrate, groups unconsciously desire to engage in acts of transgression and violation. Transgression affirms the group's need to distinguish between good and bad. One attacks the bad to preserve the boundaries of the good, which is one's group. By annihilating the other, I preserve not only myself, but the collective or group that contains me. I project into the other absolute bad, and my group wraps itself with an impenetrable armor clearly marking the boundary between clean and dirty. I and my group construct knowledge, art, and literature to fortify that boundary.

A gag rule is only as effective as the universal acceptance of principles of cooperation and negotiation make it. If, however, deeper psychological processes are at work—such as the group-logic separating clean from dirty, or phobic group reactions isolating the other—then the scope of cooperation is greatly diminished. And the conscious political and racial agenda becomes a function of what unconsciously impels the group—for example, the exclusionary legislation in Germany during the 1930s.

A constitution protective of minority rights works if it provides containment for divisive ideological expressions of preference. Beliefs, however, define what a constitution protects and what it excludes. Belief is as powerful as the sword, and when belief captures power, constitutional protections cease to exist. But to keep power and belief separate, to administer only on the basis of procedural protection, assumes belief and ideology remain subordinate to power and do not identify with it.

While Holmes's emphasis on positive constitutional restraint is admirable, the mass murderers in Germany demonstrated that the extremes of human nature are not aberrations but integral to what it means to be human. These extremes appeared in public policy and institutional action in the form of hate-driven ideology. Belief and power worked jointly to subvert constitutional restraint and to define mass murder as part of normal politics.

It may be the case the gag rule is not the problem, that reason, restraint, and belief in progress create mistaken, if not illusional, percepts regarding the power of constitutional forces to contain racism. Assaults on civil boundaries may suggest more serious contradictions than the workings of moral sentiments that disrupt understanding, unsettle communication between groups, and interfere with gag-rule functions. The wish for universal cooperation, compromise, and negotiation persistently confronts a will to destruction, an inherent aggression in the body politic, a desire or instinct for causing pain that provokes actions unthinkable within the frames established by gag rules.

Gag rules possess politically useful properties if competing interests follow the rules of the game. Such rules may on occasion restrain, through voluntary recognition, transgressive, limit-breaking acts. But they are useless against a relentless drive to destruction, violence that annihilates ethical boundaries and the constitutional protection of difference, and power that shatters cultural practices which protest the stark opposition between the dirty and the clean.

THE FRAGILE LIMITS OF PROTECTION

Take the treatment of Jewish and gypsy children during the Holocaust. What sorts of constitutional protections prevented power and belief from destroying over a million-and-a-half children? It is not likely that industrial death, the sanitizing of bodies, derives from genes inherent in the human organism. What may be part of group politics, a truly sophisticated form of human consciousness, is the capacity of technology, culture, and belief to define a collective state of mind that sees nothing wrong with putting innocent children into gas chambers. The Germans refused to obey the gag rules because they ran counter to their biological ideology.

Central to the Final Solution lay this insistence on killing children. Children carried the future; this Jewish biological future, therefore, required annihilation. In places like Auschwitz, children thrown live into burning pits pleaded with their executioners not to kill them. The Germans encouraged the setting up of *Kindergartens* to facilitate roundups (*kinderaktion*). "Special treatment" for innocent children suggests a perception of body and its fate that is absolute in its insistence on sanitation-as-death. Such actions were undertaken in moral environments that scarcely a decade earlier had been governed by constitutions, rules, implicit assumptions about gag rules and difference.

It is one thing to argue for a gag rule and claim it as a good, a desirable political end. It is an entirely different matter to argue individuals willingly gag themselves. Individuals choose to gag themselves when it is in their interest to do so. Lacking that interest, group action obeys the synthesis of ideology and desire.

The annihilation of children, its planning, came not from thugs and sadists, but from educated Germans, many of whom had received university training during the Weimar period. The agents of the Final Solution were not all deranged killers, but good citizens enthusiastically pursuing their professional commitments, and, most important, believing strongly in what they accomplished for their genetic community.

No one seemed to care for the suffering of the children. No major political, intellectual, or cultural constituencies fought on their behalf. The following is a description of a *kinderaktion* in Plaszów, a labor camp outside Kraków:

> The action was named, of all things, *die Gesundheitsaktion* [the health action] . . . the people assembled on the children's playground while the tearing away of nearly three hundred children from their trembling parents was accompanied by blaring loudspeakers, which played a sentimental song called *"mammi, kauf mir ein Pferdchen"* ("Mommy, buy me a pony").[14]

The view of the child as a menace appears in the description by a twelve-year-old boy of the destruction of a maternity ward in Lodz, shortly after his sister had given birth.

> Then as the next group of patients was being escorted to a waiting truck, we saw Esther. . . . She was pale and frightened as she stood there in her pink nightgown. . . . Soon the truck drove off and we knew we could never see our beloved Esther again. . . . There was silence for a moment. No one could figure what was going to happen next. . . .
>
> Suddenly, two Germans appeared in an upper story window and pushed it open. Seconds later a naked baby was pushed over the ledge and dropped to its death directly into the truck below. We were in such shock that at first few of us believed it was actually a live, newborn baby. . . .
>
> The SS seemed to enjoy this bloody escapade. . . . The young SS butcher rolled up his rifle sleeve and caught the very next infant on his bayonet. The blood of the infant flowed down the knife onto the murderer's arm.[15]

Similarly, in his analysis of the death marches, Goldhagen provides convincing evidence of the enthusiasm of ordinary Germans in tormenting Jews.

Agreement on limits to the game work as long as everyone complies. When the majority group, with the enthusiastic support of professional practices, rewrites the theory of constitutional protection, the system responds with actions consistent with conventional belief, in the case of the Germans, killing Jews and gypsies. In our time, we assume that rules regarding self-restraint guarantee compliance; that individuals and groups tolerate delayed gratification; that resort to legislative redress and the acceptance of compromise is more productive than the violence of armed conflict or tyranny. Ideologies and practices, however, in Germany, because of the dynamics of power, moved some distance from what at least in the Weimar Republic had been a willingness to tolerate difference. All remnants of a belief in a common humanity and common history were obliterated.

The SS officer bayonetting a baby falling from a window suggests more than one individual's savagery. It indicates a culturewide complicity in a whole new set of rules, when gagging or binding desire means destroying the passions of outrage at witnessing transgression and suppressing empathy for the victims of horrendous actions.

The saddest stories of the Holocaust are those of the bravery and courage of children adapting to the terrorizing environments that ultimately claimed their lives. Their ingenuity at surviving, their strength and courage after their parents' murders, constant starvation, and unimaginable deprivation surprised "even their executioners."[16] Empathy at the death and suffering of others should be an elementary constituent of any effective gag rule, but ideology and the practice of science in Germany decimated that dimension of human experience. What kind of culture enthusiastically produces what Mary Berg describes in her Warsaw Ghetto diary:

> There are a great number of almost naked children, whose parents have died, and who sit in rags on the streets. Their bodies are horribly emaciated; one can see their bones through their parchment-like yellow skin. This is the first stage of scurvy; in the last stage of this terrible disease, the

same little bodies are blown up and covered with festering wounds. Some of these children have lost their toes; they toss around and groan. They no longer have a human appearance and are more like monkeys than children. They no longer beg for bread, but for death.[17]

Citizens in every major profession in the Third Reich accepted the regime as sane, logical, and reasonable. A traditional ethics grounded in a respect for difference distinguishes sane from insane actions. Yet mass murder as normal politics in Germany placed ethics on a different plane.[18] When the epistemological and moral structures of Germany led to the acceptance of mass murder as a public health necessity, then ethics suffered from a debilitating myopia to the force of racism, while traditional ethics could not offer a sufficiently strong philosophical and psychological alternative to the practice of race purification. The phobia of filth had so overtaken group behavior and belief that all guidelines regarding right and wrong became subordinate to this fear.

Essential to gag rules, Holmes argues, is that "all parties must be assured that 'ultimate values'—the things they care about most—will not be dragged through the mud of contestation."[19] But what is worthy of care? People to be cared about change rapidly, as they did in Nazi Germany, to the extent that the very premise of caring underwent radical transvaluation. To care about "public health" meant caring about the health of the nation's blood. The public health professions defined care as a therapeutic cleansing of pollutants to Aryan blood and eliminating genetic embarrassments to the race. "Burying differences" came to be understood as burying bodies.

"By *postponing* the discussion of a difficult issue . . . a group or a nation may increase its capacity to solve the underlying problem later, when it can no longer be repressed."[20] Ideally, Holmes's proposition suggests a cooperative, democratic set of common recognitions, a willingness to empathize with the other. But if the concept of solving comes to be equated with killing, racism, and technological procedures for disposing of polluted flesh, the notion of postponement of difference or dispute takes on a much different meaning, again defined by belief and ideology. Postponing becomes associated with a technological set of problems: political leaders postpone action until certain kinds of machinery can be put into place. Holmes writes: "[T]he essence of liberal individualism is best expressed in the double imperative to take moral *responsibility* for one's self and to treat others as individuals, rather than as members of a group."[21] This is the highest ideal of liberal humanism. Defense of this proposition requires, however, more than a constitution. Constitutionalism implies broad acceptance for all groups within a given constitutional territory, agreement on tacit assumptions regarding restraint, boundary, and, most important, a system for containing hate.

Containing hate is modern society's most challenging task. Perhaps the problem lies in the psychological assumptions that govern liberal, democratic premises. Whatever the source for the weakness in containment, hate decimates democracy, its humanistic premises, and its moral guarantees. The twentieth century provides countless examples of hatred, sanctified by toxic power, in obliterating the belief in constitutional protection.

THE SITE
OF KILLING

What is so striking about visiting Poland fifty years after the Holocaust is the ubiquity of the death camps and the omnipresence of death. Everywhere, death seems to have been an industry like steel or coal.

To what extent did Poles contribute to or acquiesce in this process? Undoubtedly, there was a great deal of complicitous behavior; in most instances, Poles probably expressed indifference. "It's between the Jews and the Germans, leave us out of it." A young Jewish resident of Kraków spoke to me of a Catholic nun, who, during the occupation, issued a proclamation that while both Germans and Jews were historic enemies of Poland, it was Poles' Christian duty to save Jews. But he also noted that parents advised their children not to "get mixed up with the Jews." More than 3 million Polish Jews were killed, in addition to millions from other countries in camps and ghettos located on Polish territory. Poland therefore is integral to the Holocaust, and survivors still express much bitterness and anger toward the country. Survivors who remained in Poland, however, temper their condemnation and point to instances where Poles intervened to help Jews, often at the risk of their own lives. Many Poles point out that the Germans constructed camps in Poland because of economic reasons and because Poland contained the largest Jewish population in Europe. A number of Jewish survivors and Poles attest that the Poles on their own would never have engaged in anything like industrial death.

The history of Polish attacks on Jews can be characterized by sporadic pogroms. There was a tradition of considerable anti-Semitism against Jews from Polish nationalists, elements of the intelligentsia, the peasantry, and commerce and industry. The German-run newspaper in Warsaw during the occupation would print how, for example, the leather or paper or manufacturing or woodworking or retailing industries had been "de-Jewed." My Polish translator told me this word no longer exists in the Polish vocabulary. Yet there are contradictions and paradoxes. A psychiatrist told me of being hidden by a Polish woman who every morning instructed him in anti-Semitic Polish nationalist tracts. His Jewish identity survived, but he still speaks of nightmares and dreams about the images used to describe Jews.

Two children of Holocaust survivors whom I interviewed had been active in the early stages of the Solidarity movement. Both had been jailed by the Communist authorities, but not tortured or abused. Yet, they assured me, neither one of them would be appreciated today for their actions. Their very Jewishness, they said, segregated them from current participation in Solidarity politics or culture.

Each had cynical doubts about the recent Polish fascination with Jewishness. I was reminded of the comment of one informant, who associated this interest with Americans' efforts to make folk art out of the lost Indian tribes. My informants found the parallel to be intriguing, if not bizarre, although they said no Pole they knew perceived them as folk heroes like Sitting Bull.

Poles whom they associate with rarely ask them about or express interest in their religion. It has not been their experience to receive requests from young Poles wanting them to speak about their Jewish past, although they have encountered identification with Jewish objects as a form of teenage rebellion. However, it is not accompanied by any real knowledge of or commitment to Jewish life or a Jewish past.

The generation of survivors remaining in Poland live with the Holocaust as their defining identity. It frames their life and brackets existence. But for Polish Jews of the succeeding and third generation, with most likely one Jewish parent, what remains as a source of identit? Some children of survivors learn Hebrew, others make trips to Israel, but in Poland itself, nothing except the camps and monuments of death exist to define Jewish identity.

In Warsaw, the Jewish Cultural Institute, supported primarily by

private funding and small government grants, is struggling to establish a Jewish museum to commemorate Jewish life for the past 1,300
years, as a memorial to those Polish Jews who perished.[1] Yet memori-
alizing in this context presents real problems in locating the right
symbols as objects of reverence. Is it the mound of ashes and bones
overlooking the Majdanek concentration camp, the gigantic stone
urn, ringed by a rock walkway, with a huge stone mushroom shield-
ing the tons of ashes and bones that lie beneath it? Or the 800,000
pairs of shoes piled in two musty, unlit barracks in Majdanek, a stark
reminder of the magnitude of extermination? Or is it the horrible
presence of the remaining gas chambers, torture cells, dissection
tables, and crematoria ovens?

A survivor who lost his family, wife, and children at Auschwitz
finds this effort to resurrect Jewishness troubling: "Is a history of a
murdered and decimated people a fitting monument to children who
never had a chance to live, parents who never survived to see their
children bar-mitzvah'd? What sorts of memorials do justice to lives,
posterities lost to time?" He wonders what the inhabitants of those
800,000 pairs of shoes in Majdanek would want in their memory.
Would they settle for becoming an object of folk art interest, an
anthropological curiosity for touring schoolchildren?

These are difficult questions, but from a number of younger Jews
still living in Poland I persistently heard these themes in different variations, a cynicism about developing a "vibrant Jewish life" without
real, live Jews inhabiting the customs, traditions, and art. Many did
not envision a respectful memorial to the dead in making that once-
vibrant culture a series of images in a museum. A survivor assured
me that in two years following the establishment of such a museum,
one would be able to find all sorts of souvenirs of Jewish history in
shops in the popular, touristy, old town section of Warsaw, plastic
Hasidic rabbis, as one informant put it, with brightly painted side-
locks, or little wooden synagogues painted with the word "Jude," or
"Zyd" (in Polish) to put on window sills, kitchen counters, book-
shelves, and coffee tables. Many young Polish Jews fear the commer-
cialization of Jewishness and the Holocaust.

The dedication and commitment of those pursuing this
museum—this dream, as it was described to me by its most enthusiastic supporter—is striking. A museum of Jewish culture would cost

about $100 million; the Polish government is, for obvious reasons, not anxious to contribute, although the German government has indicated willingness, also for obvious reasons, to donate money. Yet, the vast majority of Polish Jews I met want to forget this horrible past and not memorialize it. It is still too painful for them, too tied into the modern currents of Polish anti-Semitism, which in itself is a cultural way of life.

It is impossible to take a position on this; nor is it my place to do so. The issues of memory and monument have a whole different set of meanings for American Jews. There was, however, something incongruous, even bizarre, in conceptualizing such a museum, to speak about it, and to be in the dank, shadowy barracks of Majdanek containing the shoes of half a million dead Jews and then to see on the side an entire bin filled with thousands of pairs of children's shoes. Nothing will bring back these people and their passions, hopes, and futures.

The remains of Auschwitz and especially Majdanek demonstrate with graphic and often grotesque clarity how Poland became a gigantic cemetery for Jews. But even cemeteries need some form of explanation, some context, and such a museum could provide a context for a remembrance for Poles who choose to think about Jews and what it once meant to be Jewish in Poland. But most Poles do not want to think about what happened, much less reflect on Jews or Jewishness. They have tired of the Holocaust and grown impatient with being accused of complicity. If crimes are to be discussed, let the subject be Soviet crimes against the Polish people, not the dead past. As one Polish historian told me: "We are now interested in detailing Soviet crimes; let us leave the Holocaust behind."

But how is it possible to put the hundreds, thousands of Jewish burial pits, the gigantic mound of ashes and bones, standing in the open in a field outside Lublin, past one's national experience? Poles today mainly speak about their past not as reflective of Polish sentiment, but as a terrible time dominated by German crimes—with some Polish participation, but also with significant Polish resistance and willingness to hide Jews. (According to one prominent survivor, the resistance made a difference to Jews only in Kraków and Warsaw.) In other places, where large extermination and labor camps had been built and ghettos established, such as Lublin, the resistance was weak or totally absent. In the small towns, Poles generally were relieved to be rid of their Jewish neighbors, particularly the nonassimilated, religious Jews who spoke Yiddish. While many Poles were disturbed by Claude Lanzmann's film *Shoah*, a significant number of my Polish informants conceded that its accuracy was unquestionable.

On balance, it is fair to say that Polish anti-Semitism figured into the death of millions of Jews. Not all Poles greeted the German policy on Jews with enthusiasm; and many Poles offered assistance to Jews *and* resistance to the Germans and suffered. The story of complicity—or as Dr. S's son put it, "dependence, not collaboration"—is not so black-and-white as to argue all Poles collaborated or minimally did nothing to save Jews. The Poles themselves endured significant losses though not on the order of the Jews. But it is disingenuous to suggest that the Nazis set up the extermination camps in Poland only because the country contained a large number of Jews. The Germans were aware of the vastness of Polish anti-Semitism. They knew that little, if any, resistance to the death camps would come from local populations. Polish resistance groups and partisans rarely had anything to do with Jewish fighters and would, on occasion, murder Jews themselves. Several Jews, for example, who escaped from the Sobibor death camp were murdered in forests by peasants and partisans.

Being at a place like Majdanek, and in the unlit barracks of shoes—three huge mesh wire bins, stretching the entire length of two barracks, as one moves down the rows, the shadows and smell become more and more pronounced; the stone parapet surrounding the urn monument; looking in and seeing a great pile of human beings turned to ashes, possibly twenty feet high at the apex—is witness to how disproportionate was the extent of suffering and loss between Poles and Jews at the hands of the Germans. In all tragic situations heroes appear, but in the case of the Holocaust, dead victims vastly outnumber all other categories of "participation." Indifferent bystanders? There were many, probably the vast majority of the Polish population during the occupation.

In Majdanek concentration camp—silence. Blue-white sky with a few high clouds, a heavy, late afternoon summer heat, empty rectangular field, circled by barbed wire fences, guard towers, a row of remaining barracks, three-tier bunks and dirty straw relics of fifty years ago. Gas chamber still stands at the foot of the camp, dark

inside, with peepholes to watch the slow dying, a row of guard barracks running perpendicular to the lower rectangle, housing exhibits
of the horror. At the very top of the rectangle, an industrial cremato-
rium, equipped with auxiliary gas chamber and dissection table. At
the very top edge, next to the field where ashes and bones were
dumped, the stone urn containing the remains of half a million dead
Jews.

An old man riding a bicycle by the camp's perimeter interrupts
the day's clashing stillness. He starts speaking excitedly with my
translator:

> During the war I smuggled meat on the road that ran by the
> camp; there were signs on the barbed wire warning us not to
> look or get too near. It was horrible in there. I knew terrible
> things were being done; the whole town knew it. You could
> smell it, burning flesh, the stench from the open latrines,
> filthy prisoners, stinking. And you could see it, the thick black
> smoke, always hanging over the camp. No words describe
> that smell; but I still remember it. Even now when I speak
> with you, I smell that stench. Of course, I would look; the
> guards didn't bother me. You couldn't miss those chimneys:
> day and night; sometimes when I made my night runs, you
> could see flames leaping out of the smoke stacks. Black soot,
> ashes; I'd have to wash them out of my hair and clothes after
> being near Majdanek. Those prisoners, I'll never forget them:
> thin, torn rags on their bodies, sometimes half naked even in
> the middle of winter, shuffling in the mud, falling down, bod-
> ies lying by the fence. . . .
>
> We all knew what was going on; but times were tough for
> us too; we had to survive. That's all we thought about. I
> needed to get the meat to my customers; so I rode my bike
> past that place.
>
> I never thought much about the Jews. It was horrible. But
> the Jews were finished and we had our own lives to think about.

Two hours later, my journey through Majdanek finished; alone in
this camp, I walk towards a Polish Catholic cemetery adjacent to the
camp, to meet my translator and find a taxi back to Lublin. The

silence of the camp unnerves me. I hear children's voices. Flowers line the entrance to the cemetery. While I am relieved to hear laughter and see kids playing, I still feel the presence of those shoes: the cemetery of shoes shrouded in musty wooden barracks standing watch in a desolate Polish field.

NOTES

Prologue

1. Daniel Jonah Goldhagen, *Hitler's Willing Executioners: Ordinary Germans and the Holocaust* (New York: Alfred A. Knopf, 1996).

2. Documents are from the Health Office of the General Government, located in the Kraków City Archives (File IZGGI).

3. This material is on microfilm in the National Library of Poland (Warsaw).

4. All excerpts taken from *Nowy Kourier*, "Warsaw News," April 28, May 1, 1942; March 22, April 8, 1943.

Chapter 1

1. Elie Wiesel, *The Town Beyond the Wall* (New York: Atheneum, 1964), p. 149.

2. Martin Broszat, Saul Friedländer, "A Controversy about the Historization of National Socialism," *New German Critique*, 44 (Spring/Summer 1988): 102–3.

3. Broszat has been criticized on the grounds that his insistence historians focus on *Alltagsgeschichte* or the common, routine, social events of day-to-day life during the Nazi period diminishes the role of the Holocaust and transforms the extremity of Nazi crimes into a secondary phenomenon of the period. For an interesting critique of Broszat, and other "revisionist" historians of the Holocaust, see Dominick LaCapra, *Representing the Holocaust: History, Theory, Trauma* (Ithaca, NY: Cornell University Press, 1994).

4. Jürgen Habermas, *The New Conservatism: Cultural Criticism and the Historians' Debate*, ed. and trans. Shierry Weber Nicholsen (Cambridge: Harvard University Press, 1989), p. 224.

5. Yehuda Bauer, *The Holocaust in Historical Perspective* (Seattle: University of Washington Press, 1978), p. 77.

6. For a discussion of indifference as a societal state of mind, see Rainier C. Bauman, "Holocaust: Moral Indifference as *the* Form of Modern Evil," in A. Rosenberg and G. E. Myers, eds., *Echoes from the Holocaust: Philosophical Reflections on Dark Time* (Philadelphia: Temple University Press, 1988).

7. For an early formulation of this concept, see Alfred Hoche and Rudolf Binding, *Die Freigabe der Vernichtung Lebensunwerten Lebens* [Release and Destruction of Lives Not Worth Living] (Leipzig, 1920). Hoche, a psychiatrist, and Binding, a lawyer, argued that euthanasia was essential since it prevented the "nation's degeneration." Paul Weindling, a modern historian of German race theory and practice, describes their project in the following terms: "If society was to ensure that life was to be of productive value, unproductive lives of 'human ballast' should be eliminated as an oppressive burden on the fit and healthy. Binding and Hoche redefined euthanasia from being a curative ending of a tormented life to being a curative value for the social organism, and refused the charge that this was murder." Paul Weindling, *Health, Race, and German Politics Between National Unification and Naziism, 1870–1945* (Cambridge: Cambridge University Press, 1989), pp. 395–96.

8. Gordon L. Horwitz, *In the Shadow of Death: Living Outside the Gates of Mauthausen* (New York: Free Press, 1990), p. 120.

9. Harold Kaplan, *Conscience and Memory: Meditations in a Museum of the Holocaust* (Chicago: University of Chicago Press, 1994), p. 55.

10. Hannah Arendt. *Eichmann in Jerusalem: A Report on the Banality of Evil* (New York: Penguin, 1964).

11. Raul Hilberg, *The Destruction of the European Jews*, vol. 1 (New York: Holmes and Meier, 1985), p. 62.

12. Ibid., p. 55.

13. Yitzhak Arad, *Belzec, Sobibor, Treblinka: The Operation Reinhard Death Camps* (Bloomington: Indiana University Press, 1986), p. 198.

14. Ibid., p. 1.

15. Ibid., p. 102.

16. Hilberg, *Perpetrators, Victims, Bystanders: The Jewish Catastrophe, 1933–1945* (New York: Harper Perennial, 1992), p. 197.

17. Gitta Sereny, *Into That Darkness: From Mercy Killing to Mass Murder* (New York: McGraw-Hill, 1974), p. 201.

18. Ibid., p. 50.

19. Ibid., p. 84.

20. Hilberg, *The Destruction of the European Jews*, vol. 1, pp. 330ff.

21. Appointed by the Germans, the *Judenräte* leaders generally complied with German demands regarding selections (the numbers of ghetto inhabitants "selected" for places like Auschwitz), resettlements, and labor and production quotas. Isaiah Trunk writes: "The German authorities forced the [Jewish] Councils to make all the preliminary preparations for 'resettlements' on their behalf: deliver data on the demography and employment of the ghetto population; prepare, in accordance with their strict guidelines, lists of suggested candidates for deportation; order the Jews to report at the places designated for 'selection'; search for deportation candidates who tried to conceal themselves and deliver them in person, or order the ghetto police to find them according to lists prepared by the Councils or given to them by the authorities." Ibid., p. 420.

22. Yitzhak Perlis, "Final Chapter: Korczak in the Warsaw Ghetto," in Janusz Korczak, *Janusz Korczak, The Ghetto Years: 1939–1942*, trans. Jerzy Bachrach and Barbara Krzywicka (New York: Holocaust Library, 1980), pp. 92–93. During the trial of Adolf Eichmann, Yitzhak Zuckerman, active in the Warsaw resistance, spoke of children starving and begging on the streets. "I would get up in the morning and find the child dead. [The children] were like hunted little animals." Yitzhak Zuckerman, *A Surplus of Memory: Chronicle of the Warsaw Ghetto Uprising*, trans. by Barbara Harshav (Berkeley: University of California Press, 1993), p. 129.

23. Ibid., pp. 190–91.

24. Hilberg, *The Destruction of the European Jews*, vol. 1, p. 267.

25. Ibid., p. 268.

26. Adam Czerniakow, *The Warsaw Diary of Adam Czerniakow: Prelude to Doom*, ed. Raul Hilberg, Stanislaw Staron, and Josef Kermisz, trans. Stanislaw Staron and the staff of Yad Vashem (New York: Stein and Day, 1979), pp. 360, 366.

27. Arnost Lustig, *Night and Hope* (Washington, D.C.: Inscape, 1976), p. 59.

28. Hermann Rauschning, *The Voice of Destruction* (New York: G. P. Putnam's Sons, 1940), pp. 251–52.

29. Harold Kaplan, *Conscience and Memory*, pp. 76, 77.

30. Zygmunt Bauman, *Modernity and the Holocaust* (Ithaca, NY: Cornell University Press, 1991).

31. Etty Hillesum, *Letters from Westerbork*, trans. Arnold J. Pomerans (London: Cape, 1987), p. 134.

32. Ibid., pp. 110–11.

33. Chaim Aron Kaplan, *The Warsaw Diary of Chaim A. Kaplan*, trans. Abraham I. Katsh (New York: Collier, 1973), pp. 220ff.

34. Ibid., p. 222.

35. Quoted in Michael Burleigh and Wolfgang Wipperman, *The Racial State: Germany 1933–1945* (New York: Cambridge University Press, 1991), p. 106.

36. Alex Bein, "The Jewish Parasite—Notes on the Semantics of the Jewish Problem, with Special Reference to Germany," in Robert Weltsch, ed., *Publications of the Leo Baeck Institute: Yearbook 9* (London: East and West Library, 1964), p. 32.

37. Ibid., p. 48.

38. Ibid., p. 13.

39. Quoted in Leon Volovici, *Nationalist Ideology and Antisemitism: The Case of Romanian Intellectuals in the 1930s*, trans. Charles Kormos (New York: Pergamon Press, 1991), p. 55.

Chapter 2

1. See Rainier C. Bauman, "Holocaust: Moral Indifference as the Form of Modern Evil"; Ian Kershaw, *Popular Opinion and Political Dissent in the Third Reich: Bavaria 1933–1945* (Oxford: Clarendon Press, 1983); Hans Mommsen, "Anti-Jewish Politics and the Implementation of the Holocaust," in Hedley Bull, ed., *The Challenge of the Third Reich: The Adam von Trott Memorial Lectures* (Oxford: Clarendon Press, 1986); John Toland, *Adolf Hitler*, vol. 1 (New York: Doubleday, 1976).

2. Quoted in Heinz Höhne, *The Order of the Death's Head: The Story of Hitler's S.S.*, trans. Richard Barry (New York: Coward-McCann, 1976), p. 326.

3. Quoted in Alexander Donat, ed., *The Death Camp Treblinka* (New York: Holocaust Library, 1979), p. 168.

4. See Philippe Lacoue-Labarthe, *Heidegger, Art and Politics* (Oxford: Basil Blackwell, 1990).

5. Chaim Kaplan, *The Warsaw Diary of Chaim A. Kaplan*, pp. 234, 247.

6. Ibid., p. 379.

7. George M. Kren and Leon Rappoport, *The Holocaust and the Crisis of Human Behavior* (New York: Holmes and Meier, 1980), p. 95.

8. Hans Frank was convicted as a war criminal and executed in 1946. The Office for the Investigation of the War Crimes against the Polish Nation is in the process of translating into Polish the entire forty-volume diary.

9. Quoted in Harold Kaplan, *Conscience and Memory*, p. 130.

10. Quoted in Saul Friedländer, *Kurt Gerstein: The Ambiguity of Good*, trans. by Charles Fullman. (New York: Alfred A. Knopf, 1969), pp. 137–38. Also, according to Poliakov, Rudolf Diels, who at various times served the Reich as the Prussian Gestapo chief, chief of police in Cologne, and chief administrative officer of the Hermann Goering Works, "informs us that, to his knowledge, the expression 'to go up in smoke' had become proverbial in Germany toward the end of the war" (p. 139).

11. Berel Lang, *Act and Idea in the Nazi Genocide* (Chicago: University of Chicago Press, 1990), p. 95.

12. Ibid., p. 96. The scientific community, popular culture, and the professions all subscribed to racial theory and ideology. The race attitudes of German genetics and biology were not confined to a small cadre of scientific elite; their findings affected medical practice, law, judicial administration, literature, film, and art. The historical research that sees the Holocaust only as a product of the Nazi Party, Party officials, and SS thugs ignores the extensive penetration of the entire culture, especially the professions, by racial ideology. For a representative selection of literature focusing exclusively on the Nazi Party and the SS see Karl Dietrich Bracker, *The German Dictatorship: The Origins, Structure, and Effects of National Socialism*, trans. Jean Steinberg (New York: Praeger, 1970); William L. Shirer, *The Rise and Fall of the Third Reich: A History of Nazi Germany* (New York: Simon & Schuster, 1960); Charles W. Sydnor, Jr., *Soldiers of Destruction: The SS Death's Head Division, 1933–1945* (Princeton: Princeton University Press, 1977); Ladislaus de Hoyos, *Klaus Barbie*, trans. Nicholas Courtin (London: W. H. Allen, 1985).

13. Lang, *Act and Idea in the Nazi Genocide*, p. 96.

14. Quoted in Robert J. Lifton, "Life Unworthy of Life: Nazi Racial Views," in Randolph L. Braham, ed., *The Psychological Perspectives of the Holocaust and of Its Aftermath* (Boulder, CO: Social Science Monographs, 1988), p. 3. See also Kriste Macrakis, "The Ideological Origins of Institutes at the Kaiser Wilhelm Gesellschaft in National Socialist Germany," in Monika Renneberg and Mark Walker, eds., *Science, Technology, and National Socialism* (Cambridge: Cambridge University Press, 1994).

15. Konrad Lorenz, "Disturbances of Species-Specific Behavior Caused by Domestication," in Benno Müller-Hill, *Murderous Science: Elimination by Scientific Selection of Jews, Gypsies, and Others, Germany 1933–1945*, trans. George R. Fraser (New York: Oxford University Press, 1988), p. 14. While German society progressively excluded Jews, gypsies, and the mentally and physically "defective," it passed laws restricting the killing and abuse of animals and legislation protecting the environment. The 1933 Law for the Protection of Animals gave animals the right not to be abused or subjected to cruelty. The 1934 Law on Hunting extended similar safeguards to game animals; hunters were required to follow scrupulous regulations in killing wild game. The 1935 Law for the Protection of Nature provided rules for the protection of flowers, trees, shrubbery, and parks. For an analysis of the "Green" movement in National Socialist ideology, see Anna Bramwell, *Blood and Soil: Richard Walther Darre and Hitler's Green Party* (Bourne End, UK: Kensal, 1985).

16. For studies that further explore these connections, see Leo Alexander, "Medical Science under Dictatorship," *New England Journal of Medicine*, 241 (1949): 39–47; Alan D. Beyerchen, *Scientists Under Hitler: Politics and the Physics Community in the Third Reich* (New Haven, CT: Yale University Press, 1977); International Auschwitz Committee, *Nazi Medicine: Doctors, Victims, and Medicine in Auschwitz* (New York: Howard Fertig, 1986); Arthur L. Caplan, *When Medicine Went Mad: Bioethics and the Holocaust* (Totowa, NJ: Humana Press, 1992).

17. Hugh Gregory Gallagher, *By Trust Betrayed: Patients, Physicians, and the License to Kill in the Third Reich* (New York: Holt, 1990), p. 4.

18. See Donald W. Light, Stephan Leibfried, and Florian Tennstedt,

"Social Medicine vs. Professional Dominance: The German Experience," *American Journal of Public Health*, 76 (1986): 78–83; Diane Paul, "Eugenics and the Left," *Journal of the History of Ideas*, 45 (1984): 567–90; and Daniel J. Kevles, *In the Name of Eugenics, Genetics and the Uses of Human Heredity* (Berkeley: University of California Press, 1985).

19. Shelia Faith Weiss, "The Race Hygiene Movement in Germany," *Osiris*, 2d ser., 3 (1987): 193–236; Paul Weindling, "Weimar Eugenics: The Kaiser Wilhelm Institute for Anthropology, Human Heredity, and Eugenics in Social Context," *Annals of Science*, 42 (1985): 303–18.

20. Müller-Hill notes that at the Wannsee conference "discussions were held to define those categories of persons who were to be killed immediately, those to be sterilized, those to be 'scrapped through labor'... and those to be 'Germanized.'" Müller-Hill, *Murderous Science*, p. 49.

21. Brigitte Schroeder-Gudehus, "The Argument for Self Government and Public Support of Science in Weimar Germany," *Minerva*, 10 (1972): 537–70.

22. For a comprehensive discussion of the entire eugenics movement, see Paul Weindling, *Health, Race, and German Politics Between National Unification and Nazism, 1870–1945* (New York: Cambridge University Press, 1989).

23. See Hoche and Binding, *Die Freigabe der Vernichtung Lebensunwerten Lebens* [Release and Destruction of Lives Not Worth Living] (Leipzig, 1920).

24. Weindling, *Health, Race, and German Politics*, p. 396.

25. For a comprehensive analysis of the role of the engineering profession in the Third Reich, see Jeffrey Herf, *Reactionary Modernism: Technology, Culture, and Politics in Weimar and the Third Reich* (New York: Cambridge University Press, 1984); and Thomas P. Hughes, "Technology," in Henry Friedlander and Sybil I. Milton, eds., *The Holocaust: Ideology, Bureaucracy, and Genocide: The San Jose Papers* (Millwood, NY: Kraus International, 1977).

26. See Robert Lewis Koehl, *RKFDV: German Resettlement and Population Policy, 1939–1945* (Cambridge: Harvard University Press, 1957); and Jeremy Noakes, "Nazism and Eugenics: The Background to the Nazi Sterilization Law of 14 July 1933," in R. J. Bullen, H. Pogge von Strandmann, and A. B. Polonsky, eds., *Ideas into Politics: Aspects of*

European History, 1880–1950 (Totowa, NJ: Barnes and Noble, 1984).

27. Weindling, *Health, Race, and German Politics*, p. 54.

28. Robert Proctor, *Racial Hygiene: Medicine Under the Nazis* (Cambridge: Harvard University Press, 1988), p. 67.

29. Ibid., p. 78.

30. Ibid., p. 79.

31. Ibid., p. 84.

32. Ibid., p. 105.

33. Ibid., p. 110.

34. B. Gebhardt, "Health Education in Germany," *American Journal of Public Health and Nation's Health*, 24 (1934): 1151.

35. Ibid. Gebhardt had presented these "findings" before the Health Officers Section of the American Public Health Association at its Sixty-third Annual Meeting in Pasadena, California, September 3, 1934.

36. Quoted in Alan M. Kraut, *Silent Travelers: Germs, Genes, and the "Immigrant Menace"* (New York: Basic Books, 1994), p. 145.

37. W. W. Peter, "Germany's Sterilization Program," *American Journal of Public Health and Nation's Health*, 24 (1934): 187.

38. Ibid., p. 189.

39. Ibid., p. 190.

40. Ibid.

41. Ibid., p. 190.

42. Ibid..

43. H. E. Kleinschmidt, "New Germany Teaches Her People: An Account of the Health Exposition of Berlin," *American Journal of Public Health and Nation's Health*, 25 (1935): 1108.

44. Ibid., p. 1109.

45. Ibid., p. 1110.

46. Ibid., p. 1111. Emphasis added.

47. Ibid.

48. Ibid., pp. 1111–112.

49. Ibid., p. 1113.

50. Ibid.

Chapter 3

1. Lucjan Dobroszycki, ed., *The Chronicle of the Łódz Ghetto: 1941–1944*, trans. Richard Lourie and Joachim Neugroschel (New

Haven, CT: Yale University Press, 1984). The Lodz Ghetto chronicles were composed by individuals officially connected to the internal record keeping of the Jewish council or Judenrat. Chaim Rumkowsky the head of the Judenrat, established a department of archives. Its charge was to record significant events in the history of the ghetto, as well as matters of daily and administrative life. These records would witness the grave conditions and peril of the ghetto community. Because of the danger in keeping such records, and the obvious need to screen its activities from German authorities and Nazi commissions inspecting the ghetto, the *Judenrat* kept the chronicles secret, even within the ghetto itself. The purpose of the chronicles, as defined by one of the leading archivists, was to serve "future scholars studying the life of a Jewish society in one of its most difficult periods." For an extensive collection of diaries, letters, and documents pertaining to the Lodz Ghetto, and life within it, see Alan Adelson and Robert Lapides, eds., *Lodz Ghetto: Inside a Community Under Siege* (New York: Penguin, 1991).

2. Ibid., p. 171.

3. Christopher R. Browning, *Ordinary Men: Reserve Police Battalion 101 and the Final Solution in Poland* (New York: Harper Perennial, 1992).

4. Norbert Troller, *Theresienstadt: Hitler's Gift to the Jews,* ed. Joel Shatzky, trans. Susan E. Cerzyak-Spatz (Chapel Hill: University of North Carolina Press, 1991), p. 147.

5. Ibid., p. 148.

6. LaCapra, *Representing the Holocaust*, p. 104.

7. Quoted in ibid., p. 109.

8. The German killers, Harold Kaplan surmises, may have been "projecting onto the Jews the alien and dangerous force they felt in themselves. . . . Hitler invented a massive ceremony of sacrifice; his passion for unity, his totalitarian spirit, required unceasing murder. Racial purity was the highest good for him, above all moral terms and at the same time 'truly' scientific." Kaplan, *Conscience and Memory*, p. 37.

9. See Robert J. Lifton, *The Nazi Doctors: Medical Killing and the Psychology of Genocide* (New York: Basic Books, 1986).

10. For further information on Pfannmüller's crimes, see ibid., p. 62.

11. Lifton, "Reflections on Genocide," p. 642.

12. Weiss, "Pedagogy, Professionalism, and Politics: Biology Instruc-

tion During the Third Reich," in Renneberg and Walker, eds., *Science, Technology, and National Socialism*, pp. 190–91.

13. Ibid., p. 193.

14. Quoted in Methchild Rössler, "'Area Research' and 'Spatial Planning,'" in Renneberg and Walker, eds, *Science, Technology, and National Socialism*, p. 131.

15. Müller-Hill, *Murderous Science*, p. 23.

16. Proctor, *Racial Hygiene*, p. 140.

17. Mario Biagioli, "Science, Modernity, and the Final Solution," in Saul Friedländer, ed., *Probing the Limits of Representation: Nazism and the "Final Solution"* (Cambridge: Harvard University Press, 1992), p. 202.

18. Ibid., pp. 192, 202.

19. Kren and Rappoport, *The Holocaust and the Crisis of Human Behavior*, p. 143.

20. For a comprehensive history of the Jewish influence in Weimar, see Donald C. Niewyk, *The Jews in Weimar Germany* (Baton Rouge: Louisiana State University Press, 1980).

21. Quoted in Proctor, *Racial Hygiene*, pp. 165–66.

22. Quoted in Müller-Hill, *Murderous Science*, p. 81.

23. Browning, *Ordinary Men*, p. 76.

24. Ibid., p. 127.

25. Goldhagen argues that Browning takes too literally testimony from former members of Battalion 101 in the "self-exculpating claims . . . to opposition, reluctance, and refusal," and misinterprets "evidence that suggests the general voluntarism and approval of the men in the Battalion for their genocidal activities." Goldhagen, *Hitler's Willing Executioners*, p. 534.

26. Quoted in Bauer, *The Holocaust in Historical Perspective*, p. 8.

27. Goldhagen, *Hitler's Willing Executioners*, p. 218.

28. John Dower, *War Without Mercy: Race and Power in the Pacific War* (New York: Pantheon, 1986).

29. See Theodor W. Adorno, Elsie Frenkel-Brunswick, Daniel J. Levinson, and R. Nevitt Sanford, *The Authoritarian Personality* (New York: Harper, 1950).

30. See Stanley Milgram, *Obedience to Authority: An Experimental View* (New York: HarperCollins, 1974).

31. Browning, *Ordinary Men*, p. 172.

32. See Craig Haney, Curtis Banks, and Philip Zimbardo, "Interper-

sonal Dynamics in a Simulated Prison," *International Journal of Criminology and Penology*, 1 (1983): 69–97.

33. For Bauman's thoughts on the Milgram experiments, see *Modernity and the Holocaust*, pp. 151–68.

34. Ervin Staub, *The Roots of Evil: The Origins of Genocide and Other Group Violence* (New York: Cambridge University Press, 1989), pp. 18, 126. For a similar argument, see George Kateb, *The Inner Ocean: Individualism and Democratic Culture* (Ithaca, NY: Cornell University Press, 1992).

35. For an elaboration of the cult of masculinity and camaraderie in German culture, see George Mosse, *The Image of Man: The Creation of Modern Masculinity* (New York: Oxford University Press, 1996); and Klaus Theweleit, *Male Fantasies,* vol. 2: *Male Bodies: Psychoanalyzing the White Terror*, trans. Stephen Conway, Erica Carter, and Chris C. Turner (Minneapolis: University of Minnesota Press, 1987).

36. Milgram, *Obedience to Authority*, p. 177.

37. Browning, *Ordinary Men*, pp. 174, 176.

38. For information on the protests of the clergy, see Proctor, *Racial Hygiene*, p. 194.

39. Ibid.

40. See Jill Stephenson, " 'Reichsbund der Kinderreichen': The League of Large Families in the Population Policy of Nazi Germany," *European Studies Review*, 9 (1979): 350–75; and Jill Stephenson, *The Nazi Organization of Women* (Totowa, NJ: Barnes and Noble, 1981).

41. Müller-Hill, *Murderous Science*, p. 23.

42. Dobroszycki, ed., *The Chronicle of the Lodz Ghetto*, pp. 166–67.

43. Ibid., p. 246.

44. Miklos Nyiszli, *Auschwitz: A Doctor's Eyewitness Account*, trans. Tibere Kramer and Richard Seaver (New York: F. Pell, 1960).

45. Proctor, *Racial Hygiene*, p. 221.

Chapter 4

1. For a comprehensive analysis of all aspects of the Auschwitz-Birkenau death camp, the largest killing center of the Final Solution, including construction, the processing of bodies, and labor inside and outside the camp, see Yisrael Gutman and Michael Berenbaum, eds., *Anatomy of the Auschwitz Death Camp* (Bloomington: Indiana University Press, 1994).

2. Peter Haas argues that the annihilation of the Jews was not a departure from the Western ethical system, but a rewriting, rethinking, and respeaking of properties attached to such concepts as good and evil. While he is correct in identifying the development of ethics and logic within Nazi ideology and racial theory, I find troubling Haas's interpretation of the philosophical development of this system and its connection with historical patterns of ethics. The Nazi system, he maintains, was indicative of the "human ability to redefine evil. . . . Nazi society had a strict, almost puritanical code of moral standards." Therefore, in his view, the Nazis do not represent the quintessentially evil or even the banality of evil, but a society redefining, within the consensus of the Western tradition, what evil is and how to conceptualize the relationship between good and evil. However, the Nazi ethos possessed a profound delusional component radically breaking from the Western ethical tradition and its approach to difference. The doing of normal politics in the context of the Third Reich was a traumatic interruption of the past with grave consequences for the ethics of tolerance, difference, and liberty, and should not be construed as the "redefinition" of ethical precepts. See Peter J. Haas, *Morality After Auschwitz: The Radical Challenge of the Nazi Ethic* (Philadelphia: Fortress Press, 1988), pp. 2–3.

3. Quoted in Saul Friedländer, *Kurt Gerstein: The Ambiguity of Good*, pp. 107–8.

4. Jean Améry, an Austrian-born half-Jew whose original name was Hans Maier, was active in the Belgian resistance. Captured by the Germans, tortured by the Gestapo, he survived Auschwitz and Bergen-Belsen, and became a widely read and respected essayist of the Holocaust. Améry committed suicide in 1978.

5. Jean Améry, *At the Mind's Limits: Contemplation by a Survivor on Auschwitz and Its Realities*, trans. Sidney Rosenfeld and Stella P. Rosenfeld (Bloomington: Indiana University Press, 1980), p. 96.

6. Josef Zelkowicz, "Days of Nightmare," Trans. Joachim, Neugroschel Dawidowicz, ed., *H. Holocaust Reader* (New York: Berhman House, 1976), pp. 299, 312.

7. Ibid., p. 314.

8. Ibid., pp. 315–16.

9. Harold Kaplan, *Conscience and Memory*, p. 28.

10. For a fuller elaboration of the structure and dynamics of delusion, see James M. Glass, *Delusion: Internal Dimensions and Political Life* (Chicago: University of Chicago Press, 1985).

11. See Bruno Bettelheim, *The Empty Fortress: Infantile Autism and the Birth of the Self* (New York: Free Press, 1967).

12. Lifton, *The Nazi Doctors*, pp. 418, 446.

13. Ibid., p. 422.

14. Peter Haidu, "The Dialectics of Unspeakability: Language, Silence, and the Narratives of Desubjectification," in Friedländer, ed., *Probing the Limits of Representation*, pp. 288–90.

15. Sigmund Freud, *Negation*, Standard Edition 19: 1925 (London: Hogarth Press, 1961), p. 237.

16. Ibid.

17. Sigmund Freud, *The Loss of Reality in Neurosis and Psychosis*, Standard Edition 19: 1924 (London: Hogarth Press, 1961), p. 185.

18. Ibid.

19. Michel Foucault in *Power/Knowledge* (New York: Pantheon, 1980) sees knowledge and power converging in the professions dealing with the treatment, discipline, education, and confinement of bodies. Foucault calls the attitudes governing how the professions work *epistèmes* (authoritative knowledge), powerful aggregations of values and perceptions that determine how bodies are perceived and treated. Power is dispersed throughout the social order and resides in the professional practices of social agents like educators, penologists, physicians, and psychiatrists. This form of social power, he argues, is a significant aspect of the exercise of power in the twentieth century and, in many respects, may possess more influence over individual life than the older concepts of state or political sovereignty.

20. Freud, *The Loss of Reality in Neurosis and Psychosis*, p. 187.

21. Fred E. Katz, *Ordinary People and Extraordinary Evil: A Report on the Beguilings of Evil* (Albany: State University of New York Press, 1993), p. 89.

22. Quoted in Andreas Hillgrüber, "War in the East and the Extermination of the Jews," in Michael R. Marrus, ed., *The Nazi Holocaust, Historical Articles on the Destruction of European Jews. 3: The "Final Solution": The Interpretation of Mass Murder*, vol. 1, p. 106.

23. Ibid., p. 107.

24. Quoted in Martin Broszat, "Hitler and the Genesis of the 'Final

Solution': An Assessment of David Irving's Theses," in Marrus, ed., *The Nazi Holocaust*, 3: vol. 1, p. 130.

25. Ibid., p. 142.

26. Ulrich Albrecht, "Military Technology and National Socialist Ideology," in Renneberg and Walker, eds., *Science, Technology, and National Socialism*.

27. Hilberg, "German Railroads/Jewish Souls," in Marrus, ed., *The Nazi Holocaust*, 3: vol. 1, p. 548.

28. Ibid., p. 550.

29. Goldhagen, *Hitler's Willing Executioners*, pp. 168–77.

30. Lawrence L. Langer, *Admitting the Holocaust: Collected Essays* (New York: Oxford University Press, 1995), p. 66.

31. Ibid., p. 68.

32. Quoted in Hillgrüber, "War in the East and the Extermination of the Jews," p. 111.

33. Ibid., p. 112.

Chapter 5

1. Bauer, *The Holocaust in Historical Perspective*, p. 57.

2. Ian Kershaw, "The Persecution of the Jews and German Popular Opinion in the Third Reich," in Marrus, ed., *The Nazi Holocaust: Historical Articles on the Destruction of European Jews, 5: Public Opinion and Relations to the Jews in Nazi Europe*, vol. 1 (Westport, CT: Meckler, 1989). See also Otto Dov Kulka, " 'Public Opinion' in Nazi Germany and the 'Jewish Question,' " in Marrus, ed., *The Nazi Holocaust*, 5: vol. 1; and Lawrence D. Stokes, "The German People and the Destruction of the European Jews," in Marrus, ed., *The Nazi Holocaust*, 5: vol. 1.

3. See Saul Friedländer, "From Anti-Semitism to Extermination: A Historiographical Study of Nazi Policies toward the Jews and an Essay in Interpretation," in Marrus, ed., *The Nazi Holocaust*, 3: vol. 1; Michael H. Kater, "Everyday Anti-Semitism in Prewar Nazi Germany: The Popular Bases," in Marrus, ed., *The Nazi Holocaust*, 5: vol. 1; and Jacob Katz, *From Prejudice to Destruction: Anti-Semitism 1700–1933* (Cambridge: Harvard University Press, 1980).

4. Hilberg, "German Railroads/Jewish Souls," in Marrus, ed., *The Nazi Holocaust*, 3: vol. 1, p. 543.

5. Ibid., pp. 535, 544.

6. Eügen Kogon, Herman Langbein, and Adelbert Rückerl, eds., *Nazi Mass Murder: A Documentary History of the Use of Poison Gas,* trans. Mary Scott and Caroline Lloyd-Morris (New Haven, CT: Yale University Press, 1994), p. 30; see also pp. 160–61.

7. Wolfgang Scheffler, "The Forgotten Part of the 'Final Solution': The Liquidation of the Ghettos," in Marrus, ed., *The Nazi Holocaust,* 5: vol. 2, p. 825.

8. Dobroszycki, ed., *The Chronicle of the Lódz Ghetto,* pp. 150–51.

9. See Broszat, "Hitler and the Genesis of the 'Final Solution'"; Mommsen, "The Realization of the Unthinkable: The 'Final Solution of the Jewish Question' in the Third Reich," in Marrus, ed., *The Nazi Holocaust,* 3: vol. 1; Browning, "A Reply to Martin Broszat Regarding the Origins of the Final Solution," in Marrus, ed., *The Nazi Holocaust,* 3: vol. 1; Browning, "Hitler and the Euphoria of Victory: The Path to the Final Solution," in David Cesarani, ed., *The Final Solution: Origins and Implementation* (New York: Routledge, 1994); Hilberg, "The Bureaucracy of Annihilation," in François Furet, ed., *Unanswered Questions: Nazi Germany and the Genocide of the Jews* (New York: Schocken Books, 1989)

10. Saul Friedländer, "From Anti-Semitism to Extermination," p. 318.

11. Browning, "Nazi Resettlement Policy and the Search for a Solution to the Jewish Question, 1939–1941," in Marrus, ed., *The Nazi Holocaust,* 3: vol. 1; Philip Friedman, "The Lublin Reservation and the Madagascar Plan: Two Aspects of Nazi Jewish Policy During the Second World War," in Marrus, ed., *The Nazi Holocaust,* 5: vol. 2.

12. Saul Friedländer, "From Anti-Semitism to Extermination," p. 327.

13. See David Bankier, "German Public Awareness of the Final Solution," in Cesarani, ed., *The Final Solution*; Goldhagen, *Hitler's Willing Executioners,* pp. 80–128.

14. Müller-Hill, "The Idea of the Final Solution and the Role of Experts," in Cesarani, ed., *The Final Solution,* p. 63.

15. Ibid., p. 68.

16. Hanna Lévy-Haas, *Inside Belsen,* trans. Ronald Taylor (Sussex, UK: Harvester Press, 1982), pp. 54–55.

17. Ibid., p. 70.

18. Ibid., p. 41.

19. Ibid., p. 43.

20. Ibid., p. 39.

21. *Trials of War Criminals Before the Nuremberg Military Tribunals,* Control Council Law No. 10, 2 vols. (Nuremberg: October 1946–April 1949), (Washington, D.C.: Government Printing Office, 1949–1952), vol. 1, p. 49.

22. Ibid., p. 50.

23. International Auschwitz Committee, *Nazi Medicine,* pt. 1, pp. 104–5.

24. Ibid., p. 113.

25. *Trials of War Criminals Before the Nuremberg Military Tribunals,* vol. 1, p. 580.

26. Ibid., p. 585.

27. Ibid., pp. 589–90.

28. Ibid., p. 572.

29. Ibid., p. 640.

30. Ibid., p. 648.

31. Ibid., p. 402ff.

32. Ibid., p. 447ff.

33. Cf. ibid., p. 403–5.

34. Ibid., p. 406.

35. See, for example, the jaundice experiments conducted at Sachsenhausen and Buchenwald concentration camps, ibid., p. 494ff. The following memo is typical of communications regarding medical experiments:

> Hauptsturmfuehrer Professor Dr. Dresel, Director of the Hygienic Institute of the University of Leipzig, has cultivated a virus from persons suffering from hepatitis and succeeded in transplanting it on animals.
>
> It is necessary to make experiments on human beings in order to determine the fact that this virus is indeed the effective virus for hepatitis epidemica. The plenipotentiary for research on epidemics in the Reich Research Council therefore addressed himself to me with the request to carry out the above experiments.
>
> I am asking you to obtain authorization from the Reich Leader SS to carry out the necessary experiments on 20 suitable prisoners who have hitherto never suffered from hepatitis epidemica, at

the typhus experimental station of the concentration camp in Buchenwald.

Trials of War Criminals Before the Nuremberg Military Tribunals, vol. 1, pp. 496–97.

36. Müller-Hill, "Genetics after Auschwitz," in Marrus, ed., *The Nazi Holocaust, 5*: vol. 2, p. 667.

37. Ibid., p. 669.

38. Ibid., p. 673.

39. For an insightful analysis of Nazi medical experiments and the Nuremberg trials, see George J. Annas and Michael A. Grodin, *The Nazi Doctors and the Nuremberg Code: Human Rights in Human Experimentation* (New York: Oxford University Press, 1992).

40. *Trials of War Criminals Before the Nuremberg Military Tribunals*, vol. 2, p. 840.

41. Ibid., pp. 473, 474.

42. Ibid.

43. Ibid., pp. 556–58.

44. When manpower in sufficient numbers was not forthcoming through normal channels, the Jaegerstab [hunting staff] did not shrink from other methods of obtaining its labor. When necessary, the Jaegerstab recruited its own labor, either directly or by engineering "snatching" expeditions for the seizure of manpower arriving on transports from the East. . . .

The Jaegerstab was no mere discussion group. As an agency with absolute authority over fighter production, the Jaegerstab acted by orders and directives. The Jaegerstab fixed hours of labor and conditions of work. It was the Jaegerstab, for example, which established the 72-hour work week in the aircraft industry. In addition to its jurisdiction over fighter production, the Jaegerstab was charged with the program for the decentralization of the German aircraft industry, both to above-ground bombproof installations and to subterranean installations. Much of the labor employed in both phases of the project was concentration camp labor. . . . The testimony of Dorsch shows that these Jews [from Auschwitz] were used on the construction projects, that the conditions under which they lived were intolerable, and that the death rate on the project was excessive.

From the prosecutor's summary of the case against Erhard Milch, *Trials of War Criminals Before the Nuremberg Military Tribunals*, vol. 2, pp. 703, 704.

45. Ibid., p. 558.

46. Ibid., pp. 577–78.

47. Ibid., p. 579.

48. Ibid., p. 580.

49. Ibid., p. 618.

50. Troller, Theresienstadt, pp. 153–54.

51. *Trials of War Criminals Before the Nuremberg Military Tribunals*, vol. 2, p. 478; *See also* "Extracts from Stenographic Minutes of the Fifty-third Conference of the Planning Board, 16 February 1944," pp. 478–84.

52. Ibid., from"Opinion and Judgment of the United States Military Tribunal II Regarding Charges Brought Against Erhard Milch," pp. 789.

53. Lifton, *The Nazi Doctors*, pp. 418–65.

54. Hoess et al., *KL Auschwitz Seen by the SS*, pp. 240–41.

55. Ibid.

56. Lang, *Act and Idea in the Nazi Genocide*, p. 53.

Chapter 6

1. Quoted in Hillgrüber, "War in the East and the Extermination of the Jews," p. 114.

2. Quoted in Lifton, "Reflections on Genocide," p. 651.

3. Quoted in Arad, *Belzec, Sobibor, Treblinka*, p. 130.

4. Yitzhak Arad, Shmuel Krakowski, and Shmuel Spector, *The Einsatzgruppen Reports: Selections from the Dispatches of the Nazi Death Squads' Campaign Against the Jews, July 1941–January 1943* (New York: Holocaust Library, 1989), p. 119; see also Alfred Streim, "The Tasks of the SS *Einsatzgruppen*," in Marrus, ed., *The Nazi Holocaust*, 3: vol. 2.

5. Ibid., p. 123.

6. Ibid., p. 132.

7. Ibid., pp. 149, 151.

8. Broszat, "Hitler and the Genesis of the 'Final Solution,'" p. 161.

9. Horwitz, *In the Shadow of Death*, p. 146.

10. Dobroszycki, *The Chronicle of the Lódz Ghetto*, p. 50.

11. Müller-Hill, *Murderous Science*, p. 96.

12. Ibid., p. 101.

13. Lifton, "Reflections on Genocide," p. 642.

14. Lang, *Act and Idea in the Nazi Genocide*, p. 92.

15. Amery, *At the Mind's Limits*, p. 52.

16. International Auschwitz Committee, *Nazi Medicine*, pt. 3, pp. 191–92.

17. Freud, *Neurosis and Psychosis*, Standard Edition 19: 1924 (London: Hogarth Press, 1961), p. 151.

18. Quoted in Kogon et al., eds., *Nazi Mass Murder*, pp. 40–41.

19. Quoted in Götz Aly, Peter Chroust, and Christian Pross, *Cleansing the Fatherland: Nazi Medicine and Racial Hygiene*, trans. Belinda Cooper (Baltimore: Johns Hopkins University Press, 1994), p. 266.

20. Ibid., p. 267.

21. Ibid., p. 269.

22. Quoted in Herf, *Reactionary Modernism*, p. 163.

23. Ibid., pp. 163, 193.

24. Ibid., p. 207.

25. See Kershaw, *Popular Opinion and Dissent in the Third Reich*; Mommsen, "Anti-Jewish Politics and the Implementation of the Holocaust."

26. Kershaw, *Popular Opinion and Dissent in the Third Reich*, p. 360.

27. Moishe Postone, "Anti-Semitism and National Socialism: Notes on the German Reaction to the Holocaust," *New German Critique*, 19 (1980): 97–115.

28. Quoted in Hans Peter Bleuel, *Sex and Society in Nazi Germany*, ed. Heinrich Fraenkel, trans. J. Maxwell Brownjohn (New York: Lippincott, 1973), p. 224. Himmler confided to a medical aide: "I have long been considering whether it might not be expedient to castrate every homosexual at once." In 1934, a Professor Lothar Tirala, teaching in Munich, maintained that homosexuality demonstrated a "moral pathology" and that it was incumbent upon German society to utilize "all possible means to suppress such sick perversions in the body of our people." A physician writing for the Office of Racial Policy in the summer of 1938 maintained that homosexuals were "enemies of the state to be eliminated." Many in the medical and political community saw homosexuals, like Jews and gypsies, as constituting a genetic health risk to the larger society. See Proctor, *Racial Hygiene*, pp. 212-14; also see Claudia Schoppmann, *Days of Masquerade: Life Sto-*

ries of Lesbians During the Third Reich, trans. Allison Brown (New York: Columbia University Press, 1996); and Richard Plant, *The Pink Trian-gle: The Nazi War Against Homosexuals* (New York: Holt, 1988).

29. Quoted in Herf, *Reactionary Modernism*, p. 138.

30. See Calvin Goldschneider and Alan S. Zuckerman, *The Transfor-mation of the Jews* (Chicago: University of Chicago Press, 1984), pp. 77ff.

31. Mosse, *George L. Masses and Man: Naturalist and Fascist Perceptions of Reality* (New York: Howard Fertig, 1980). Mosse shows how exclu-sive and deeply embedded anti-Semitism had been in German cul-ture; see also Saul Friedländer, *Nazi Germany and the Jews*, vol. 1: *The Years of Persecution, 1933–1939* (New York: HarperCollins, 1997).

32. Ibid., p. 225.

33. For elaboration on this idea, see Karl A. Schleunes, *The Twisted Road to Auschwitz: Nazi Policy Toward German Jews, 1933–1939* (Urbana: University of Illinois Press, 1970), pp. 102ff.

34. Ibid., p. 109.

35. For an account of the horror of Treblinka, see Samuel Willen-berg, *Surviving Treblinka*, ed. Wladyslaw T. Bartoszewski, trans. Naf-tali Greenwood (Oxford: Basil Blackwell, 1989).

36. Julia Kristeva, *Powers of Horror: An Essay on Abjection*, trans. Leon S. Roudiez (New York: Columbia University Press, 1982). For Kris-teva, the power of abjection lies in its psychological horror. To suffer abjection is to experience its presence as an overwhelming degrada-tion, a transfiguration of boundary, a breaking down of limits and the knowledge that the self is being overtaken by brutality, barbarity, and ultimately death.

37. Ibid., p. 17.

38. Ibid., p. 5.

39. Ibid., pp. 2–4.

40. Ibid., p. 4.

41. Ibid.

42. Ibid., p. 16.

43. Note how the psychoanalytic theorist Thomas Ogden describes this process: "[T]he experience of surfaces touching one another is a principal medium through which connections are made and organiza-tion achieved in this psychological mode." Ogden refers to a primitive sense of self he calls the "autistic-contiguous position," which depends on the distinction and feel of surfaces, skin, and the sense of

surface as threatening, friendly, rigid, flexible, and so on. "The word *contiguous* thus provides the necessary antithesis to the connotations of isolation and disconnectedness carried by the word *autistic*." A sense of threat or danger from surfaces forces the self back into an autistic position; a sense of receptivity or pleasure moves the self towards a "contiguous" relation with another's surfaces or skin. Thomas Ogden, *The Primitive Edge of Experience* (Northvale, NJ: Jason Aronson, 1989), p. 50.

Chapter 7

1. Jankiel Wiernik, "A Year in Treblinka," in Alexander Donat, ed., *The Death Camp Treblinka* (New York: Holocaust Library, 1979), p. 163.

2. Charlotte Delbo, *None of Us Will Return*, quoted in Langer, *Admitting the Holocaust: Collected Essays* (New York: Oxford University Press, 1995), p. 31.

3. Vamik Volkan, *The Need to Have Enemies and Allies: From Clinical Practice to International Relationships* (Northvale, NJ: Jason Aronson, 1988).

4. For a comprehensive discussion of this phenomenon, and its interpretation through psychoanalytic perspectives, see Kristeva, *Strangers to Ourselves*, trans. Leon S. Roudiez (New York: Columbia University Press, 1991).

5. Freud, *The Interpretation of Dreams*, pt. 2, Standard Edition 5: 1911 (London: Hogarth Press, 1953), pp. 612–13.

6. Melanie Klein, *Contributions to Psychoanalysis 1921–1945* (London: Hogarth Press, 1948), p. 238.

7. Ibid., p. 251.

8. Freud speaks of *"phantasying*, which begins already in children's play." Later in childhood it is "continued as *day-dreaming*," a mental operation that "abandons dependence on real objects." Freud also warns against "undervaluing the importance of phantasies in the formation of symptoms on the ground that they are not actualities." Fantasies have the power to replace reality entirely, thereby leading to the possibility of psychotic distortion. Freud, *Formulations on the Two Principles of Mental Functioning*, Standard Edition: 12, 1911 (London: Hogarth Press, 1958), pp. 222, 225.

9. Zygmunt Bauman, *Modernity and the Holocaust*, p. 89.

10. For Yehuda Bauer, the uniqueness of the Holocaust lies in the

fact that "for the first time in history a sentence of death had been pronounced on anyone guilty of having been born, and born of certain parents. . . . The Jew . . . a devil and a parasite . . . was the personification of evil and thus not human at all." Yehuda Bauer, *The Holocaust in Historical Perspective,* p. 32. Saul Friedländer argues that this perception of the Jew as innately diseased is a "psychotic delusion" that permeated "Nazi theory and practice." For a similar perspective, see Amos Elon, *The Israelis: Founders and Sons* (New York: Holt, Rinehart, and Winston, 1971), p. 266. For Jean Amery the danger lies in losing a sense of the uniqueness of the Holocaust amid a century of violence. He fears "everything will be submerged in a general 'Century of Barbarism.'" Amery, *At the Mind's Limits,* p. 80.

11. Mommsen, "Anti-Jewish Politics and the Implementation of the Holocaust," pp. 130–38.

12. Zygmunt Bauman, *Modernity and the Holocaust,* p. 109.

13. Mommsen, "Anti-Jewish Politics and the Implementation of the Holocaust," p. 118.

14. Quoted in Harold Kaplan, *Conscience and Memory,* p. 60.

15. Zygmunt Bauman, *Modernity and the Holocaust,* p. 177.

16. Ibid., p. 130. Kren and Rappoport, *The Holocaust and the Crisis of Human Behavior,* p.130.

17. Ibid., pp. 131–32.

18. Ibid., p. 139.

19. Arendt, *Eichmann in Jerusalem,* p. 106.

20. Jean-Jacques Rousseau, *Discourse on the Origins of Inequality* (London: Dent, 1990).

21. Zygmunt Bauman, *Modernity and the Holocaust,* pp. 186–87.

22. Ibid., p. 189.

23. Hilberg, *Perpetrators, Victims, Bystanders,* p. 72.

24. Quoted in Arad, *Belzec, Sobibor, Treblinka,* p. 52.

25. Zygmunt Bauman, *Modernity and the Holocaust,* p. 193.

26. Hilberg, "The Significance of the Holocaust," in Henry Friedlander and Sybil Milton, eds., *The Holocaust: Ideology, Bureaucracy, and Genocide,* p. 99.

27. Paul Celan, "Todesfuge," in Langer, ed., *Art from the Ashes: A Holocaust Anthology* (New York: Oxford University Press, 1995), p. 601.

Chapter 8

1. Kristeva, *Powers of Horror*, p. 53.

2. Ogden, *The Primitive Edge of Experience*, p. 56.

3. Freud, *Totem and Taboo*, Standard Edition 13: 1913 (London: Hogarth Press, 1950).

4. Harold Kaplan, *Conscience and Memory*, p. 88.

5. Ibid., pp. 88–89.

6. Haidu, "The Dialectics of Unspeakability," p. 293.

7. Kristeva, *Powers of Horror*, p. 109.

8. Ibid.

9. Goldhagen makes this point from a different perspective using data from the death marches of late 1944 and 1945 and the brutalization of prisoners in slave labor camps in *Hitler's Willing Executioners*, pp. 283–323.

10. Améry, *At the Mind's Limits*, p. 25.

11. Ibid., p. 73.

12. Ibid., p. 74.

13. Ibid.

14. Ibid., p. 87.

15. Didier Anzieu, *The Skin Ego: A Psychoanalytic Approach to the Self*, trans. Chris Turner (New Haven, CT: Yale University Press, 1989).

16. James M. Glass, *Shattered Selves: Multiple Personality in a Postmodern World* (Ithaca, NY: Cornell University Press, 1993).

17. Bodily experience and psychical percepts, Freud's argument in *The Ego and the Id*, interpenetrate one another: "A person's own body, and above all its surface, is a place from which both external and internal perceptions may spring. . . . The ego is first and foremost a bodily ego; it is not merely a surface entity, but is itself the projection of a surface. . . . [T]he ego is ultimately derived from bodily sensations, chiefly from those springing from the surface of the body. It may thus be regarded as a mental projection of the surface of the body." Freud, *The Ego and the Id,* Standard Edition 19: 1924 (London: Hogarth Press, 1961).

18. Anzieu, *The Skin Ego*, p. 108.

19. Thomas Ogden argues that primitive fears against feeling invaded by holes in the skin or by penetration of surfaces derive from

preverbal perceptions in infancy, when all experience is assimilated through the skin. Resonances from this period remain within the self and may assert themselves through phobic aversion. Further, these archaic memories, or disruption of skin surfaces, may condition adult experiences of otherness. This "failing sense of bodily cohesion," symptomatic of severe emotional anxiety, gives us a glimpse of psychological processes that are at the foundation of all human life. Ogden, *The Primitive Edge of Experience*, p. 70.

20. For a comprehensive analysis of the psychoanalysis of groups and political theory, see C. Fred Alford, *Group Psychology and Political Theory* (New Haven, CT: Yale University Press, 1995).

21. Ogden, *The Primitive Edge of Experience*, p. 56.

Chapter 9

1. Anzieu, *The Skin Ego*, p. 123.

2. Troller, *Theresienstadt*, pp. 83, 86.

3. Dobroszycki, *The Chronicle of the Lódz Ghetto*, p. 282.

4. Trunk, *Judenrat*, p. 84.

5. Höhne, *The Order of the Death's Head*, p. 387.

6. Quoted in Browning, *The Path to Genocide: Essays on Launching the Final Solution* (New York: Cambridge University Press, 1992), p. 158. See also Browning's "The German Bureaucracy and the Holocaust," in Alex Grobman and Daniel Landes, eds., *Genocide: Critical Issues of the Holocaust: A Companion to the Film*, Genocide. (Los Angeles: Simon Wiesenthal Center, 1983).

7. Charles G. Roland, *Courage Under Siege: Starvation, Disease, and Death in the Warsaw Ghetto* (New York: Oxford University Press, 1992), pp. 130–31.

8. Mordecai Lenski, "Problems of Disease in the Warsaw Ghetto," *Yad Vashem Studies* 3 (1975): 285.

9. Quoted in Burleigh and Wipperman, *The Racial State*, p. 101.

10. Quoted in Roland, *Courage Under Siege*, pp. 135–36.

11. Hilberg, "The Bureaucracy of Annihilation," p. 120. Also see Browning's "The Decision Concerning the Final Solution," in Marrus, ed., *The Nazi Holocaust: Historical Articles on the Destruction of European Jews*, vol. 1 (Westport, CT: Meckler, 1989); and David F. Crew, *Naziism and German Society, 1933–1948* (New York: Routledge, 1994).

12. Ibid., p. 131.

13. Browning, *The Path to Genocide*, p. 143.

14. Quoted in Alexander Mitscherlich and Fred Mielke, *The Death Doctors*, trans. James Cleugh (London: Elek Books, 1962), p. 265; see also Max Weinreich, *Hitler's Professors: The Part of Scholarship in Germany's Crimes Against the Jewish People* (New York: Yiddish Scientific Institute [YIVO], 1946).

15. Gallagher, *By Trust Betrayed*, pp. 6–7.

16. Aly et al., *Cleansing the Fatherland*, pp. 82–83.

17. Ibid., pp. 16–17.

18. Ibid., p. 89.

19. Ibid., p. 92.

20. Ibid., p. 93.

21. Ibid. There is, however, disagreement in the historical literature over the extent of popular protest. Unlike Proctor, for example, Gallagher finds, after the actions became known, significant popular disenchantment with the T–4 program and considerable questioning of its aims, methods, and justifications.

22. Medical surveillance of the nation's "health" and the notion of physicians as guardians of public health go back to the eighteenth century and the concept of the "medical police" formulated by Johann Peter Frank (1745–1841), a German physician and professor of medicine. It is not too long a step from Frank's notion of medicine as overseer of the nation's hygienic and moral welfare to the Nazi physician standing guard over the biological future. See George Rosen, *From Medical Police to Social Medicine: Essays on the History of Health Care* (New York: Science History Publications, 1974), pp. 120–58.

23. Quoted in Aly et al., *Cleansing the Fatherland*, p. 208.

24. Ibid., p. 210.

25. Ibid., p. 213.

26. Ibid., p. 215.

27. Ibid., p. 218.

28. Ibid., pp. 219–20.

29. From an interrogation with Allied officers in July 1945, ibid., p. 224.

30. Ibid., p. 228.

31. Browning, *The Path to Genocide*, p. 161.

Chapter 10

1. Harold Kaplan, *Conscience and Memory*, p. 106.

2. Saul Friedländer, *Memory, History, and the Extermination of the Jews of Europe* (Bloomington: Indiana University Press, 1993), p. 104.

3. Ibid., p. 107.

4. Jürgen Habermas addresses a polarity implicit in what has come to be called the "historians' debate": those who see the Final Solution and what it signifies as exception or extraordinary lapse in human behavior versus those who speak of it as part of a continuum of normal human experience. "Something happened there [Auschwitz], that no one could previously have thought even possible. It touched a deep layer of solidarity among all who have a human face. Until then—in spite of all the quasi-natural brutalities of world history—we had simply taken the integrity of this deep layer for granted. At that point a bond of naiveté was torn to shreds—a naiveté that as such had nourished historical continuities." Habermas, *The New Conservatism*, pp. 251–252.

5. Note how Eric L. Santner describes Saul Friedländer's critique of the historicization of the Holocaust and the importance Broszat and other revisionist historians attach to "pleasure in historical narration" (the need to find and be empathic toward complacency and normality in the life of ordinary Germans): "The gist of [Friedländer's] critique, as I understand it, is the claim that the events in question—Nazism and the 'Final Solution'—mark a shattering of the regime of normal social and psychological functioning and therewith a crossing over into a realm of psychotic experience that may be inaccessible to empathic interpretation, that may not be redeemable within an economy of narrative pleasure." Santner himself, in a footnote discussing published correspondence between Broszat and Friedländer, refers to "the psychotic layer of these events." Eric L. Santner, "History Beyond the Pleasure Principle: Some Thoughts on the Representation of Trauma," in Saul Friedländer, ed., *Probing the Limits of Representation*, pp. 149, 365.

6. Saul Friedländer, *Memory, History, and the Extermination of the Jews of Europe*, p. 105.

7. The stakes in the historians' debate, and the uniqueness of the Holocaust, touch on modern German politics. Charles Mairer observes:

The central issue has been whether Nazi crimes were unique, a legacy of evil in a class by themselves, irreparably burdening any concept of German nationhood, or whether they are comparable to other national atrocities, especially Stalinist terror. Uniqueness, it has been pointed out, should not be so important an issue; the killing remains horrendous whether or not other regimes committed mass murder. Comparability cannot really exculpate. In fact, however, uniqueness is rightly perceived as a crucial issue. If Auschwitz is admittedly dreadful, but dreadful as only one specimen of genocide—as the so-called revisionists have implied— then Germany can still aspire to reclaim a national acceptance that no one denies to perpetrators of other massacres, such as Soviet Russia. But if the Final Solution remains noncomparable— as the opposing historians have insisted—the past may never be "worked through," the future never normalized, and German nationhood may remain forever tainted, like some well forever poisoned.

Charles Mairer, *The Unmasterable Past* (Cambridge: Harvard University Press, 1988), p. 1.

8. Saul Friedländer, *Memory, History, and the Extermination of the Jews of Europe*, p. 105.

9. Ibid., p. 110.

10. Ibid.

11. Ibid.

12. Ibid.

13. Ibid., pp. 110–11.

14. Ibid. Kren and Rappoport take a somewhat different point of view than Friedländer: "If one keeps at the Holocaust long enough, then sooner or later the ultimate personal truth begins to reveal itself: one knows, finally, that one might either do it, or be done to. If it could happen on such a massive scale elsewhere, then it can happen anywhere; it is all within the range of human possibility, and like it or not, Auschwitz expands the universe of consciousness no less than landings on the moon." Kren and Rappoport, *The Holocaust and the Crisis of Human Behavior*, p. 126.

15. Bauer, "Genocide: Was It the Nazis' Original Plan?" in Marrus, ed., *The Nazi Holocaust, 3*: vol. 1.

16. In his *In the Shadow of Death,* Horwitz shows how seemingly normal citizens can, in a matter of hours, transform into tormentors of human beings regarded as "life unworthy of life."

17. Terrence Des Pres, *The Survivor: An Anatomy of Life in the Death Camps* (New York: Pocket Books, 1977).

18. Troller, *Theresienstadt,* p. 44.

19. Ibid.

Chapter 11

1. Sara Nomberg-Przytyk, *Auschwitz: True Tales from a Grotesque Land,* ed. Eli Pfefferkorn and David H. Hirsch, trans. Roslyn Hirsch (Chapel Hill: The University of North Carolina Press, 1985), p. 69.

2. Emmanuel Ringelblum, *Notes from the Warsaw Ghetto: The Journal of Emmanuel Ringelblum,* trans. Jacob Sloan (New York: Schocken, 1975), p. 174.

3. From Eügen Heimler, "Children of Auschwitz," quoted in George Mikes, *Prison: A Symposium* (London: Routledge and Kegan Paul, 1963), p. 12.

4. George Eisen, *Children and Play in the Holocaust: Games Among the Shadows* (Amherst: University of Massachusetts Press, 1988), p. 60.

5. Dobroszycki, *The Chronicle of the Lódz Ghetto,* pp. 165–67.

6. Ibid., pp. 307–9.

7. Joseph Zelkowicz, "Days of Nightmare," in Lucy S. Dawidowicz, ed., *A Holocaust Reader* (New York: Behrman House, 1976), p. 309.

8. Ibid., pp. 311, 315.

9. For the initial formulation of this concept, see Bettelheim, *The Empty Fortress.*

10. Langer, *Admitting the Holocaust,* pp. 49–50.

11. Stephen Holmes, *Passions and Constraint: On the Theory of Liberal Democracy* (Chicago: University of Chicago Press, 1995).

12. Wilfred Bion, *Experience in Groups, and Other Papers* (New York: Basic Books, 1961).

13. Alford, *Group Psychology and Political Theory.*

14. Eisen, *Children and Play in the Holocaust,* p. 17.

15. Ben Edelbaum, "Growing Up in the Holocaust," quoted in Eisen, *Children and Play in the Holocaust,* pp. 17–18.

16. Ibid., p. 22.

17. Mary Berg, *Warsaw Ghetto Diary*, quoted in Eisen, *Children and Play in the Holocaust*, p. 25.

18. For an analysis of the danger psychotic thinking presents for a democratic ethics, see Glass, *Psychosis and Power: Threats to Democracy in the Self and the Group* (Ithaca, NY: Cornell University Press, 1995).

19. Holmes, *Passions and Constraint*, p. 217.

20. Ibid., p. 222.

21. Ibid., p. 269.

Epilogue

1. The institute collects documents, photographs, and artifacts relating to the Holocaust and to Jewish culture and religion prior to the occupation. Its archive collections contain materials, particularly the diaries of Emmanuel Ringelblum, which are invaluable as descriptions of life in the Warsaw Ghetto.

REFERENCES

Adelson, Alan, and Robert Lapides, eds. *Lódz Ghetto: Inside a Community Under Siege*. New York: Penguin, 1991.

Adorno, Theodore W., Elsie Frenkel-Brunswick, Daniel J. Levinson, and R. Nevitt Sanford. *The Authoritarian Personality*. New York: Harper, 1950.

Albrecht, Ulrich. "Military Technology and National Socialist Ideology." In Monika Renneberg and Mark Walker, eds., *Science, Technology, and National Socialism*. Cambridge: Cambridge University Press, 1994.

Alexander, Leo. "Medical Science Under Dictatorship." *New England Journal of Medicine*, 241 (1949): 39–47.

Alford, Charles F. *Group Psychology and Political Theory*. New Haven, CT: Yale University Press, 1994.

Aly, Götz, Peter Chroust, and Christian Pross. *Cleansing the Fatherland: Nazi Medicine and Racial Hygiene*. Trans. Belinda Cooper. Baltimore: Johns Hopkins University Press, 1994.

Améry, Jean. *At the Mind's Limits: Contemplation by a Survivor on Auschwitz and Its Realities*. Trans. Sidney Rosenfeld and Stella P. Rosenfeld. Bloomington: Indiana University Press, 1980.

Annas, George J., and Michael A. Grodin. *The Nazi Doctors and the Nuremberg Code: Human Rights in Human Experimentation*. New York: Oxford University Press, 1992.

Anzieu, Didier. *The Group and the Unconscious*. Trans. Benjamin F. Kilborne. Boston: Routledge and Kegan Paul, 1984.

———. *The Skin Ego: A Psychoanalytic Approach to the Self*. Trans. Chris Turner. New Haven, CT: Yale University Press, 1989.

Arad, Yitzhak. *Belzec, Sobibor, Treblinka: The Operation Reinhard Death Camps*. Bloomington: Indiana University Press, 1986.

Arad, Yitzhak, Shmuel Krakowski, and Shmuel Spector. *The Einsatz-*

gruppen Reports: Selections from the Dispatches of the Nazi Death Squads' Campaign Against the Jews, July 1941–January 1943. New York: Holocaust Library, 1989.

Arendt, Hannah. *Eichmann in Jerusalem: A Report on the Banality of Evil*. New York: Penguin, 1964.

Bagioli, Mario. "Science, Modernity, and the Final Solution." In Saul Friedländer, ed., *Probing the Limits of Representation*. Cambridge: Harvard University Press, 1992.

Bankier, David. "German Public Awareness of the Final Solution." In David Cesarani, ed., *The Final Solution: Origins and Implementation*. New York: Routledge, 1994.

Bauer, Yehuda. "Conclusion: The Significance of the Final Solution." In David Cesarani, ed., *The Final Solution: Origins and Implementation*. New York: Routledge, 1994.

———. "Genocide: Was It the Nazis' Original Plan?" In Michael R. Marrus, ed., *The Nazi Holocaust: Historical Articles on the Destruction of European Jews. 3: The "Final Solution": The Implementation of Mass Murder*, vol. 1. Westport, CT: Meckler, 1989.

———. *The Holocaust in Historical Perspective*. Seattle: University of Washington Press, 1978.

Bauman, Rainer C. "Holocaust: Moral Indifference as the Form of Modern Evil." In Alan Rosenberg and Gerald E. Myers, eds., *Echoes from the Holocaust: Philosophical Reflections on a Dark Time*. Philadelphia: Temple University Press, 1988.

Bauman, Zygmunt. *Modernity and the Holocaust*. Ithaca, NY: Cornell University Press, 1991.

Bein, Alex. "The Jewish Parasite—Notes on the Semantics of the Jewish Problem, with Special Reference to Germany." In Robert Weltsch, ed., *Publications of the Leo Baeck Institute: Yearbook 9*. London: East and West Library, 1964.

Bettelheim, Bruno. *The Empty Fortress: Infantile Autism and the Birth of the Self*. New York: Free Press, 1967.

Beyerchen, Alan D. *Scientists Under Hitler: Politics and the Physics Community in the Third Reich*. New Haven, CT: Yale University Press, 1977.

Bion, Wilfred R. *Experience in Groups and Other Papers*. New York: Basic Books, 1961.

Blacker, C. P. "Eugenic Experiments Conducted by Nazis on Human Subjects." *Eugenics Review*, 44 (1952): 9–19.

Bleuel, Hans Peter. *Sex and Society in Nazi Germany*. Ed. Heinrich Fraenkel. Trans. J. Maxwell Brownjohn. New York: Lippincott, 1973.

Bracker, Karl Dietrich. *The German Dictatorship: The Origins, Structure, and Effects of National Socialism*. Trans. Jean Steinberg. New York: Praeger, 1970.

Braham, Randolph L., ed. *The Psychological Perspectives of the Holocaust and of Its Aftermath*. Boulder, CO: Social Science Monographs, 1988.

Bramwell, Anna. *Blood and Soil: Richard Walther Darre and Hitler's Green Party*. Bourne End, UK: Kensal, 1985.

Bridenthal, Renate, Atima Grossman, and Marian Kaplan, eds. *When Biology Became Destiny: Women in Weimar and Nazi Germany*. New York: Monthly Review Press, 1984.

Broszat, Martin. "Hitler and the Genesis of the 'Final Solution': An Assessment of David Irving's Theses." In Michael R. Marrus, ed., *The Nazi Holocaust: Historical Articles on the Destruction of European Jews. 3: The "Final Solution": The Implementation of Mass Murder*, vol. 1. Westport, CT: Meckler, 1989.

Browning, Christopher R. "The Government Experts." In Henry Friedlander and Sybil I. Milton, eds., *The Holocaust: Ideology, Bureaucracy, and Genocide: The San Jose Papers*. Millwood, NY: Kraus International, 1980.

———. "The Government Experts." In Michael R. Marrus, ed., *The Nazi Holocaust: Historical Articles on the Destruction of European Jews. 3: The "Final Solution": The Implementation of Mass Murder*, vol. 1. Westport, CT: Meckler, 1989.

———. "Hitler and the Euphoria of Victory: The Path to the Final Solution." In David Cesarani, ed., *The Final Solution: Origins and Implementation*. New York: Routledge, 1994.

———. "Nazi Resettlement Policy and the Search for a Solution to the Jewish Question, 1939–1941." In Michael R. Marrus, ed., *The Nazi Holocaust: Historical Articles on the Destruction of European Jews. 3: The "Final Solution": The Implementation of Mass Murder*, vol. 1. Westport, CT: Meckler, 1989.

———. *Ordinary Men: Reserve Police Battalion 101 and the Final Solution in Poland*. New York: Harper Perennial, 1992.

———. *The Path to Genocide: Essays on Launching the Final Solution*. New York: Cambridge University Press, 1992.

———. "A Reply to Martin Broszat Regarding the Origins of the Final Solution." In Michael R. Marrus, ed., *The Nazi Holocaust: Historical Articles on the Destruction of European Jews. 3: The "Final Solution": The Implementation of Mass Murder,* vol. 1. Westport, CT: Meckler, 1989.

Bull, Hedley, ed. *The Challenge of the Third Reich: The Adam von Trott Memorial Lectures.* Oxford: Clarendon Press, 1986.

Burleigh, Michael, and Wolfgang Wipperman. *The Racial State: Germany 1933–1945.* New York: Cambridge University Press, 1991.

Caplan, Arthur L. *When Medicine Went Mad: Bioethics and the Holocaust.* Totowa, NJ: Humana Press, 1992.

Celan, Paul. "Todesfuge." In Lawrence L. Langer, ed., *Art from the Ashes: A Holocaust Anthology.* New York: Oxford University Press, 1995.

Cesarani, David, ed. *The Final Solution: Origins and Implementation.* New York: Routledge, 1994.

Crew, David F. *Naziism and German Society, 1933–1948.* New York: Routledge, 1994.

Czerniakow, Adam. *The Warsaw Diary of Adam Czerniakow: Prelude to Doom.* Ed. Raul Hilberg, Stanislaw Staron, and Josef Kermisz. Trans. Stanislaw Staron and the staff of Yad Vashem. New York: Stein and Day, 1979.

Dawidowicz, Lucy S. *The War Against the Jews, 1933–1945.* New York: Holt, Rinehart, and Winston, 1975.

de Hoyos, Ladislaus. *Klaus Barbie.* Trans. Nicholas Courtin. London: W. H. Allen, 1985.

Delbo, Charlotte. *None of Us Will Return.* Trans. John Githens. New York: Grove Press, 1968.

Des Pres, Terrence. *The Survivor: An Anatomy of Life in the Death Camps.* New York: Pocket Books, 1977.

Dobroszycki, Lucjan, ed. *The Chronicle of the Lódz Ghetto: 1941–1944.* Trans. Richard Lourie and Joachim Neugroschel. New Haven, CT: Yale University Press, 1984.

Donat, Alexander, ed. *The Death Camp Treblinka.* New York: Holocaust Library, 1979.

Dower, John. *War Without Mercy: Race and Power in the Pacific War.* New York: Pantheon, 1986.

Eisen, George. *Children and Play in the Holocaust: Games Among the Shadows.* Amherst: University of Massachusetts Press, 1988.

Elon, Amos. *The Israelis: Founders and Sons*. New York: Holt, Rinehart, and Winston, 1971.

Fein, Helen. *Accounting for Genocide: National Responses and Jewish Victimization During the Holocaust*. New York: Free Press, 1979.

Foucault, Michel. *Power/Knowledge*. New York: Pantheon, 1980.

Freud, Sigmund. *The Ego and the Id*. Standard Edition: 19, 1924. London: Hogarth Press, 1961.

―――. *Formulations on the Two Principles of Mental Functioning*. Standard Edition: 12, 1911. London: Hogarth Press, 1958.

―――. *The Interpretation of Dreams*, pt. 2. Standard Edition: 5, 1911. London: Hogarth Press, 1958.

―――. *The Loss of Reality in Neurosis and Psychosis*. Standard Edition: 19, 1924. London: Hogarth Press, 1961.

―――. *Negation*. Standard Edition: 19, 1925. London: Hogarth Press, 1961.

―――. *Neurosis and Psychosis*. Standard Edition: 19, 1924. London: Hogarth Press, 1961.

―――. *Totem and Taboo*. Standard Edition: 13, 1913. London: Hogarth Press, 1950.

―――. *The Uncanny*. Standard Edition: 17, 1919. London: Hogarth Press, 1955.

Friedländer, Henry, and Sybil I. Milton, eds. *The Holocaust: Ideology, Bureaucracy, and Genocide: The San Jose Papers*. Millwood, NY: Kraus International, 1980.

Friedländer, Saul, "A Controversy About the Historization of National Socialism," *New German Critique* 44 (Spring/Summer 1988): 85-126.

―――. "From Anti-Semitism to Extermination: A Historiographical Study of Nazi Policies Toward the Jews and an Essay in Interpretation." In Michael R. Marrus, ed., *The Nazi Holocaust: Historical Articles on the Destruction of European Jews*. 3: *The "Final Solution": The Implementation of Mass Murder*, vol. 1. Westport, CT: Meckler, 1989.

―――. *Kurt Gerstein: The Ambiguity of Good*. Trans. Charles Fullman. New York: Knopf, 1969.

―――. *Memory, History, and the Extermination of the Jews of Europe*. Bloomington: Indiana University Press, 1993.

―――. *Nazi Germany and the Jews*. Volume 1: *The Years of Persecution 1933–1939*. New York: HarperCollins, 1997.

―――. ed. *Probing the Limits of Representation: Nazism and the "Final*

Solution." Cambridge: Harvard University Press, 1992.

Friedman, Philip, "The Lublin Reservation and the Madagascar Plan: Two Aspects of Nazi Jewish Policy During the Second World War." In Michael R. Marrus, ed., *The Nazi Holocaust: Historical Articles on the Destruction of European Jews.* 3: *The "Final Solution": The Implementation of Mass Murder, Public Opinion, and Relations to the Jews in Nazi Europe,* vol. 2. Westport, CT: Meckler, 1989.

Furet, François, ed. *Unanswered Questions: Nazi Germany and the Genocide of the Jews.* New York: Schocken, 1989.

Gallagher, Hugh G. *By Trust Betrayed: Patients, Physicians, and the License to Kill in the Third Reich.* New York: Holt, 1990.

Gebhardt, B. "Health Education in Germany." *American Journal of Public Health and Nation's Health,* 24 (1934): 1148–51.

Glass, James M. *Delusion: Internal Dimensions and Political Life.* Chicago: University of Chicago Press, 1985.

———. *Psychosis and Power: Threats to Democracy in the Self and the Group.* Ithaca, NY: Cornell University Press, 1995.

———. *Shattered Selves: Multiple Personality in a Postmodern World.* Ithaca, NY: Cornell University Press, 1993.

Goldhagen, Daniel Jonah. *Hitler's Willing Executioners: Ordinary Germans and the Holocaust.* New York: Knopf, 1996.

Goldscheider, Calvin, and Alan S. Zuckerman. *The Transformation of the Jews.* Chicago: University of Chicago Press, 1984.

Graham, Loren R. "Science and Values: The Eugenics Movement in Germany and Russia in the 1920s." *American Historical Review,* 82 (1977): 1133–64.

Gutman, Yisrael, and Michael Berenbaum, eds. *Anatomy of the Auschwitz Death Camp.* Bloomington: Indiana University Press, 1994.

Haas, Peter J. *Morality After Auschwitz: The Radical Challenge of the Nazi Ethic.* Philadelphia: Fortress Press, 1988.

Haberer, Joseph. *Politics and the Community of Science.* New York: Van Nostrand Reinhold, 1969.

Habermas, Jürgen. *The New Conservatism: Cultural Criticism and the Historians' Debate.* Ed. and trans. Shierry Weber Nicholsen. Cambridge: Harvard University Press, 1989.

Haidu, Peter, "The Dialectics of Unspeakability: Language, Silence, and the Narratives of Desubjectification," In Saul Friedländer, ed.,

Probing the Limits of Representation. Cambridge: Harvard University Press, 1992.

Haney, Craig, Curtis Banks, and Philip Zimbardo. "Interpersonal Dynamics in a Simulated Prison." *International Journal of Criminology and Penology*, 1 (1983): 69–97.

Herf, Jeffrey. *Reactionary Modernism: Technology, Culture, and Politics in Weimar and the Third Reich*. New York: Cambridge University Press, 1989.

Hilberg, Raul. "The Bureaucracy of Annihilation." In François Furet, ed., *Unanswered Questions: Nazi Germany and the Genocide of the Jews*. New York: Schocken, 1989.

———. *The Destruction of the European Jews*. 2 vols. New York: Holmes and Meier, 1985.

———. "German Railroads/Jewish Souls." In Michael R. Marrus, ed., *The Nazi Holocaust: Historical Articles on the Destruction of European Jews. 3: The "Final Solution": The Implementation of Mass Murder*, vol. 1. Westport, CT: Meckler, 1989.

———. *Perpetrators, Victims, Bystanders: The Jewish Catastrophe, 1933–1945*. New York: Harper Perennial, 1992.

———. "The Significance of the Holocaust." In Henry Friedlander and Sybil I. Milton, eds., *The Holocaust: Ideology, Bureaucracy, and Genocide*. Millwood, NY: Kraus International, 1980.

Hillesum, Etty. *Letters from Westerbork*. Trans. Arnold J. Pomerans. London: Cape, 1987.

Hillgrüber, Andreas. "War in the East and the Extermination of the Jews." In Michael R. Marrus, ed., *The Nazi Holocaust: Historical Articles on the Destruction of European Jews. 3: The "Final Solution": The Implementation of Mass Murder*, vol. 1. Westport, CT: Meckler, 1989.

Hoche, Alfred, and Rudolf Binding. *Die Freigabe der Vernichtung Lebensunwerten Lebens* [Release and Destruction of Lives Not Worth Living]. Leipzig, 1920.

Hoess, Rudolf, Pery Broad, and Johann Paul Kremer. *KL Auschwitz Seen by the SS*. Ed. Jadwiga Bezwinska, Donata Czech. Trans. Constantine Fitzgibbon and Krystyna Michalik. New York: Howard Fertig, 1984.

Höhne, Heinz. *The Order of the Death's Head: The Story of Hitler's S.S.*. Trans. Richard Barry. New York: Coward-McCann, 1976.

Holmes, Stephen. *Passions and Constraint: On the Theory of Liberal*

Democracy. Chicago: University of Chicago Press, 1995.

Horwitz, Gordon L. *In the Shadow of Death: Living Outside the Gates of Mauthausen*. New York: Free Press, 1990.

Hughes, Thomas P. "Technology." In Henry Friedlander and Sybil I. Milton, eds. *The Holocaust: Ideology, Bureaucracy, and Genocide: The San Jose Papers*. Millwood, NY: Kraus International, 1980.

International Auschwitz Committee. *Nazi Medicine: Doctors, Victims, and Medicine in Auschwitz*. New York: Howard Fertig, 1986.

Kaplan, Chaim Aron. *The Warsaw Diary of Chaim A. Kaplan*. Trans. Abraham I. Katsh. New York: Collier, 1973.

Kaplan, Harold. *Conscience and Memory: Meditations in a Museum of the Holocaust*. Chicago: University of Chicago Press, 1994.

Kateb, George. *The Inner Ocean: Individualism and Democratic Culture*. Ithaca, NY: Cornell University Press, 1992.

Kater, Michael H. "Everyday Anti-Semitism in Prewar Nazi Germany: The Popular Bases." In Michael R. Marrus, ed., *The Nazi Holocaust: Historical Articles on the Destruction of European Jews. 5: Public Opinion and Relations to the Jews in Nazi Europe*, vol. 1. Westport, CT: Meckler, 1989.

Katz, Fred E. *Ordinary People and Extraordinary Evil: A Report on the Beguilings of Evil*. Albany: State University of New York Press, 1993.

Katz, Jacob. *From Prejudice to Destruction: Anti-Semitism 1700–1933*. Cambridge: Harvard University Press, 1980.

Kershaw, Ian. "The Persecution of the Jews and German Popular Opinion in the Third Reich." In Michael R. Marrus, ed., *The Nazi Holocaust: Historical Articles on the Destruction of European Jews. 5: Public Opinion and Relations to the Jews in Nazi Europe*, vol. 1. Westport, CT: Meckler, 1989.

———. *Popular Opinion and Political Dissent in the Third Reich: Bavaria 1933–1945*. Oxford: Clarendon Press, 1983.

Kevles, Daniel J. *In the Name of Eugenics: Genetics and the Uses of Human Heredity*. Berkeley: University of California Press, 1985.

Klein, Melanie. *Contributions to Psychoanalysis 1921–1945*. London: Hogarth Press, 1948.

Kleinschmidt, H. E. "New Germany Teaches Her People: An Account of the Health Exposition of Berlin." *American Journal of Public Health and Nation's Health*, 35 (1935): 1108–13.

Koehl, Robert Lewis. *RKFDV: German Resettlement and Population Pol-*

icy, 1939–1945. Cambridge: Harvard University Press, 1957.

Kogon, Eügen, Herman Langbein, and Adelbert Rückerl, eds. *Nazi Mass Murder: A Documentary History of the Use of Poison Gas.* Trans. Mary Scott and Caroline Lloyd-Morris. New Haven, CT: Yale University Press, 1994.

Korczak, Janusz. *The Ghetto Years: 1939–1942.* Trans. Jerzy Bachrack and Barbara Krzywicka. Intro. Yitzhak Perlis. New York: Holocaust Library, 1980.

Kraut, Alan M. *Silent Travelers: Germs, Genes, and the "Immigrant Menace."* New York: Basic Books, 1994.

Kren, George M., and Leon Rappoport. *The Holocaust and the Crisis of Human Behavior.* New York: Holmes and Meier, 1980.

Kristeva, Julia. *Powers of Horror: An Essay on Abjection.* Trans. Leon S. Roudiez. New York: Columbia University Press, 1982.

———. *Strangers to Ourselves.* Trans. Leon S. Roudiez. New York: Columbia University Press, 1991.

Kulka, Otto Dov. "'Public Opinion' in Nazi Germany and the 'Jewish Question.'" In Michael R. Marrus, ed., *The Nazi Holocaust: Historical Articles on the Destruction of European Jews. 5: Public Opinion and Relations to the Jews in Nazi Europe,* vol. 1. Westport, CT: Meckler, 1989.

LaCapra, Dominick. *Representing the Holocaust: History. Theory, Trauma.* Ithaca, NY: Cornell University Press, 1994.

Lacoue-Labarthe, Philippe. *Heidegger, Art and Politics.* Oxford: Basil Blackwell, 1990.

Lang, Berel. *Act and Idea in the Nazi Genocide.* Chicago: University of Chicago Press, 1990.

Langer, Lawrence L. *Admitting the Holocaust: Collected Essays.* New York: Oxford University Press, 1995.

———. *Art from the Ashes: A Holocaust Anthology.* New York: Oxford University Press, 1995.

———. *Holocaust Testimonies: The Ruins of Memory.* New Haven, CT: Yale University Press, 1991.

Lenski, Mordecai. "Problems of Disease in the Warsaw Ghetto." *Yad Vashem Studies* 3 (1975): 283–93.

Lévy-Hass, Hanna. *Inside Belsen.* Trans. Ronald Taylor. Sussex, UK: Harvester Press, 1982.

Lifton, Robert J. "Life Unworthy of Life: Nazi Racial Views." In Randolph L. Braham, ed., *The Psychological Perspectives of the Holocaust and of Its Aftermath*. Boulder, CO: Social Science Monographs, 1988.

————. *The Nazi Doctors: Medical Killing and the Psychology of Genocide*. New York: Basic Books, 1986.

————. "Reflections on Genocide." In Michael R. Marrus, ed., *The Nazi Holocaust: Historical Articles on the Destruction of European Jews. 3: The "Final Solution": The Implementation of Mass Murder*, vol. 2. Westport, CT: Meckler, 1989.

Light, Donald W., Stephan Leibfried, and Florian Tennstedt. "Social Medicine vs. Professional Dominance: The German Experience." *American Journal of Public Health*, 76 (1986): 78–83.

Lustig, Arnost. *Night and Hope*. Washington, D.C.: Inscape, 1976.

Macrakis, Kriste. "The Ideological Origins of Institutes at the Kaiser Wilhelm Gesellschaft in National Socialist Germany." In Monika Renneberg and Mark Walker, eds., *Science, Technology, and National Socialism*. Cambridge: Cambridge University Press, 1994.

Mairer, Charles. *The Unmasterable Past*. Cambridge: Harvard University Press, 1988.

Marrus, Michael R., ed. *The Nazi Holocaust: Historical Articles on the Destruction of European Jews. 3: The "Final Solution": The Implementation of Mass Murder*. 2 vols. Westport, CT: Meckler. 1989.

————. *The Nazi Holocaust: Historical Articles on the Destruction of European Jews. 5: Public Opinion and Relations to the Jews in Nazi Europe*. 2 vols. Westport, CT: Meckler, 1989.

Mikes, George. *Prison: A Symposium*. London: Routledge and Kegan Paul, 1963.

Milgram, Stanley. *Obedience to Authority: An Experimental View*. New York: HarperCollins, 1974.

Mitscherlich, Alexander, and Fred Mielke. *The Death Doctors*. Trans. James Cleugh. London: Elek Books, 1962.

Mommsen, Hans. "Anti-Jewish Politics and the Implementation of the Holocaust." In Hedley Bull, ed., *The Challenge of the Third Reich: The Adam von Trott Memorial Lectures*. Oxford: Clarendon Press, 1986.

————. "The Realization of the Unthinkable: The 'Final Solution of the Jewish Question' in the Third Reich." In Michael R. Marrus, ed., *The Nazi Holocaust: Historical Articles on the Destruction of Euro-*

pean Jews. 3: The "Final Solution": The Implementation of Mass Murder, vol. 1. Westport, CT: Meckler, 1989.

Mosse, George L. *The Image of Man: The Creation of Modern Masculinity*. New York: Oxford University Press, 1996.

———. *Masses and Man: Nationalist and Fascist Perceptions of Reality.* New York: Howard Fertig, 1980.

Müller-Hill, Benno. "Genetics After Auschwitz." In Michael R. Marrus, ed., *The Nazi Holocaust: Historical Articles on the Destruction of European Jews. 5: Public Opinion and Relations to the Jews in Nazi Europe*, vol. 2. Westport, CT: Meckler, 1989.

———. "The Idea of the Final Solution and the Role of Experts." In David Cesarani, ed. *The Final Solution: Origins and Implementation*. New York: Routledge, 1994.

———. *Murderous Science: Elimination by Scientific Selection of Jews, Gypsies, and Others, Germany 1933–1945*. Trans. George R. Fraser. New York: Oxford University Press, 1988.

Niewyk, Donald C. *The Jews in Weimar Germany*. Baton Rouge: Louisiana State University Press, 1980.

Noakes, Jeremy. "Nazism and Eugenics: The Background to the Nazi Sterilization Law of 14 July 1933." In R. J. Bullen, H. Pogge von Strandmann, and A. B. Polonsky, eds., *Ideas into Politics: Aspects of European History, 1880–1950*. Totawa, NJ: Barnes and Noble, 1984.

Nomberg-Przytyk, Sara. *Auschwitz: True Tales from a Grotesque Land*. Ed. Eli Pfefferkorn and David H. Hirsch. Trans. Roslyn Hirsch. Chapel Hill: University of North Carolina Press, 1985.

Nyiszli, Miklos. *Auschwitz: A Doctor's Eyewitness Account*. Trans. Tibere Kramer and Richard Seaver. New York: F. Fell, 1960.

Ogden, Thomas H. *The Primitive Edge of Experience*. Northvale, NJ: Jason Aronson, 1989.

Paul, Diane. "Eugenics and the Left." *Journal of the History of Ideas*, 45 (1984): 567–90.

Peter, W. W. "Germany's Sterilization Program," *American Journal of Public Health and Nation's Health*, 24 (1934): 187–91.

Plant, Richard. *The Pink Triangle: The Nazi War Against Homosexuals*. New York: Holt, 1988.

Postone, Moishe. "Anti-Semitism and National Socialism: Notes on the German Reaction to the Holocaust." *New German Critique*, 19 (1980): 97–115.

Proctor, Robert. *Racial Hygiene: Medicine Under the Nazis*. Cambridge: Harvard University Press, 1988.

Rauschning, Hermann. *The Voice of Destruction*. New York: G. P. Putnam's Sons, 1940.

Renneberg, Monika, and Mark Walker, eds., *Science, Technology, and National Socialism*. Cambridge: Cambridge University Press, 1994.

Ringelblum, Emmanuel. *Notes from the Warsaw Ghetto: The Journal of Emmanuel Ringelblum*. Trans. Jacob Sloan. New York: Schocken, 1975.

Roland, Charles G. *Courage Under Siege: Starvation, Disease, and Death in the Warsaw Ghetto*. New York: Oxford University Press, 1992.

Rosen, George. *From Medical Police to Social Medicine: Essays on the History of Health Care*. New York: Science History Publications, 1974.

Rossler, Methchild. "'Area Research' and 'Spatial Planning.'" In Monika Renneberg and Mark Walker, eds., *Science, Technology, and National Socialism*. Cambridge: Cambridge University Press, 1994.

Rousseau, Jean-Jacques. *Discourse on the Origins of Inequality*. London: Dent, 1990.

Santner, Eric L. "History Beyond the Pleasure Principle: Some Thoughts on the Representation of Trauma." In Saul Friedländer, ed., *Probing the Limits of Representation: Nazism and the "Final Solution."* Cambridge: Harvard University Press, 1992.

Scheffler, Wolfgang. "The Forgotten Part of the 'Final Solution': The Liquidation of the Ghettos." In Michael R. Marrus, ed., *The Nazi Holocaust: Historical Articles on the Destruction of European Jews. 5: Public Opinion and Relations to the Jews in Nazi Europe*, vol. 1. Westport, CT: Meckler, 1989.

Schleunes, Karl A. *The Twisted Road to Auschwitz: Nazi Policy Toward German Jews, 1933–1939*. Urbana: University of Illinois Press, 1970.

Schoppmann, Claudia. *Days of Masquerade: Life Stories of Lesbians During the Third Reich*. Trans. Allison Brown. New York: Columbia University Press, 1996.

Schroeder-Gudehus, Brigitte. "The Argument for Self Government and Public Support of Science in Weimar Germany." *Minerva*, 10 (1972): 537–70.

Sereny, Gitta. *Into That Darkness: From Mercy Killing to Mass Murder*. New York: McGraw-Hill, 1974.

Shirer, William L. *The Rise and Fall of the Third Reich: A History of Nazi Germany*. New York: Simon & Schuster, 1960.

Sombart, Werner. *The Jews and Modern Capitalism*. Trans. Mortimer Epstein. London: T. F. Unwin, 1913.

Staub, Ervin. *The Roots of Evil: The Origins of Genocide and Other Group Violence*. New York: Cambridge University Press, 1993.

Stephenson, Jill. *The Nazi Organization of Women*. Totowa, NJ: Barnes and Noble, 1981.

————. "'Reichsbund der Kinderreichen': The League of Large Families in the Population Policy of Nazi Germany." *European Studies Review*, 9 (1979): 350–75.

Stokes, Lawrence D. "The German People and the Destruction of the European Jews." In Michael R. Marrus, ed., *The Nazi Holocaust: Historical Articles on the Destruction of European Jews. 5: Public Opinion and Relations to the Jews in Nazi Europe*, vol. 1. Westport, CT: Meckler, 1989.

Streim, Alfred. "The Tasks of the SS *Einsatzgruppen*." In Michael R. Marrus, ed., *The Nazi Holocaust: Historical Articles on the Destruction of European Jews. 3: The "Final Solution": The Implementation of Mass Murder*, vol. 2. Westport, CT: Meckler, 1989.

Sydnor, Charles W., Jr. *Soldiers of Destruction: The SS Death's Head Division, 1933–1945*. Princeton: Princeton University Press, 1977.

Theweleit, Klaus. *Male Fantasies*. Volume 2: *Male Bodies: Psychoanalyzing the White Terror*. Trans. Stephen Conway, Erica Carter, and Chris C. Turner. Minneapolis: University of Minnesota Press, 1987.

Toland, John. *Adolf Hitler*, vol. 1. New York: Doubleday, 1976.

Trials of War Criminals Before the Nuremberg Military Tribunals. Control Council Law No. 10. 2 vols. Nuremberg: October 1946–April 1949. Washington, D.C.: Government Printing Office, 1949–1952.

Troller, Norbert. *Theresienstadt: Hitler's Gift to the Jews*. Ed. Joel Shatzky. Trans. Susan E. Cernyak-Spatz. Chapel Hill: University of North Carolina Press, 1991.

Trunk, Isaiah. *Judenrat: The Jewish Councils in Eastern Europe Under Nazi Occupation*. New York: Stein and Day, 1977.

Volkan, Vamik. *The Need to Have Enemies and Allies: From Clinical Practice to International Relationships*. Northvale, NJ: Jason Aronson, 1988.

Volovici, Leon. *Nationalist Ideology and Antisemitism: The Case of Romanian Intellectuals in the 1930s*. Trans. Charles Kormos. New York: Pergamon Press, 1991.

Weindling, Paul. *Health, Race, and German Politics Between National Unification and Nazism, 1870–1945*. New York: Cambridge University Press, 1989.

———. "Weimar Eugenics: The Kaiser Wilhelm Institute for Anthropology, Human Heredity, and Eugenics in Social Context." *Annals of Science*, 42 (1985): 303–18.

Weinreich, Max. *Hitler's Professors: The Part of Scholarship in Germany's Crimes Against the Jewish People*. New York: Yiddish Scientific Institute (YIVO), 1946.

Weiss, Shelia Faith. "Pedagogy, Professionalism, and Politics: Biology Instruction During the Third Reich." In Monika Renneberg and Mark Walker, eds., *Science, Technology, and National Socialism*. Cambridge: Cambridge University Press, 1994.

———. "The Race Hygiene Movement in Germany," *Osiris*, 2d ser., 3 (1987): 193–236.

Wiernik, Jankiel. "A Year in Treblinka." In Alexander Donat, ed. *The Death Camp Treblinka*. New York: Holocaust Library, 1979.

Wiesel, Elie. *The Town Beyond the Wall*. Trans. Stephen Becker. New York: Atheneum, 1964.

Willenberg, Samuel. *Surviving Treblinka*. Ed. Wladyslaw T. Bartoszewski. Trans. Naftali Greenwood. Oxford: Basil Blackwell, 1989.

Zelkowicz, Joseph. "Days of Nightmare." In Lucy S. Dawidowicz, ed., *A Holocaust Reader*. New York: Behrman House, 1976.

Zuckerman, Yitzhak. *A Surplus of Memory: Chronicle of the Warsaw Ghetto Uprising*. Trans. Barbara Harshav. Berkeley: University of California Press, 1993.

INDEX

Abel, Wolfgang, 41

Abjection, 120–22, 124, 132, 140, 216n36

Adler, Teresa, 48

Alford, Fred, 181

Aly, Götz, 156–57

Améry, Jean, 67–68, 113, 140–41, 208n4

American Journal of Public Health and Nation's Health, 43–44

American Medical Association, xiv

Ancestry, certificates testifying to, 39

Ansbach, 159

Anti-Semitism, xiii, 19, 54, 80, 193; eliminationist, xiv; and group identity, 82, 83, 112, 115, 119; and Hitler, 16–17, 37, 115; and the indifference thesis, 85, 86; Kershaw on, 162; and the phobic group, 112, 115, 119; and popular media, 60

Anxiety, vii, 132, 135, 146, 148

Anzieu, Didier, 141, 144–45, 147–48

Arad, Yitzhak, 8

Arendt, Hannah, 72, 163; on animal pity, 130, 132; on the banality of evil, 7, 140–41; on bureaucratic mentality, 7, 69, 82, 165; and the "functionalist" argument, 81; and Hilberg, 9

Aryan race, 31, 38, 62–63, 145, 186;

and the Blood Protection Law, 50–52; and the definition of the *Kultur*-group, 140; and extermination centers, 160; and the identification of non-Aryans, 40; medical treatment of, xvii–xviii, 51, 53; and the phobic group, 118, 122; and the Sterilization Law, 39; Auschwitz concentration camp, xiv, 8, 12, 26, 81, 103, 167; acts of resistance in, 169; and the Auschwitz self, 74, 105–7; Broszat on, 4; commandant of, 30; construction of, 86; and economic conditions, 173; Friedländer on, 167; intelligentsia sent to, 52; Katz on, 79; killing of newborns at, 113–14; medical experiments at, 63, 92, 96, 98; murder of children at, 183; number of bodies processed in, 67; personal effects of Jews from, 15–16; and the phobic group, 113–14, 117, 119–20; physicians at, 73–74, 107; remains of, 192; sale of Jewish female subjects from, 65; selections at, 129–30; survivors of, 13, 48–49, 67, 113–14, 124, 128–30, 140–41, 171–72, 174; transportation of Jews to/from, 17, 90–91; and the uniqueness of the Holocaust, 123, 124, 128–30, 162–63; Wiesel on, 3